Preface

P ricing seldom is an area that business managers talk about with great enthusiasm. Price is often the centerpiece of strained relations with a good customer; the weapon competitors are using to steal market share; and the source of conflicts within the company as those with the spreadsheets, pro forma income statements, and knowledge of costs have different pricing ideas from the customer contact people.

In our discussions with executives in general management and across the various functional areas in the firm, we continually hear that pricing is a big headache—and one that is getting worse by the day as markets globalize. Many firms have given up—"we determine our costs and take our industry's traditional margins" or "the market sets the price and we have to figure out how to cope with it." Others have a different attitude, proactively using price as a key tool to achieve their business and financial aims. These "power pricers" have discovered the highly leveraged effect of price and built the capacity to practice pricing in a way which transforms the bottom line.

Power pricers think and act differently from everyday pricers. In our various capacities as case study developer, consultant, researcher, and teacher we have had the opportunity to work with power pricers around the world in industries ranging from pharmaceuticals to industrial machinery to automobiles to snack foods. We understand what makes them stand out: their attitudes, thought processes, and actions. And we have observed their successes—not small improvements but major transformations of the bottom line. This is a book about how to become a "power pricer."

We joined together as an international team on this book to be sure we could capture the practices of the worldwide leaders. We consistently rely on these firms to develop our underlying ideas and exemplify practices worthy of emulation. Our approach though is not simply to describe interesting pricing strategies but rather, aided by our understanding of the underlying economics, to weave these best practice examples together into a framework for advancing your own pricing program.

At the outset, we note that becoming a power pricer is not without certain costs. Investments must be made in mechanisms to assemble the necessary fact base and to rethink what it means to manage price. We set out these processes. Our objective is to provide proven, implementable pricing practice prescriptions.

Our research showed us that various aspects of pricing responsibility are typically diffused across the organization. Consequently, our intent is to present a set of pricing ideas useful to general managers, finance and accounting, and marketing and sales executives alike.

There have been many contributors to our thinking. We both spend lots of time "in the field" working with and learning from managers in companies. We owe these managers a great debt for sharing their problems, attempted solutions, and judgments of success or failure. While not "in the field" we each sit in an exciting intellectual environment: Dolan at Harvard Business School and Simon at Simon, Kucher & Partners. Our colleagues there have been subjected to the initial formation of lots of the ideas in this book—and also some ideas that are not in the book because they exposed us to the frailty of the ideas. We thank them both for sorting the ideas worth cultivating and those that were not, and for helping us to grow and articulate the ones in the former set.

The logistics of writing a book with authors working in two quite different environments have been eased by modern communication technology; but, still, our assistants combined an uncommon amount of talent and good cheer during this project. As authors, we created many issues but they were always resolved with competence and style by Sheila Linehan at Harvard Business School and Ingrun Rodewald at

Simon, Kucher. Thanks also to Robert Wallace at The Free Press for his enthusiasm for this book when it was nothing more than an idea and also to Bob, Dewey Brinkley, and the rest of The Free Press team for all the help along the way.

We dedicate this book to our wives, Kathleen Splaine-Dolan and Cecilia Simon, who both regularly insisted "one book by the two of you together will be better—plus it will be more fun to write it that way." They were right. This joint effort led to many ideas that would not have developed if each of us had gone off on a solo adventure. So, we thank them for their insight and encouragement throughout this collaboration.

Robert J. Dolan
Boston, Massachusetts

Hermann Simon
Koenigswinter, Germany and
Cambridge, Massachusetts

PART I

Foundations

1

Introduction

INTRODUCTION

"We have to get our prices up." This is a common refrain in businesses around the world today as competitive pressures have sliced margins. Often, however, the exhortation which follows is an unrealistic one—for example, "Boost prices, sales volume, and profitability each by ten percent in the next year!" Opportunities to do this are rare; but opportunities to improve profit dramatically by better pricing are the norm.

Consider the CEO of a $10-billion company meeting with the marketing managers of his various divisions. "Get me a nickel, get me a dime—every day. Find a way to convince the customer that we are worth it. Pick up these nickels and dimes all around the world—every day—they drop right to our bottom line—and pretty soon we are talking big improvements to our net income." What about this dime? Does it really mean "big improvements to our net income"? Suppose your average price is $10 per unit. Now add a dime to it, to make the price $10.10, a 1% improvement in average price realization. Not necessarily by getting the price on every single order to improve by 1%—but some 2%, some 5%—just average out to 1% and hold your sales volume.

What would that be worth to you? How much leverage is there in that? How much would it improve your net income?

If you worked at Coca-Cola, the 1% price realization improvement would boost net income by 6.4%; at Fuji Photo, 16.7%; at Nestle, 17.5%; at Ford, 26%; at Philips, 28.7%. In some companies, it would be the difference between a profit and a significant loss. Given a cost structure typical of large corporations, a 1% boost in price realization yields a net income gain of 12%.[1] In short, it's worth some effort to figure out how to do it. In fact, it's worth a lot of effort in data collection, analysis, creative thinking, and willingness to experiment. Yet most firms just don't. A 1994 survey found only 12% of firms doing "any serious pricing research" and one-third of these had no strategy for using the research results.[2] Our general experience squares with these survey findings. Many firms abrogate pricing responsibility—"the market sets the price" or "we have to match our competitor"; others use an inappropriate rule of thumb such as taking a standard mark-up on cost. These firms leave "nickels and dimes" and in some case thousands of Deutschmarks, Swiss francs, yen, dollars, and other currencies with customers around the world because they do not understand and capture the value they create for individual customers.

The cost of such lack of sophistication in pricing is growing day by day. Customers and competitors operating globally in a generally more complex marketing environment are making mundane thinking about pricing a serious threat to the firm's financial well-being. Managers are feeling this pricing pressure. Figure 1-1 presents the results of a recent (1995) survey in which we asked 186 managers (57 from the United States and 129 from Europe) representing a broad range of industries to rank 13 marketing issues on a scale ranging from 1 = low problem pressure to 5 = high problem pressure. Pricing tops the list at a 4.3 rating overall. This is indicative of the importance for company financial performance of "pricing right" and the difficulty of getting it right. The reasons for the increasing difficulty of doing a good job on pricing can be summarized in two words: interdependence and information.

Interdependence comes in two forms: products and markets. The days of Coca-Cola being an "anytime, anywhere" drink (as Coke ads proclaimed) and for anybody (ads showed everyone from little children to Mom and Dad to grandparents drinking Coke) are gone. Now, it's Classic Coke, Coke, Diet Coke, Cherry Coke, Caffeine Free Coke, etc., etc. The single product has evolved into a varied product line for differ-

FIGURE 1-1

Managers' Rating of Marketing Issues

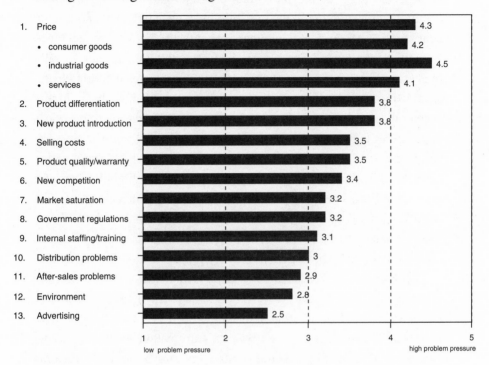

ing tastes. This represents one form of product proliferation—"horizontal" in the sense that all Coke products are on the same inherent quality level; i.e., whether Coke is better than Diet Coke is determined by the individual consumer's tastes.

"Vertical" product proliferation in the form of "good, better, best" strategies are common as well. AlliedSignal's Autolite spark plugs come in three grades: carbon, platinum, and double platinum. Kodak markets three grades of consumer film: Funtime Film "for casual picture-taking," its mainstay Gold Film, and a high-performance Royal Gold Film that they advertise as "extra clear and extra sharp for extra special moments." Similarly, firms offer complementary products. Intuit markets not only its Quicken home-finance software but also the checks to put in the system, a Quicken credit card, and electronic bill-paying services. The razor and blades, cameras and film, hardware and software, products and technical support scenario of tied, complementary products is commonplace.

This trend to offering interdependent products complicates pricing—because the price of the individual elements cannot be set independently. A product's role in the portfolio must be established and pricing considered at the product line rather than at the individual product level.

Market interdependence also is impacting pricing. Pricing is relatively simple when markets can be separated and a price individually determined for each. Historically, pricing has tended to be a highly decentralized decision with individual country managers setting prices in pursuit of their own objectives. However, today, as products are standardized across the world and global brands become the norm, treating markets individually risks shrinking worldwide profitability, because gray markets are emerging as third parties buy, sell, and ship around the world to take advantage of differences in prices. Second, individual customers have moved to worldwide procurement, further narrowing the flexibility of pricing managers as they try to set prices across markets.

The second related cause of complexity is information: better information creating smarter, more powerful customers. Buying services emerge as intermediaries for end users in industries such as automobiles because of their ability to access and process data. Information technology allows for international tracking and transmittal of pricing information, creating the need for harmonized world pricing. Buying groups have formed in a wide variety of situations from independent funeral home operators sharing information and pooling casket purchases to major corporations joining with one another to negotiate ticket prices with airline companies. For many companies, purchasing has become a strategic function. The acrimonious situation starting in the mid-1990s and continuing for years involving General Motors in the United States and Volkswagen in Germany was not about the "defection" of a great car designer or marketer, but rather about Volkswagen's spiriting away of GM's Vice President of Worldwide purchasing manager, Ignacio Lopez, and GM's allegation that Lopez took supplier pricing information with him.

The forces of interrelatedness and information have created more complex price schedules. No longer able to charge customers different prices just because of their geographic separation, firms attain price customization by applying the *same pricing schedule* to all customers, fully aware that because of the specific terms and conditions of sale different prices are received in the end.

Finally, all of this occurs in an environment of increasing competitive diversity. Coke now faces not only Pepsi, but also President's Choice, a "brand" of Loblaw's, the Canadian supermarket chain. Kodak film competes not only against Fuji and Agfa, but also against viable quality products manufactured by 3M and sold under private labels. Industry leaders in high technology continue to battle one another on technological innovation grounds; but they now also face firms with "rapid imitation" rather than innovation strategies. Eight hundred different car models vie for the consumer's attention in Germany, where traditional suppliers from throughout Europe, the United States, and Japan have been joined by cars from Korea, Malaysia, and Mexico.

The net result of this is that being simply "good" in your pricing thinking has become very costly. Customary rules of thumb are inadequate in dealing with this environment. Becoming astute in pricing analysis and judgment can pay big dividends. The goal of this book is to help your firm attain maximum financial performance by improving its pricing thinking and to show how that improved thinking can translate into improved net price realization. We do not describe good pricing practice. Rather, we specify the practices of those who have moved pricing to a higher level, the "power pricers" who have transformed their bottom line by pricing. This chapter begins by looking at some power pricers and then sets out the book's plan to help you attain this level of pricing sophistication and resulting profit improvement.

BECOMING A POWER PRICER

Four dimensions help to define the power pricer:

1. viewpoint on pricing
2. fact files to support pricing
3. tools and scope of analysis
4. determination and implementation

Viewpoint on Pricing

The three profit drivers are sales volume, price, and costs. Specifically:

Profit = sales volume × price − costs

Sales volume inevitably gets everyone's attention. What actions are we going to undertake to move product? What investments are required in sales force, advertising, and production capacity? Sales volume is seen as a controllable outcome of company actions. Recently, the "costs" part of the equation has received the spotlight in many companies as companies like AT&T are "rightsized" and processes are "reengineered" in an attempt to "get the costs out." The attitude is that sales volume and costs can and should be managed vigorously. Pricing, however, is often the third front in the battle for profitability, as the scarce resources of management time, energy, and imagination are siphoned off to the first two fronts of sales volume and costs. The power pricer does not treat price like a third front; rather, he brings it to the fore. The power pricer believes price can be managed as effectively as other profit drivers and recognizes the extraordinary leverage that price offers.

The power pricer does not let "the market" or "the competition" set his price. His viewpoint is that given a customer's wants, his offering and its presentation, along with competitive products and prices, create a value for his product. He coordinates this "value creation" with pricing, his "value extraction" activity, and understands the system relationship among his profit drivers. Price is a key element of his profit system and he does not give up control of it to someone or something else; nor does he see it as less manageable than the other profit drivers.

Fact Files

A power pricer has data that are more *accurate, timely, relevant,* and *disaggregated* than everyday pricers. There is precision in what he does. He understands what is happening now—not just what happened two months ago; he knows a product's value to the customer—not just its cost, and he understands what's happening at the individual account or key market segment level—not just at a broad market aggregate.

Figure 1-2 shows the central role of perceived customer value in pricing. Starting at the top of the diagram, the firm's initial analysis has two components—*competitive analysis* (left) to identify differentiation opportunities, and *consumer analysis* (right) to identify consumer wants and important segmentation of the market. Based on this, decisions are made that create the perceived value of the firm's offering in the marketplace: first the target market is selected, and then the value-creating elements of the marketing mix assembled, i.e., the product itself, communication efforts to support its marketing and distribution to create convenient availability, and other support.

These efforts in concert with the offerings of competitors determine the *value* that a customer perceives in the firm's product. This perceived value is the maximum price the customer will pay. Knowing these values for members of his target market shows the power pricer the trade-off between price and sales volume. These values vary by customer. The power pricer understands this variation and the source of it. This requires data on customers' viewpoints and competitors' performance and pricing.

The dotted line at the bottom of Figure 1-2 shows that the firm's price may impact competitive offerings—either their prices or their value creation activities. The power pricer understands his competitor's cost structure, capabilities, and business model and systematically tracks competitors' actions and reactions. He takes advantage of his experience in the marketplace, carefully observing and generalizing from market activities to develop a deep understanding of how the market works.

FIGURE 1-2

Schematic of Value and Pricing Process

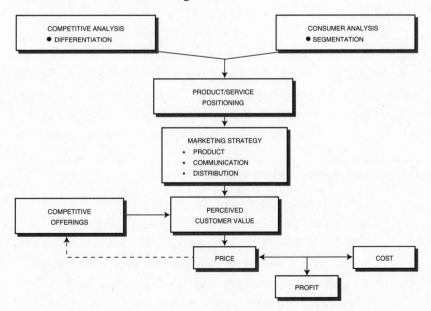

His pricing fact file also has relevant internal data, e.g., production, marketing, and service costs information—reflecting both current levels and trends. Recent work on activity-based costing has shown the criticality of this information. In many cases, understanding the true costs of serving an account results in recognizing that a price increase is warranted.[3] Even if the price increase results in a lost sale, the firm may be better off because the revenue received from the account does not cover the true cost of the activities associated with servicing it.

In short, good pricing decisions require facts about one's own cost of doing business, the consumer's evaluation processes, and competitive activity.

Tools and Scope of Analysis

Building from the fact files, the power pricer undertakes a systematic analysis of customers and competitors to enable him to assess the outcome of alternative pricing scenarios. The first question is what sales level will a price generate? Then follows a consideration of the profitability impact. Tools such as break-even analysis and market simulations are used to assess the advisability of a price increase or decrease. The scope of the analysis extends beyond customer reaction to competitive reaction and the impact of price on industry profitability, not just market share.

The power pricer maps out the likely evolution of the industry and understands how today's pricing actions impact future price levels—understanding, for example, that a low price used to build share today may undermine the future profitability of the industry because price increases will be hard to implement. In short, he defines the price problem right—focusing on long-term profitability, not on short-term market share.

Determination and Implementation

Managing price is not an easy task. The power pricer assembles a team from throughout the organization to do the job. If CEO-level involvement is needed to sell through a price decision to a major customer, the CEO becomes part of the price management team. The fact file is assembled by broad participation of functional people in touch with the right data. Technologists, sales people, market researchers, manufacturing and operations, and financial analysts all typically have data to be brought together in a coordinated way. Pricing right is a priority and the company is determined to get the value to which it is entitled.

Pricing goals are clearly understood and holders of final pricing authority have incentives which are aligned with these goals. The power pricer with a profitability goal, for example, does not delegate pricing authority to a sales force compensated on sales volume.

THE MISTAKES AVOIDED

These characteristics of a power pricer enable him to avoid three common costly pricing errors:

1. A firm focusing on customer value does not make the error of divorcing pricing from the rest of the marketing mix. For the power pricer, value creation through product, communication, and distribution goes hand in hand with value extraction through pricing. Often, a firm identifies itself as having a "pricing problem" when, in fact, the problem is that the necessary value creation foundation was never laid down properly.
2. The fact file at a disaggregate level helps overcome the tendency to too much uniformity in:
   a. prices across customers
   b. prices over time
   c. gross margin percentages across products

The value that customers place on a product can vary tremendously; failing to customize pricing to that situation "leaves a lot of money on the table." Although it is not always easy to implement a pricing schedule to adapt fully to customer-value variation, big profit opportunities are often lost through failing to understand the value variation or being insufficiently insightful about what to do about it. Often, "finding the optimal price" is the wrong way to define the problem. But properly seeing it as "defining the optimal pricing structure" yields big profit opportunities.

While it is generally not a good idea to be changing prices every day, our experience is that prices on average are too sticky, i.e., they have too much inertia. Customer wants and competitive offerings are always changing. Costs are dynamic as well. Price change reviews should be *reg-*

ularly scheduled to review prices in light of such changes to keep the price-value equation from getting seriously unbalanced in either direction.

Finally, uniformity in gross margin percentage across products is common and typically stems from the cost-driven pricing rule, a failure to understand the customer-value side. Understanding value and costs at the appropriately disaggregate level allows more precise and profitable matching of prices and value.

3. The attributes of a power pricer preclude him from not learning about the underlying drivers of the marketplace. The everyday pricer sees things changing all the time in the marketplace and believes history therefore irrelevant. The power pricer's understanding is deeper. He knows that changes in easily observable behavior are manifestations of an underlying, stable reality, and he seeks to grasp the underlying reality and drivers of change. Continual learning is thus a by-product of his participation in the marketplace.

PARAGONS OF PRICING PRACTICE

Throughout the book, we will introduce detailed examples of power pricers at work in each chapter. Here we briefly offer a few examples of power pricing strategies.

Pricing and Marketing Strategy: Swatch

Swatch watch pricing exemplifies the integration of pricing with the overall marketing strategy. Swatch's idea of a low-priced Swiss-made watch to capture part of the low-priced-watch market segment was based on making a watch not as a way to tell time—just about all watches can do that—but as a way to feel and express the "joy of life."

As noted by the head of Swatch's design labs,[4] Swatch's pricing at an unchanging $40 for a basic model was to be "a simple price, a clean price. Price has become a mirror for the other attributes we try to communicate. It helps set us apart from the rest of the world. A Swatch is not just affordable, it's approachable. Buying a Swatch is an easy decision to make, an easy decision to live with." The price message at $40 is different from that at $37.50—or the message if there is a $50 list price but the product is usually found on sale at 20% off. The $40 constant price says, "You can't make a mistake, don't worry, have some fun." The message developed in the watch design and advertising is enhanced by the pricing policy. The pricing message does not fight against the message of the rest of the marketing mix; rather, the implementation of the value extraction activity complements the value creation activity.

The Value Perspective: Glaxo

Glaxo introduced its ulcer medication Zantac after market incumbent Tagamet. The conventional wisdom was that as the "second one in" Glaxo should price 10% below the incumbent. However, Chief Executive Sir Paul Girolami understood that Zantac had superiority over Tagamet in featuring fewer drug interactions and side effects and more convenient dosing. If adequately communicated to the marketplace, this performance superiority provided the basis for a price premium over Tagamet. Thus, Glaxo introduced Zantac at a significant price premium over Tagamet and still gained the market leadership position. In addition, as the product established itself in the market and became more proven, price was increased with the increase in perceived customer value.[5]

Customizing Price and Service Based on Segment Value: Bugs Burger

Bugs Burger Bugs Killer's price was about ten times that of other firms that do battle with rodents on a commercial property. Bugs got his price premium because he focused on a particularly quality-sensitive segment of the market (hotels and restaurants) and gave them what they valued most: guaranteed pest *elimination* rather than control. Recognizing the superior value provided to this chosen segment, he let that guide his pricing. This enabled him to train and compensate service technicians in a way that allowed him to deliver his extermination service. Thus the value provided drove the price, which in turn funded the activities necessary to provide the value.

Customizing Price Based on Segment Cost and Competitive Situation: Progressive Insurance

Progressive Insurance has been hailed as "the prince of smart pricing" by *Fortune* magazine.[6] Progressive wins in the automobile insurance game by collecting and analyzing loss data better than anyone else. Its understanding of costs to serve various types of customers enable it to serve the high-risk customer. These are the best customers for Progressive because no one else wants to insure them due to their poor driving record. Free of competition and armed with a solid understanding of costs, Progressive is quite profitable because it prices recognizing the value it provides to this customer base, a group unserved by others.

Defining the Problem Right: Deutsche Bahn AG

Train riders in Germany were conditioned to paying for each trip based on distance traveled. One simply chose a first-class or second-class cabin and paid the applicable per-kilometer price—which almost always made it more economical to drive if, as many travelers did, one considered only the fuel cost for the trip. Then in 1993 the BahnCard was instituted, which allowed people to pay an up-front fee and then receive a 50% discount on each trip—driving the incremental cost of a train trip below the cost of driving. Now three million BahnCards are sold each year. Understanding the basic issue and then thinking creatively about optimizing the pricing structure—not just the price per km—enabled Deutsche Bahn to increase volume and profit significantly. (This example is developed extensively in chapter 7.)

Determination: A German Multinational

A large division of a DM 20 billion German multinational believed a price increase was both necessary due to cost pressure and justified by the value the firm delivered to the customer. However, its product was a significant item in the cost structure of its customers. Consequently, it feared that key accounts would react quite negatively and might desert the company. The CEO of the company became involved in personally calling on customers to sell the price increase. This helped to sell the increase but also provided a signal to the organization on the effort to be made to obtain prices justified by the value provided.

These exemplars of pricing illustrate just a few of the routes to superior profitability through pricing excellence. This book is designed to map out the path to becoming a power pricer. The remaining three chapters of Part I set down the necessary foundation. Chapter 2, "Price, Costs, and Profit: Economic Underpinnings of Pricing," expands the profit drivers discussion above and establishes the economic framework; Chapter 3, "Price Response Estimation," presents the various methods of estimating customers' response to price—a necessary part of the power pricer's fact file. Chapter 4, "Pricing and Competitive Strategy," balances chapter 3's consideration of the customer by focusing on required competitive analysis. It discusses competitive positioning, competitive reaction, and industry profitability.

Part II is entitled "Breakthrough Pricing Concepts" and contains seven chapters designed to move one from everyday pricing to profit-maximizing power pricing. It presents creative ways to conceptualize and analyze pricing issues.

Chapter 5, "Price Customization," demonstrates the principle and value of customizing prices to customers based on their values. Chapters 6–11 present implementable ways of achieving customization in practice.

Chapter 6, "International Pricing," discusses how to manage price across geographic markets in the face of parallel imports and free information flows.

Chapter 7, "Nonlinear Pricing," establishes the benefits of plans of the type discussed above for the Deutsche Bahn AG in which average price paid depends upon total quantity purchased. The various methods for implementing these plans are presented.

Chapter 8, "Product-Line Pricing," shows how to develop an understanding of the interrelationship among the company's products and price accordingly in pursuit of maximum overall profitability.

Chapter 9, "Price Bundling," shows when and how to construct packages of individual products and price them appropriately.

Chapter 10, "Time Customization of Prices: The Short Term," shows how to customize prices over time through a temporary discount or sale policy.

Chapter 11, "Time Customization of Prices: The Long Term," presents a framework for dealing with saturating of markets and identifying a proactive approach to managing price over the product life cycle.

Part III is "Implementation in the Organization." Chapter 12, "Organizing for Power Pricing," addresses organization and proper location of pricing authority issues for effective pricing, and chapter 13, "Becoming a Power Pricer: Checking Your Pricing IQ," provides a procedure to apply to make a self-assessment of the quality of your pricing thinking. The "Pricing IQ Scorecard" also pinpoints areas to focus improvement programs on.

Throughout, we rely on examples of real firms to capture and exemplify best thinking. Our focus is on those techniques and frameworks which have proven themselves in practice, i.e., techniques power pricers are using today throughout the world to boost their profitability. In some cases, to protect the confidentiality of situations, we use a disguised company or product name, and specific data may be rounded off in a way that retains the substance of the argument. To signal the reader to disguised situations, we use all capital letters for the company or product name in those cases.

2

Price, Costs, and Profit

Economic Underpinnings of Pricing

INTRODUCTION

This chapter shows how price affects profit and describes major price determinants. In principle and in theory the economic underpinnings of price are simple, but in practice they are more subtle, due to the multiple effects of price on profit.

It is obvious that price directly affects the unit profit margin. A higher price yields a higher margin per unit sold, and thus a higher profit for a given sales volume. However, a higher price typically implies a lower sales volume, thus producing an offsetting impact on profit. Price may also impact cost: e.g., a higher sales volume resulting from a lower price may induce a decrease in unit costs due to economies of scale or learning. Or a lower price may attract new buyers who remain loyal in the future, and thus increase future profits. These issues will be addressed in subsequent chapters. Here we focus on the more direct and current influences of price on profit.

Figure 2-1 shows the profit system in a simple hierarchical form. Scanning downward, at the first level profit drivers are sales revenue and costs. The sales revenue is, in turn, price times sales volume. Costs have variable and fixed components. Variable costs change with the

FIGURE 2-1

The Drivers of Profit

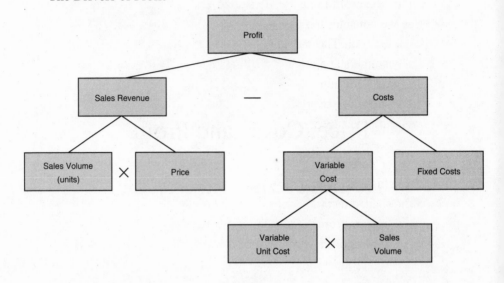

sales volume but fixed costs do not. The cost of an additional unit is referred to as marginal cost.

WHAT THIS CHAPTER WILL DO

This chapter addresses the following questions:

1. How do price changes affect profit?
2. How do customers respond to price changes?
3. Which factors affect the price decision and how?
4. How can conflicting objectives like profit and volume be reconciled when making pricing decisions?
5. What is the role of variable and fixed costs in pricing?

Knowing the answers to these questions will help the manager to:

1. fully understand and correctly judge the effects of price
2. consider the right factors in making price decisions
3. base price decisions on the customers' perceived value rather than on cost
4. deal with practical conflicts in pricing

THE IMPACT OF PRICE CHANGES

To illustrate the profit impact of a specific price and possible changes in that price we consider the case of a product we call POWERSTAR, an electric power tool. The manufacturer sells the product directly to professional customers at a price of $100. The worldwide annual sales volume is around 1 million units. The variable unit cost or marginal cost of the product is $60, so that the unit contribution—the difference between price and variable unit cost—is $40. Thus, each unit sold contributes $40 to the recovery of fixed costs and to profit.

The upper part of Figure 2-2 illustrates this situation, in which the company achieves a sales revenue of $100 million ($100 times 1 million units). The shaded rectangle represents the total contribution of $40 million, which results from 1 million units each of which contributes $40. The total contribution can always be represented as a rectangle since it is obtained as the product of unit contribution and sales volume.

The fixed costs such as plant and administration for POWERSTAR are estimated at $30 million; subtracting this from the total contribution of $40 million yields a profit of $10 million or 10% of the sales revenue. Alternatively, the profit can be calculated by taking the total costs of $90 million ($60 million variable costs plus $30 million fixed costs) and subtracting them from the sales revenue of $100 million. Total costs per unit are $90 and the unit profit margin (to be distinguished from the unit contribution) is $10. The return on sales of 10% is a relatively typical magnitude for industrial products of this kind.

POWERSTAR management questioned whether the current $100 price yielded the highest possible profit and suggested considering alternative prices in the range of plus or minus 20% from the current price. As a first step, management wanted to know the sales volume required to maintain the $10 million profit with alternative prices.

We first consider a 20% price cut alternative. An $80 price and unchanged variable unit costs of $60 reduce the unit contribution from $40 to $20. Thus, POWERSTAR now has to sell twice as many units as at a price of $100 to achieve the same total contribution and profit. With 2 million units sold at $80, sales revenue would increase to $160 million. We show the $80 price scenario in the middle of Figure 2-2. Since the profit contribution is unchanged, the surface of the shaded rectangle is

FIGURE 2-2

The Effect of Price on POWERSTAR's Profit

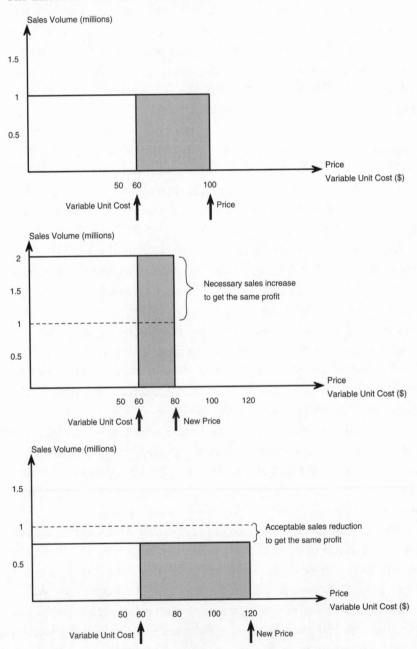

the same as in the upper part of Figure 2-2. While the price reduction is only 20%, the reduction in unit contribution is 50%. The sales increase required to compensate for this smaller margin accordingly is 100%. Such a 100% increase in sales volume due to a 20% price change was seen as unrealistic to management. In addition capacity was insufficient to manufacture the higher volume. A capacity expansion would have induced higher fixed costs.

The 20% price-increase scenario is summarized at the bottom of Figure 2-2. Unit contribution increases to $60, thereby requiring only 667,000 units to be sold to generate $10 million profit, a 33.3% decrease in volume. If sales decline by less than 33.3%, the price increase would drive profit up. For example, if 750,000 units were sold at $120, profit would increase from $10 million to $15 million. Thus POWERSTAR management judged the price-increase scenario worthy of more investigation.

As we see, price decreases and increases have highly leveraged effects. A seemingly small price reduction can have a large negative impact on unit contribution, requiring a tremendous increase in sales volume to generate the same profit. A small-percentage price increase can have a strong positive effect on unit contribution, creating a large acceptable decrease in sales volume while still retaining the profit level.

The POWERSTAR case is somewhat typical for industrial products where variable costs often amount to 50% or more of price and are high relative to fixed costs. Such service industries as hotels, airlines, and telecommunications, in contrast, typically have relatively low variable but high fixed costs. Similar cost structures characterize industries such as software and pharmaceuticals, where R&D accounts for the bulk of costs and unit variable costs tend to be very low.

Cost structure has a strong impact on the price-profit relationship. For example consider SUPRACOM, a new entrant in the telecom market in a European country. It runs its own network in its domestic market but has to buy capacity from third parties for its international services. Its variable cost for domestic traffic is 5 cents per minute; for international traffic, SUPRACOM has to pay 40 cents per minute to its foreign suppliers.

SUPRACOM's price per minute is 40 cents for domestic and 60 cents for international traffic, yielding per-minute contributions of 35 cents for domestic and 20 cents for international service. To cope with increasing competitive pressures the company was considering price cuts of 10 cents a minute for both services. What increases in sales volume would be required in each service to leave its profit unchanged? Per the analysis above, the required sales volume increases for international and domestic service are 100% and 40% respectively.

The 10-cent price cut requires a much stronger sales increase for international service because the international-unit contribution is cut to half while the domestic-unit contribution declines only by 28.5%. In general, a much greater increase in sales volume is required to offset the negative effect of a price cut if variable costs are high.

In judging price decrease advisability, one must consider available capacity. In 1994 Lufthansa offered flights on domestic routes at DM 99 ($66). In spite of severe availability restrictions, demand exploded; allotted capacities were sold out for up to five months. In light of the limited available capacity, the new price was too low and profit opportunities were lost. We suspect that this often happens in the airline and similar service businesses when prices are cut by 50% or more. The volume increase required to compensate for the reduction in unit contribution may well exceed the available capacities.

Figure 2-3 puts the considerations on price and sales volume changes into a more general perspective. The horizontal axis depicts variable unit cost as a percentage of current price. The vertical axis shows the required increase in sales volume (upward) and the acceptable decrease in sales volume (downward) to return the same profit. We consider price increases and decreases of 10% and of 20%.

We first consider the price-decrease curves, seen in the upper part of the figure. The 20% price-cut curve shows that, with a variable unit cost of 60%, such a cut requires a 100% increase in sales volume (point A). This corresponds to the POWERSTAR case. If the price cut is only 10% the required sales increase shrinks to 33% (point B). This comparison reveals how strongly profit will react to price changes if variable unit cost is relatively high. The curves get steeper the higher the variable unit cost is. For variable unit cost of 80% of current price, a volume increase of 100% is required to offset a price reduction of only 10% (point C).

In contrast, the 10% and 20% price-increase curves, seen in the lower part of Figure 2-3, are much flatter and closer together. This shows that the acceptable decreases in sales volume react less sensitively to variations in variable unit cost and price.

FIGURE 2-3

Increases and Decreases in Sales to Return Same Profit

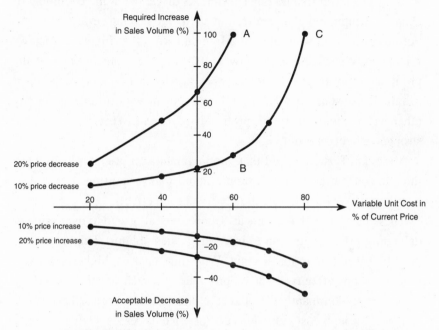

To be read as follows: With variable units cost of 60% a 20% price decrease requires a 100% volume increase (Point A); a 10% price decrease requires only a 33% volume increase (Point B).

Figure 2-3, which can easily be expanded to include price changes of other magnitudes, can be used as a simple decision-support tool for considering price changes. While it says nothing about customers' "reactions" to price changes it identifies what those changes must be to maintain profit. In our experience, exhibits of this type can have a strong impact on managers, particularly those considering a price cut. The curves make the implications of a price change transparent and point to volume effects which may not be likely to materialize in reality.

Break-even analysis is another simple way to look at the interaction of price, costs, and profit. Break-even analysis determines for a given price the sales volume at which profit becomes zero or, in other words, where total contribution equals fixed costs. It shows how sensitively the break-even volume reacts to price changes. However, because it only tells the manager which combination of price and volume is required to break even and does not address which high price yields the highest profit, its utility is limited.

COMPARISON OF PROFIT DRIVERS

Price drives profit like no other factor. As discussed at the beginning of chapter 1, improved price realization has a high leverage effect on profit. Following an idea suggested by Marn and Rosiello,[1] Figure 2-4 shows for the POWERSTAR case how a 10% improvement in each of the profit drivers of Figure 2-1 impacts profit. All other factors are assumed to remain constant. A 10% price improvement with no change in any other value yields a 100% profit improvement. This is by far the strongest effect on profit.

Marn and Rosiello[2] hold that "improvements in price typically have three to four times the effect on profitability as proportionate increases in volume." We have frequently observed such effects.

These data show that efforts are often better allocated to increasing or defending price levels than to increasing sales volume. This is particularly true if unit margins are thin. With thin margins, higher sales volume does not effectively drive profit up. In such a situation efforts should be predominantly directed at improving the margins. This can be achieved through cost reductions and/or price increases.

FIGURE 2-4

Comparison of Profit Drivers

A 10% Improvement in...   ... Leads to a Profit Increase of...

	Profit Driver		Profit			
	Old	New	Old	New		
Price	$100	$110	$10m	$20m		100%
Variable Unit Cost	$60	$54	$10m	$16m		60%
Sales Volume	$1m	$1.1m	$10m	$14m		40%
Fixed Costs	$30m	$27m	$10m	$13m		30%

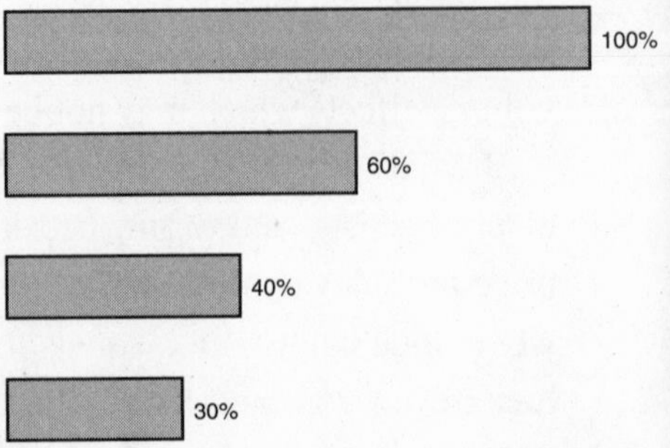

To be read as follows: A 10% improvement in price brings price up to $110; with everything else unchanged; this increases profit by 100% to $20 million.

A price increase typically does depress sales volume somewhat—but this does not always happen. For example, a leading agrochemical company had adjusted its prices downward to competitive levels. Later, unhappy with the resulting thin margins, the firm gave consideration to possible price increases; this led to a thorough value analysis, which showed that farmers valued the firm's insecticide at 20% more than competitive levels. The analysis proved correct as a 20% price increase was implemented with no sales volume decline—yielding a fivefold profit increase! In another case an office-products company eliminated some of its discounts, effectively increasing its prices by 5%. The profit level doubled, as the sales volume change was minimal.

PRICE AND THE CUSTOMER

Price is the economic sacrifice a customer makes to acquire a product or a service. The customer always compares this sacrifice with his perception of the product's value. Price and value are the cornerstones of every economic transaction.

In essence, a customer buys a product or service only if its perceived value—measured in money terms—is greater than the price. If selecting from several alternatives, the customer prefers the one offering the highest net value, i.e., the greatest differential of perceived value over price. These simple considerations of price and value help us to understand how the customer reacts to a specific price and to price changes.

Figure 2-5 illustrates the situation for an individual consumer. We assume his perceived value and his willingness to pay for one can of a soft drink is $1, shown as his "maximum price."

If the price is less than $1, the sales volume to this consumer is 1; if the price is higher than $1, the sales volume is 0. All pricing situations essentially reduce to this simple model—the "atomic building stone" of pricing. It can incorporate various situations. For a second can of the soft drink, the maximum price at the same time will probably be lower than $1. The maximum price may vary over time or across individuals. Such variations lead us to the issues of dynamic pricing, market segmentation, and price customization. They suggest that different prices should be asked at different times or from individual customers who differ in their maximum prices.

FIGURE 2-5

The "Atomic Building Stone" of Pricing

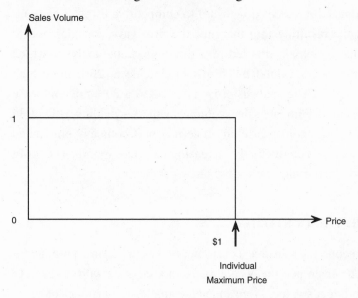

It is useful to distinguish two situations: "yes:no" and "variable quantity." In the "yes:no" situation, depending on the price the customer buys one unit of the good or none at all. "Yes:no" describes situations like the purchase of a video cassette recorder, a personal computer, a mobile phone, or a car. If the consumer has one unit, he does not need another. In contrast, in the "variable quantity" case depending on the price, the customer may buy one or several units. This describes purchases of goods like minutes of use of a mobile phone, variety-driven items like ties, and consumables like soft drinks. Usually, successive units of a good have decreasing incremental value for a customer.

A firm considering pricing should understand the behavior that best describes its customers. But there is an important similarity in the two situations when the firm considers the overall response to a price in that customers typically differ from one to another in their willingness to pay. This leads us to an overall market response curve relating price to quantity sold, which shows a negative slope—the higher the price quoted to the market, the smaller the total sales volume. We call this relationship the price response curve. The price response curve for POWERSTAR, an electric power tool, is shown in Figure 2-6. The methods to actually deter-

FIGURE 2-6

Price Response Curve—The Case of POWERSTAR (Electric Power Tool)

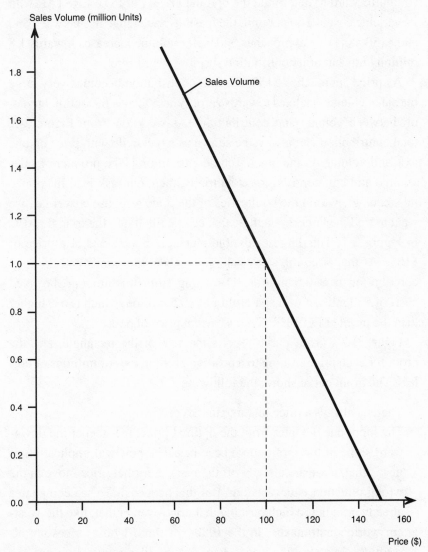

mine this curve are the subject of chapter 3. In the case of POWERSTAR the curve was determined by a market study which revealed that a price increase of 10% would lead to a sales volume reduction of about 20%. The relationship was essentially linear. For example, at a price of $80, 1.4 million units would be sold, about 40% more than the current volume.

THE OPTIMAL PRICE

Once we know the price response curve, as shown in Figure 2-6, it is straightforward to determine the optimal price. For POWERSTAR with its variable cost of $60 per unit, the feasible price range lies between $60 and $150. As price approaches $60, sales volume increases towards 1.8 million units but unit contribution shrinks toward zero.

As price approaches $150, the unit contribution becomes very large but sales volume declines towards zero. Where then is the optimal trade-off between volume and contribution? As we know from Figure 2-2, total contribution can always be shown as a rectangle with price on one axis and volume on the other. Total contribution is the product of sales volume and unit contribution. Pictorially, then, our task is to maximize this rectangle within the boundaries of the price response curve; i.e., we want to find the largest rectangle that can be fitted into the triangle ABC in Figure 2-7. This largest possible rectangle is obtained at a price of $105.[3] At this price the sales volume is 0.9 million units and the total contribution is $40.5 million. Deducting from this amount the fixed costs of $30 million we get a profit of $10.5 million, which is 5% higher than the profit at POWERSTAR's current price of $100.

Figure 2-7's profit curve reports the size of the rectangle, i.e., the profit for each price leading to a positive profit in tens of millions of dollars. The profit curve shows the following.

- There is always a price that maximizes profit.
- The more one deviates from the optimal price, the steeper the downward slope of the profit curve becomes. The practical implication of this is that, if we are already off the mark, a further price move in the wrong direction is devastating. But this happens! We see companies already pricing too high pushing that price even higher, like the Western world's automakers in the 1980s, or those whose prices are already too low slashing prices even further, like a typical airline in a price war.
- A price which is too high (e.g., $120 for POWERSTAR) is as bad as a price which is too low (e.g., a price of $90). Often managers delude themselves by thinking that if you are wrong, it does not hurt too much as long as you are wrong on the high side. This is a misperception.

Note that fixed costs have *not* played a role in our discussion of the optimal price. Figure 2-7 makes clear why this is the case. Fixed costs are simply deducted from the total contribution. If we drew them into the figure they would represent a horizontal line at $30 million; they would be equal for all prices considered, and therefore have no influence on the optimal price. Fixed costs at $20 million instead of $30 million

FIGURE 2-7

The Optimal Price for POWERSTAR (Electric Power Tool)

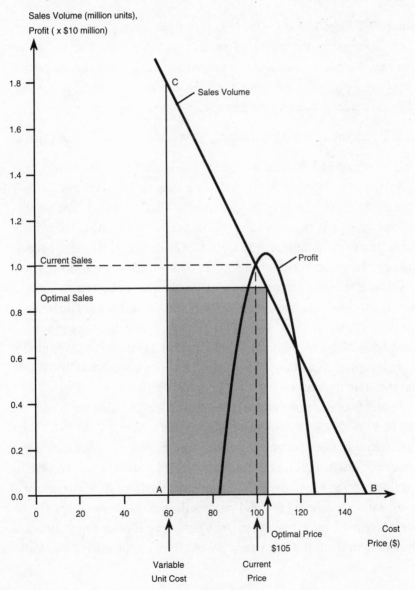

would not influence the shape of the profit curve and the optimal price would remain the same; however, the level of profit would shift upward by $10 million.

The same can be said of any sunk costs, such as for R&D expenditures or market introduction. They should not influence the optimal price.

PRICE ELASTICITY

Figure 2-7 helps introduce the concept of price elasticity, an extremely useful measure of the impact of price changes on sales volume. As we just saw, the response of sales volume to price is a major determinant of the optimal price. Price elasticity is defined as the ratio of the percentage change in sales volume to the percentage change in price, i.e.,

Price Elasticity = % Change in Sales Volume ÷ % Change in Price

In the POWERSTAR case depicted in Figure 2-7, at the current price of $100 a price increase of 10% causes a sales volume decrease of 20%. Hence, the price elasticity in this case is –2(–20%/10%). The relative volume change is twice as large as the relative price change. Formally, according to the definition, price elasticity has a negative sign, because volume change and price change go in opposite directions. However, in business discussions, the opposite movement of price and quantity is well understood and managers may simply talk of the absolute value of the price elasticity. The values of the price elasticity vary strongly across products, competitive situations, and individual customers; we provide more information on this in chapter 3. The price elasticity is also different at different points on the price response curve.

In practice, if a price elasticity less than 1 is found, a price increase can immediately be recommended, since this means that the percentage of decrease in sales volume is smaller than the percentage of increase in price. For instance, if a price increase of 10% reduces sales volume by only 5% (price elasticity = 0.5), implementing the 10% increase will boost sales revenue by 5% and profit will increase even more. The reverse is true for price reductions; they never pay if price elasticity is less than 1, as in the following case: "After Miller cut its price 20%, Miller

High Life sales jumped 9%."[4] Despite the unit sales increase, sales revenue would be 12.8% lower after the price cut, since .80 (price) x 109 (volume) = 87.2, which is 12.8% less than 100.

A SPECIAL CASE: OPTIMIZATION WITH PRICE THRESHOLDS

In the preceding analysis, we have explicitly considered the price response curve with a smooth trade-off between price and volume. In practice we sometimes encounter a pricing requirement for a "yes:no" situation for an individual customer. If the price is lower than this customer's maximum willingness to pay or what we call his maximum price, he will buy one unit of the product. If the price is higher, he will not buy. The price response curve, as shown in Figure 2-5, consists of two horizontal sections. Obviously the price that yields the highest profit—where the marginal cost is lower than the customer's maximum price—is exactly the maximum price. Any price below this figure would mean a profit sacrifice.

If customers were all the same with regard to their maximum prices, we could apply this thinking to the whole market. The aggregate price response curve then has the same structure as the individual response curve. In this case, price response is measured by one single parameter, the maximum price, instead of a whole curve. As long as cost is below this maximum price, that is exactly the price we would like to charge. Figure 2-8 illustrates this situation.

For some products the assumption of homogeneous maximum prices may not be too far off the mark. Lingua Video, a company which sells foreign-language videos, sets its prices along these lines. Its managing director explains, "We assume that our customers have maximum prices which they are willing to pay. We estimate that these prices are typically defined by round figures like DM 50, DM 60, or DM 100 depending on the perceived value of the film. To be on the safe side, we typically set our prices just below these round figures." In Lingua Video's catalogue almost all prices end with a 9: DM 49, DM 59, or DM 99.

Maximum price-oriented price setting offers an explanation for the prevalence of "odd prices" that are just below a round figure. If the assumption on homogeneity of maximum prices is close enough to real-

FIGURE 2-8

Price Optimization with Price Thresholds

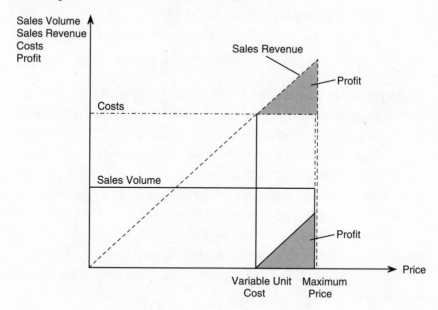

ity it is a simple and reasonable method for setting prices. One should, however, make sure that this critical assumption holds; this can be done only through understanding each individual's price thresholds.

PROFIT, VOLUME, OR BOTH?

To this point, we have generally assumed that the firm was trying to maximize profit. Indeed, empirical studies have shown this to be the most common goal. But there are also theories that suggest other goals, such as sales maximization, and Japanese companies are said to often strive for market-share rather than direct-profit goals.[5]

In fact complex and often unclear systems of goals are not unusual. A prevalent conflict is between profit and volume goals. Most practitioners love to have higher prices but they hate to lose volume or market share. For example, we once advised a pharmaceutical company to increase its prices and accept market share loss in a small European country where it had low prices. Increasing prices would prevent unwanted shipment from the low-cost country (parallel imports) into the large German market, where its prices were higher. While accepting that this would lead to higher company profits, the management was very reluctant to give up the market-share points in the smaller market.

Many firms have explicit volume or market-share goals. In the auto industry, for example, marketing plans usually prescribe a certain number of cars to be sold. In the computer industry plant capacity is set according to volume goals, and capacity utilization thresholds exist. In service industries occupancy rates are a critical indicator of success. Given these industry and company norms, profit is hardly ever the only goal being pursued in pricing decisions. A mixture of profit and volume goals is more typical for business practice.

Managers usually don't like to trade off volume and profit. They want both an increase in profit *and* an increase in volume. But what Hudson[6] writes on Escom, then No. 3 in the European PC market, applies to most companies: "Escom has proven a basic business law: You can increase market share or you can increase profit, but it's tough to do both at the same time." It is, however, not impossible!

Juergen Walker, Senior Vice Presiden, Business Management and Controlling, at Mercedes-Benz Passenger Cars, suggested to us a diagram to capture this situation. The diagram, as shown in Figure 2-9, has profit growth on the vertical axis and volume growth on the horizontal axis. The intersection of the two coordinates describes the status quo. The upper right quadrant (Quadrant I) denotes the "manager's dream" where both profit and volume increase. In Quadrant II profit increases but volume decreases, and the reverse is true for Quadrant IV; a trade-off between profit and volume growth has to be made in these two quadrants. Quadrant III, the "manager's nightmare," can be avoided. However, few managers seem to appreciate how difficult it is to move into Quadrant I from the origin. Simultaneous pursuit of volume and profit growth may be a good guide for product development. But for price actions it can be unrealistic and frustrating. Figure 2-10, the "Pricing Goal Matrix," is helpful in setting realistic pricing goals.

Figure 2-10 now relates these quadrants to specific price situations. The curves in the four quadrants show the situation underlying the growth and profit possibilities. Quadrant I can indeed happen only if one undertakes a price cut *and* the current price is higher than the optimal

FIGURE 2-9

Profit Growth, Volume Growth, or Both?

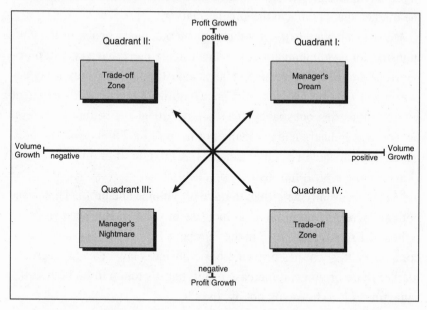

price. That is, to fall into Quadrant I, a particular kind of mistake must have been made in the past.

Eurodisney, the theme park near Paris, fits this description. In the early 1990s the park started with high prices, which were not well accepted by European consumers. The number of visitors and hotel occupancy remained low for the first three years and very high losses were incurred, bringing the company to the verge of bankruptcy. The *Wall Street Journal Europe* commented that Eurodisney "didn't get the pricing structure right" and that "prices were often criticized as being too high." In early 1994 prices were reduced by about 30% and, according to the article, Eurodisney "now does represent good value for money."[7] The price repositioning indeed worked; attendance at the park increased strongly, and in late 1995 Eurodisney announced that it had become profitable.[8] Another example is Fielmann, the German market leader in eyeglasses and No. 2 in the world, whose price cutting boosted its market share to over 30% in Germany and increased its profitability at the same time.

Quadrant I is also the domain of Intel and its chief executive officer, Andrew Grove. *Fortune* magazine[9] described their strategy in 1994:

"Pushing down prices faster is also part of Grove's master plan. He argues that what Intel gives up in profit margins it can more than make up in volume."

However, Quadrants II and IV are more typical in practice; i.e., either profit increases or volume increases, but not both. In Quadrant II the current price is below the optimum. Thus an increase of the price brings profit up, but volume down. A maker of industrial paint experienced this situation when they initiated a price increase. Some customers who were only willing to buy at very low prices switched to other suppliers. Volume went down by about 20% but profit went up. A loss of $8 million in revenues entailed a profit improvement of $14 million due to better unit contribution margins. Many managers, however, have serious difficulties with this situation because it suggests a weakening of their market position. They are fixated on volume or market-share goals and neglect the

FIGURE 2-10

Price, Profit Growth, and Volume Growth: The Pricing Goal Matrix

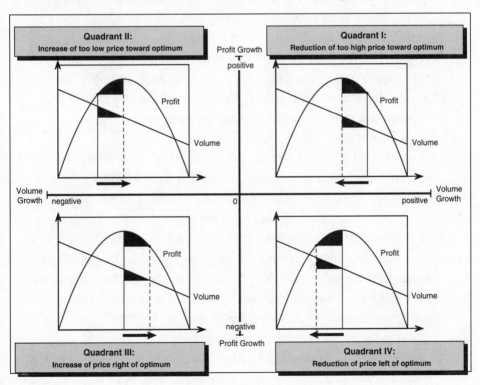

profit implications. But sometimes it is reasonable to raise prices and sacrifice volume in order to increase profit.

In Quadrant IV we encounter the opposite situation. If a price which
is at or below the optimum is reduced, sales volume increases but profits
decline. This situation is typical when market share is to be built or defended. A typical case is the price cut of Philip Morris for its Marlboro
brand in the American market in April 1993. (This situation is discussed
in detail in chapter 4.) After Marlboro had experienced a major decline
in market share due to an increasing price premium over private label
cigarettes and resulting share losses to them, Philip Morris cut the price
per pack from $2.25 to $1.85, causing a same-day stock-market value
decline of $13 billion. But in the aftermath Marlboro's share recovered
and the brand again strengthened its leadership position.

A similar move occurred a decade earlier in the German cigarette
market. In January 1983, Reemtsma Cigarettenfabriken cut the price of
its West brand from DM 3.80 to DM 3.30, the first such move for a
branded product in the West German cigarette market since World War
II. Within four months West's market share rocketed from 0.6% to 10%,
corresponding to an annual sales revenue increase from DM 150 million to DM 2.2 billion.[10]

As can be seen from the profit curve in Quadrant IV, the situation can
become quite dangerous if the price reductions lead to further and further deviations from the optimum. Due to shrinking unit contributions,
the downward slope of the profit curve steepens rapidly with increasing
distance from the optimum.

Quadrant III is the "nightmare situation" where both profit and volume shrink because a price that is already too high is further increased.
This has happened to quite a few German machinery companies. Their
prices were already too high and not competitive. When several currencies such as the U.S. dollar and the Italian lira were devaluated in 1993,
the German products became even more expensive to customers who
operate in these currencies. Sales volumes of the machines declined,
sometimes by as much as 50%, and several of the companies went into
bankruptcy. Again it should be observed that the downward slope of the
profit curve can become very steep if prices are much too high.

Figure 2-10, the Pricing Goal Matrix, has proved to be a valuable tool
for the analysis of a firm's pricing situation in relation to its profit and

volume goals. To make the right price move, we must know where the price currently stands and how sales respond to price changes. Depending on whether the current price is above, close to, or below the optimum, different actions are indicated. It may be that both a profit and a volume increase are possible. But usually the two goals are in conflict and pursuit of growth in both through price actions can be foolhardy. The matrix can help us to make a conscious and informed trade-off between the objectives of volume growth and profit growth.

ADDITIONAL COST CONSIDERATIONS

We have already seen that variable costs play a crucial role in shaping the optimal price. However, one must be careful not to let availability of cost data overwhelm more subjective customer value judgments.

Cost-Plus Pricing

In practice, one of the most popular price setting methods is "cost-plus pricing," wherein unit costs are determined and a mark-up is applied to yield price. Markups can be based on industry tradition, individual experiences, or rules of thumb. The following quotes reflect this kind of pricing behavior: "Products must be sold for about two and a half times what they cost to make," from an electronics journal, and "In a restaurant, food is marked up three times direct cost, beer four times, and liquor six times."[11] Wied-Nebbeling[12] found that about 70% of the firms in her survey apply some version of cost-plus pricing.

This method has several practical advantages. It is simple and easy to apply. It is based on hard cost data and seemingly copes with market uncertainty. In some instances, financial and accounting people, who are often involved in pricing decisions, prefer to think in cost-plus terms and are more likely to accept a price recommendation substantiated this way than to be guided by "soft" market response data. Under competitive aspects, cost-plus pricing can amount to a silent collusion and optimal pricing behavior if competitors have similar cost structures and apply the same markups.

On the other hand, there are strong arguments against this kind of pricing. It is foolish not to explicitly consider the demand side in setting prices. The customer's willingness to pay is not determined by the costs of a product but by its performance and resulting value to this customer. If cost-plus pricing is based on full costs—as is often the case in practice—the fixed costs determine price, which is logically wrong as we have seen in connection with Figure 2-7. The fixed costs affect neither the shape of the profit curve nor the location of the optimal price; therefore they must not be considered in setting this price. This fundamental principle is ignored in full cost-plus pricing. The method has the fatal flaw that a reduction in sales leads to higher prices—because the fixed costs have to be distributed over fewer units, so that the fixed costs per unit increase.

In spite of its popularity in practice, cost-plus pricing is not an acceptable method for the power pricer as it ignores the central factor of the customer's perceived value.

Cost-Based Price Floors

While costs alone are not sufficient to set optimal prices, they can be useful in determining lower price limits, i.e., price floors below which a product should not be sold. It is useful to distinguish between long-term and short-term price floors. In the long term, the price must obviously cover the full unit costs of a product. Otherwise the seller cannot make a profit and will not survive. Therefore, the long-term price floor is determined by the total (fixed plus variable) unit costs. A higher sales volume, however achieved, leads to lower fixed costs per unit sold, and thus reduces the long-term price floor. This is often what is meant when people talk of economies of scale in connection with pricing. Fixed costs do not influence the optimal price but they do determine the long-term price floor.

In the short term, a product can be sold if its price exceeds the variable unit cost, thereby providing a positive contribution to the fixed costs.

The case of a hotel lends itself to an illustration of the difference between long-term and short-term price floors. At an average occupancy rate of 60% the full costs per room in this hotel are $110. Therefore the long-term price floor for the (average) price is $110. Only if an average price greater than $110 per night is realized will the hotel be profitable at the assumed occupancy. The variable or marginal cost per room per night is approximately $20 (cleaning, sheeting, administration, etc.). The short-term price floor is $20. Each customer who pays more than $20 per night contributes positively to profit. Therefore, this hotel rents rooms on weekends for $80, which is a reasonable policy even though an average price of $80 would drive it out of business.

If there are capacity bottlenecks and existing capacity can be employed for a different business, the opportunity costs determine the price floor. Opportunity costs are profits which are forgone if capacity is used for one business and not another. If our hotel has an agreement with a travel agent who can fill the hotel to capacity by sending in additional guests on short notice at $50, the short-term price floor for "walk-in" business changes from $20 to $50. If the hotel accepted a guest at $25 in this situation it would forgo a profit contribution of $25 ($50 − $25).

The discussion on price floors can be summarized as follows:

- long-term price floor   full unit cost
- short-term price floor
  - with uniform price   variable unit cost
  - with differentiated price   marginal cost
  - with limited capacity   opportunity cost

Fixed Costs and Price

We have argued that fixed costs normally do not affect the optimal price. If, however, the price decision ultimately involves a shift in the fixed costs (which in reality makes them by definition "variable") they have to be included in the price considerations and they can influence the optimal price after all.

We again use the case of POWERSTAR for an illustration. In Figure 2-7 we have seen that the optimal price in the current situation is $105 and the optimal sales volume is 900,000 units, generating a profit of $10.5 million. The company is considering an investment in new manufacturing facilities, which would involve a higher degree of automation and an elimination of costly labor. Variable unit cost would decline by one third, from $60 to $40, while fixed costs would increase by 60%, from $30 million to $48 million. We can employ the reasoning of Figure 2-7 (and Note 3) to determine the new optimal price at $95. The reduction in variable unit cost of $20 ($60 minus $40) is translated into a price reduction of $10 compared to the current optimum. At a price of $95 and a variable unit cost of $40, POWERSTAR achieves a unit contribution of $55 and sells 1.1 million units, yielding a total contribution of $60.5 million ($55 × 1.1 million). Deducting the increased fixed cost of $48 million, a profit of $12.5 million is obtained. This profit is 19% higher than the currently optimal profit of $10.5 million. Therefore, profit maximization suggests making the plant investment and reducing the price to $95. In the context of the Pricing Goal Matrix of Figure 2-10 we are in Quadrant I, where both volume and profit can be increased. The decision is, however, not confined to a price change but requires a major manufacturing investment. The new situation involves further aspects of risk and price competitiveness.

The case illustrates that variable and fixed costs can hardly be seen in isolation. Lower variable costs are often associated with higher fixed costs (and vice versa). While this does not affect the principle that fixed costs should not influence the optimal price in a given situation, the example shows that more comprehensive pricing considerations are necessary when new investments are involved. Similar considerations have to be applied to new product development while the R&D costs have not yet been committed but still depend on the decision to be made.

SUMMARY

In this chapter we have looked at the fundamental economics of price and cost and their impact on profit. Price, cost, and volume are the profit drivers. In summary:

- Price and price changes have a very strong impact on profit. In order to neutralize the profit effect of a price change, the percentage change in unit contribution must be offset by an according percentage change in volume. A 20% price cut may mean a 50% reduction of the unit contribution, which would then require a 100% volume increase to keep profit constant.
- The structure of variable and fixed costs has a very strong influence on the profit impact of a price change. The higher the variable unit cost (or marginal cost) is relative to the price, the stronger is the profit impact of a price change.

- Under the assumption that all other variables remain unchanged, and for a typical industrial cost structure, price changes have a stronger effect on profit than changes in the other profit drivers.
- A customer's willingness to pay for a product is essentially determined by his needs and financial situation on the one hand and his perception of the product's value on the other hand.
- It is useful to distinguish between a "yes:no" and a "variable quantity" demand situation. However, in each case an individual price response can be measured and added across customers to yield an aggregate response curve with a negative slope. Price elasticity is a convenient measure of sensitivity of demand to price and is defined as the ratio of the percentage change in sales volume to the percentage change in price.
- In order to determine the price which yields the highest profit, both the price response and the costs must be known.
- In pricing decisions, both profit and volume objectives may have to be taken into account. If the pricer knows price response and cost curves, he can make a conscious trade-off between these two often incompatible goals.
- While popular in practice, cost-plus pricing is hardly an acceptable method for the power pricer, since it does not satisfactorily consider the demand effects of price.
- Costs can be used to determine long- and short-term price floors. The long-term price floor is defined by total unit costs, while the short-term price floor is equal to variable unit, marginal, or opportunity costs.
- All costs that depend on a pricing decision have to be included in this decision. All costs that do not depend on it have to be excluded. Thus, fixed costs do not influence the optimal price.

Power pricing starts with a better understanding of the economic underpinnings of cost and value. In this chapter we have tried to lay out a practice-oriented foundation of the relevant concepts, which we shall pursue further and investigate more deeply in the following chapters.

3

Price Response Estimation

INTRODUCTION

The information requirements for pricing decisions can be quite extensive. For example, a leading agrochemical company planned to sell a new insecticide, NETEX, to different market segments of farmers in different countries. The NETEX pricing process had started, as usual, with the accountant's cost estimates. Soon it became apparent that the various parties involved—accounting and finance, product management, sales and top management—had conflicting views on the proper price.

Highly influential accountants and finance people argued for the cost-plus and unit margin approach and preferred a "healthy" margin. Their separation from their customers made them uncomfortable with the "soft" information marketing provided. Product management, on the other hand, favored a low price to achieve quick market penetration and high sales volume. Sales management supported this position, seeing a high price as an obstacle to concluding deals. "Value is difficult to communicate," the sales manager said. Top management tended towards a slight premium over competition consistent with the general price position of the company's product line.

NETEX had several applications with different requirements, customer characteristics, and competitive alternatives. This complicated the situation, as it seemed that each proponent could cite some anecdotal evidence to support his or her position. The debate raised more questions than answers. How important is price to farmers and dealers, relative to such product and service attributes as efficacy, spectrum, safety, delivery, and information? How does NETEX's performance compare with that of competitive products on these attributes? How do market segments of farmers differ in purchasing volume, attribute importance ratings, perceptions, short lists of approved suppliers, preferences, and price elasticities? What is the structure of the market and where are competitors positioned? These all seemed to be important questions on which the company was insufficiently informed.

Consequently, a comprehensive study was undertaken to consider the issues summarized in Figure 3-1. Primary data were collected through personal interviews with farmers and dealers in several countries.

The new information, along with analytical tools to summarize the data in an insightful way, put the pricing discussion on a rational, fact-based plane. While not every member of the team accepted every finding, the analysis provided a common base for further discussion. The study increased the time to arrive at the price decision, but it decreased the overall time to implementation. In this sense, management time was more efficiently allocated.

The price structure turned out to be complex, with a set of highly differentiated price schemes. For example, for one major application the perceived value of NETEX was above that which customers ascribed to competitors. This favored a premium price for NETEX. However, NETEX was also sold to a broad market where such a price premium was not justified.

Consequently the company developed a slightly modified version, optimized around the high-value segment's needs, called NETEX-FORTE, to sell at a higher markup in the segment. In certain developing countries NETEX's perceived value was relatively low, mostly because farmers there did not appreciate the product's superior safety and environmental characteristics. The company did not introduce the product in those countries because the price attainable there could, via reimports, jeopardize the price in other, more important markets. In another field NETEX had to be used with a second, much cheaper product. By combining this agent with NETEX to become NETEX-Combi, the company saved farmers an additional spraying and raised the product's perceived

FIGURE 3-1

Framework for Pricing Information in the NETEX Case

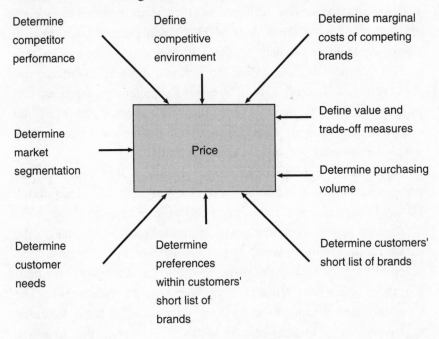

value. The company could set a lucrative price for the combination. The study also influenced the overall price structure. The company found that light users were much less price sensitive than heavy users, so it offered significant quantity rebates and a bonus system. It introduced a seasonal price scheme that reflected variations in orders.

With a few exceptions, the structural characteristics of the NETEX pricing strategy were no surprise for the team members who were close to the market, but even the best experts were surprised about the extent of price and perceived value differentials. The profit potentials inherent in these differentials could not have been fully exploited without the analyses. This case illustrates that better information is an indispensable foundation for more powerful pricing.

WHAT THIS CHAPTER WILL DO

This chapter addresses the following questions:

1. How does customers' response to price enter into the causal chain between price and profit?

2. Which methods for price response estimation are available and how should they be applied?
3. How can value measures be translated into price decisions?
4. What do we know about empirical magnitudes of price elasticity?

Knowing the answers to these questions will help you to

1. fully understand the systems context and the information require- ments of pricing
2. select proven methods and the right experts to estimate price response and avoid the pitfalls of these methods
3. make a well-informed and powerful price decision

THE SYSTEMS CONTEXT OF PRICE RESPONSE ESTIMATION

The essential—and sometimes the most difficult—part of the informa- tion needed to make power pricing decisions is the price response curve introduced in chapter 2. Figure 3-2 puts this information into a systems context. Our own price in conjunction with competitive prices impacts sales volume; volume, in turn, impacts costs. Price times volume yields sales revenue. Sales revenue minus costs equals profit.

Figure 3-2 tells us that there is no way around a quantitative estima- tion of price response, marked by the black arrows. Only if we know, in quantitative terms, how customers respond to our own price and to com- petitive prices can we make a rational price decision.

Figure 3-2 also underlines the fact that cost-plus pricing starts at the wrong point; it turns causality upside down. The power pricer has to start with the customers and learn how they respond to potential suppli- ers' prices and price changes. Even an excellent company like Boeing has had to learn this lesson. A customer's view was: "Boeing has settled on a radical new strategy. Rather than clinging to its own notions of a so- called fair price [in our view cost induced], Boeing has started offering planes for what it thinks the airlines will pay."[1] This is tantamount to a new price response-driven approach to pricing.

Price response estimates can be represented in different forms:

• as numbers for specific price points
• as a table

- as a mathematical function or model
- as a graphical curve

The form used is secondary to the quantification as such. We mainly favor graphical representations in this book, but often a mathematical model underlies the curves. The graphical form is also recommended for managers' use of these concepts, because by revealing structures it both fosters individual understanding and facilitates group discussion.

How well are practitioners informed on the various factors appearing in Figure 3-2? If our experience with a well-respected U.S.-based multinational company is a good guide, managers know costs pretty well, but are weak on customer response to price.

Interviews with managers from various divisions and functions yielded the data in Figure 3-3 on self-perceptions of being "well informed." More than 80% of the respondents think that they are well informed on variable and fixed costs. Their information level on competitive prices is also high; three quarters of them feel well informed. But the percentage of respondents who are well informed about product value to customer is markedly lower (61%). And when customers' response to price is concerned, "informedness" drops off considerably. Only 21% feel well informed on the critical question of customers' acceptance of various price levels.

FIGURE 3-2

The Systems Context of Price Response Estimation

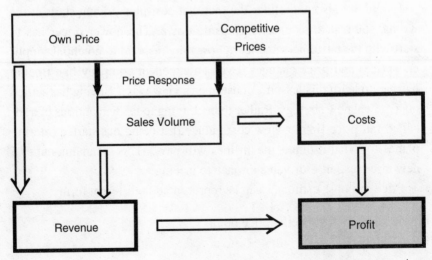

FIGURE 3-3

Information of Managers on Price-Relevant Factors (Self-Evaluations)

Percentage of Respondents Who Think They Are Well Informed on . . .

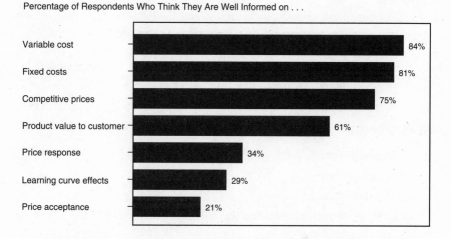

Such lack of information or misjudgment of price response can be disastrous. Mercury One-2-One, a British cellular phone service operator, launched a campaign in 1993 offering free calling service from 7 P.M. to 7 A.M., its "off-peak" time. The campaign was successful beyond any expectation, attracting over 300,000 new customers. But many of those new customers only used the phone during the night and never during the day when they would have had to pay. So great was the boost in evening call volume that it became the peak time. The "zero" price offering has turned into an economic nightmare for Mercury, particularly since the free night service was guaranteed indefinitely for those customers.

In another marketing crusade, Mercury offered free service on Christmas Day 1994. Call volume was about ten times the daily average and generated more than 33,000 hours of free calls, jamming the networks. The average call lasted nearly 90 minutes, with India and Pakistan the most-called destinations. As noted by the *Wall Street Journal*,[2] "For Mercury, the holiday generosity has produced a big-time hangover."

When Mercedes-Benz introduced its SLC roadster starting at around DM 90,000 in the early 1990s, it heavily underestimated consumers' willingness to pay, receiving more orders than it could fulfill within an acceptable time. A gray market developed, wherein lucky recipients of the car were able to resell it to others at prices much higher than the official new-car price of Mercedes. Over time, Mercedes has substantially increased the price to align demand and capacity. And today Mercedes is a heavy user of sophisticated methods to estimate price response.

METHODS FOR PRICE RESPONSE ESTIMATION

While guidelines can be developed by considering the experience of analogous products, we strongly recommend analyzing the specific context. There are four major approaches whose application and careful execution have proven useful in practice:

1. expert judgment
2. customer surveys
3. price experiments
4. analysis of historical market data

No one method is inherently superior to the others for all situations. Each has advantages and disadvantages. Consequently we now present each in turn—emphasizing those with the richest potential for accurate price response estimation. In particular, we discuss a customer survey based method called conjoint measurement in depth, due to our perceptions of its power and proven track record.

Expert Judgment

The idea of systematically tapping the knowledge of experts to estimate marketing response goes back to Little's conceptualization of "decision calculus" in 1970.[3] In some cases, such as a breakthrough innovation or a new competitive situation, it may be the only practical method for price response estimation. For details, and to examine how such a process ideally works, we consider an example of a new consumer nondurable, which was to be introduced in three European regions. Managers from the three markets were selected as the best experts for the price response estimates and asked to provide three estimates or points on the price response curve:

- the lowest realistic price and the first year's sales volume expected at this price
- the highest realistic price and the associated sales volume
- the expected sales volume at the "medium" price

The top part of Figure 3-4 shows the consensus estimates for the individual regions. Since a uniform price was to be set in all regions, the estimated sales volumes were aggregated yielding the estimated response curve shown in the lower part of the figure. The variable unit cost of the product was $.55. With this information, we are able to calculate the estimated total contribution for each price as shown. The highest contribution is attained at a price of around $1.30–1.35, yielding a contribution of about $55 million in the first year. If the price were set instead at $1.50 (as initially proposed by central management, prior to collecting the systematic judgments representing the regions' viewpoint), a profit of about $6 million would be forgone in the first year.

Experience from several hundred applications of this method generates the following guidelines:

1. Develop a questionnaire specifically designed for the situation at hand.
2. Interview at least ten experts if possible and expect large discrepancies in the estimates of the experts.
3. Discuss the possibly divergent results in a meeting with all respondents; a consensus should be reached. This leads to better results than simply calculating averages from the individual estimates.
4. Enlist participation of experts representing different functions and hierarchical levels in the organization. It is important to have a full array of viewpoints represented, e.g., the sales force, marketing, general management.
5. Have a neutral outsider conduct the interviews since the subject of price response estimates is political. For example, acceptance of a given price response curve begins to develop expectations within the company about the sales volume the sales force should deliver.
6. Utilize computer support to facilitate the estimation process.

Expert judgment is a simple and typically low-cost method. It can be applied in multiproduct situations where more expensive methods would prove prohibitive. For example, it was the best alternative for a manufacturer of fastening and assembly products who sold seven product lines, each with many variants. Traditionally prices were set through a standard cost-plus procedure with uniform markups. Applying expert judgment to seven product categories and three customer groups

FIGURE 3-4

Price Response Estimate Based on Expert Judgment

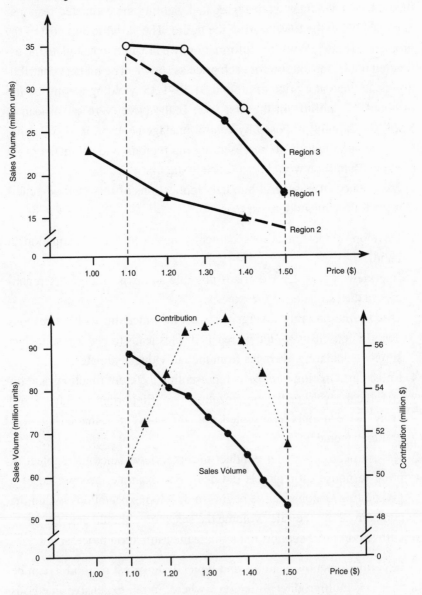

revealed that price response was highly variable across product-market segments. A new pricing system took these differences into account, and profits increased by 15%.

The major limitation of expert judgment is that it relies on internal sources of information. The judgment of managers, marketing experts, and sales people may or may not be consistent with what customers think and how they behave. In our projects, we usually find that the experts know their markets and customers relatively well and a consensus view emerges based on sharing of data. But in some cases, the expert judgments are far off the mark. Thus, if expert judgment is the sole method applied, a considerable degree of uncertainty remains. Expert judgment is also limited when it comes to estimating price response on an individual customer level; it works well only in business-to-business markets with very few customers. In such a case, extensive contact with each individual customer creates in-depth knowledge. However, in markets with many customers, managers usually think in terms of aggregate demand and cannot reliably estimate the price response of individual customers or segments. The only way to get to this information is a customer survey.

Customer Surveys

There are two fundamentally different methods to extract price response estimates from customers:

A. Directly ask customers how they would respond to certain prices, price changes, or price differentials.
B. Infer the response from an analysis of data on customers' expressed preference for one product over another.

Direct Price Response Surveys

In a direct price response survey, the respondent is asked a series of questions of the following kind:

- What is the likelihood you would buy this product at a price of $25?
- At what price would you definitely buy this product?
- How much would you be willing to pay for this product?
- How much of this product would you buy at a price of $0.99?
- At which price difference would you switch from product A to product B?

We now demonstrate this method for a personal computer. Customers in a Vobis store (Vobis is the largest computer retailer in Europe) were shown a specific personal computer and asked: "What is the maximum

FIGURE 3-5

Price Response Estimate for a Personal Computer Based on a Direct
Customer Survey

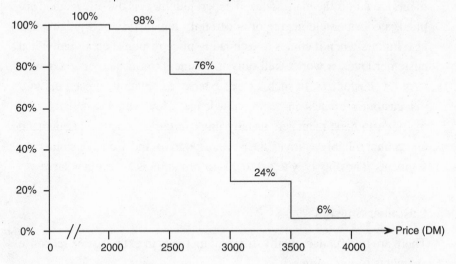

price you would be willing to pay for this computer?" The respondent
had only to give his or her maximum price. Figure 3-5 shows the result
of this survey. We observe a strong price threshold at DM 3,000 and another at DM 2,500, suggesting a price just below DM 3,000 or DM
2,500, depending of course on the cost situation.

A questioning survey that directly impacted senior management's
planning of a product introduction was Kodak's analysis of the instant
camera market. Respondents were provided a description of a new generation of instant cameras and then asked several questions to stimulate
consideration of the pros and cons of these cameras in order to simulate
an actual purchase situation.

Respondents were then presented prices of $150, $80, and $40 and
asked to indicate their purchase intention on a seven-point scale, from
"Definitely Not Buy" to "Definitely Would Buy." The results are shown
in Table 3-1.

Kodak used a "top-three box" to summarize the data, considering as
"probable buyers" those choosing any one of the top three scale values.
The price response curve thus estimated is shown in Figure 3-6.

TABLE 3-1

Purchase Intention for Instant Camera

	Stated Price		
	$150	**$80**	**$40**
1. Definitely Would Buy	4%	5%	15%
2.	—	—	2%
3. Probably Would Buy	7%	14%	30%
4.	1%	2%	4%
5. Probably Not Buy	22%	24%	18%
6.	2%	2%	1%
7. Definitely Not Buy	65%	54%	30%

When Kodak finally introduced a camera at a suggested retail price of $39.95, its president cited these data in his report to shareholders: "In research we did on instant pictures, we found that $40 was the dividing line at which respondents really turned on to the idea of buying an instant camera. We have been working ever since to get the combination."

FIGURE 3-6

Price Response Curve for Instant Cameras as Estimated Through Direct Questioning

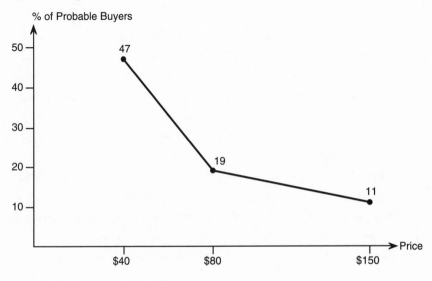

Subsequently, the survey data proved to be indicative of the true situation as instant-camera sales boomed with these low price offerings.

The direct-survey method was very popular in the sixties (see for example Gabor and Granger,[4] Abrams,[5] Adam[6]). The method is simple, easily understood, and inexpensive, but has important limitations.

- The direct questioning about price can induce unrealistically high price consciousness in respondents.
- The price is viewed in isolation, while in reality the customer weighs product attributes (value) and price against each other.
- Price involves a potential prestige effect. Respondents may be reluctant to admit that they cannot afford a premium product or that they "buy cheap." Under these circumstances, they would overstate their willingness to pay. This bias is pretty well understood now and it is often possible to adjust for it.

Nevertheless, due to these dangers, sole reliance on a direct customer survey is not recommended. Rather it can be employed in connection with other approaches to cross-check results. According to our experience, the direct-survey method is more useful for industrial than for consumer goods. Generally, however, there are better methods based on preferences to measure customers' price response. Among these, conjoint measurement plays a prominent role.

Preference-Based Inference: Conjoint Measurement

Conjoint measurement is a relatively new but powerful procedure which has been widely applied for both consumer and industrial products and services. It has been used in the pricing and design of products ranging from computer hardware and software to hotels, clothing, automobiles, and information services, to name just a few areas. Conjoint measurement calibrates the value of a product and its attributes in money (dollars, Deutschmarks, etc.) terms.

Its superiority stems from the fact that the questions posed to respondents replicate the realistic scenario of a customer facing an array of competitive alternatives with different features and prices and having to choose among them.

From these choice data, a mathematical procedure derives each customer's individual value of the product's attributes and their levels as well as the effects of alternative prices. Many variants of the conjoint method exist; below we describe the most popular version. (For details on other methods see Dolan[7] for a "manager's guide" and for more technical details Green and Srinivasan,[8] Wittink, Vriens, and Burhenne,[9] and Johnson.)[10]

An Automobile Industry Example. A German automobile company used conjoint measurement as input to the design and pricing of its new LION model. The questions of interest were such as: What is the value of our brand to customers? How much is the customer willing to pay for a higher-powered engine? How do fuel consumption and environmental performance relate to price acceptance?

The project to answer these extremely relevant yet difficult questions proceeded through the following seven steps:

1. Management decided that five key attributes which it wanted to investigate were: (a) brand, (b) engine power, (c) fuel consumption, (d) environmental performance, and (e) price. This is a critical feature of conjoint: a product needs to be meaningfully described by a set of attributes. These attributes can be a mix of tangibles—like horsepower or the engine—and intangibles like brand name.

2. For each product attribute, three realistic levels were determined whose value to the customer should be investigated. Table 3-2 shows the five attributes and their levels. In general, conjoint measurement can handle any number of levels for an attribute; the number of levels need not be the same for each attribute. Besides LION, a second German brand and one Japanese brand were included in the anaysis. The three levels of environmental performance were described in detail to the respondents.

3. In order to have representative data, survey respondents were pre-screened for interest in a car in the price bracket DM 50,000 to DM 70,000. The interviews were administered to all respondents using laptop computers.

4. In the interview, the computer program develops alternative "product profiles" and confronts the respondent with two profiles at a time from which he or she has to choose, e.g., as shown in Figure 3-7. The

TABLE 3-2

Conjoint Measurement Design for LION Case

Attribute	Attribute Levels		
Brand	LION	German	Japanese
Engine power (HP = horsepower)	150	200	250
Fuel consumption* (liters per 100 km)	12	14	16
Price (DM)	50,000	60,000	70,000
Environmental performance	Fulfills minimum environmental requirements	Exceeds environmental requirements	Sets new standards in environmental performance

* In Europe fuel consumption is measured in liters per 100 km not in miles per gallon.

advantage of using laptop computers and a computer program is that the program adapts the pairs presented to the answers given. This leads to great efficiency in obtaining needed data.

The respondent compares profiles A and B of Figure 3-7. A choice between A and B means trading off one thing to get another. Specifically, profile A with brand LION fulfills only minimum environmental requirements, has high fuel consumption and a high price, but its engine is very powerful. Profile B's brand is "Japanese"; it's better than profile A in environmental requirements, fuel consumption, and price, but has a much less powerful engine. Depending on his or her personal preferences, the customer makes a choice. Based on this and previous choices, the computer program selects another choice pair to present.

Each such choice by the respondent reveals something about his or her preference structure because the choice pairs are designed to include an implicit trade-off judgment which is revealed via the choice. In a realistic survey, we usually need ten to twenty such comparisons to be able to calculate the value of each attribute level for a single respondent. The typical interview time varies between 30 and 60 minutes.

5. Based on these data, the mathematical program provides the relative importance to the customer of the five attributes. In the LION case we obtained the following average "importance weights" (sum of weights = 100%).

Brand	30%
Engine power	28%
Price	20%
Fuel consumption	12%
Environmental performance	10%

These "importance weights" vary from individual to individual. The individual weights provide an excellent base for market segmentation. Here we confine ourselves to consideration of the average weights.

Brand proves to be the most important product attribute with a weight of 30%. Environmental performance is least important with only 10%. The relative unimportance of environmental performance was a revelation to management, because in a direct question survey respondents had attributed high importance to environmental performance. But due to conjoint's presentation of the reality of having either to pay a higher price or to accept less engine power for better environmental performance, the customers' true attitudes were revealed.

FIGURE 3-7

Example of a Paired Comparison in LION Case

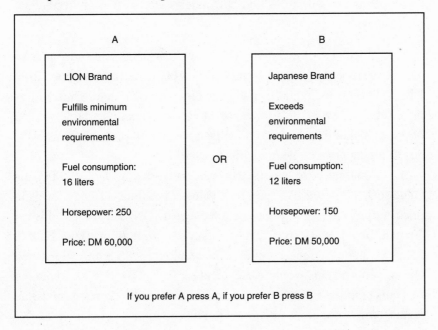

Second, we obtain the value of each attribute level. The big advantage of conjoint measurement is that these values can be translated into price terms. Thus, we can relate them directly to price and determine how much a customer is willing to pay for higher engine power or less fuel consumption. Here we touch the very core of the price-value relation. Figure 3-8 gives the values for all attribute levels in the LION case. The vertical value scales are comparable across all attributes.

6. For each attribute, the lowest value is set to zero. The new LION brand is clearly less valuable than the established German brand, but has a higher value than the Japanese brand. The value of engine power increases with higher horsepower (HP), but the relationship is nonlinear. The major increase in value, and thus in willingness to pay, is between 150 and 200 HP. Going further to 250 HP adds only a smaller marginal value, which has to be set against the higher costs of a stronger engine. Reducing fuel consumption from 14 liters per 100 kilometers to 12 liters/100km adds little marginal value. As mentioned above, to the surprise of management, the same is true for environmental performance. Even setting totally new standards (which would probably be very costly) would only add 35 value points, meaning that the consumer is not willing to trade off much to get better environmental performance.

The "price" panel in Figure 3-8 shows that price sensitivity is high between prices of DM 50,000 and DM 60,000. If we increase price from DM 50,000 to DM 60,000 value goes down by 65 points. Thus, in this price interval DM 10,000 correspond to 65 value points. The low value of prices higher than DM 60,000 tells us that it will probably be dangerous to set the price higher than this threshold.

If we confine ourselves to the price range below DM 60,000, the value scale allows us to express the values of various attribute levels in price terms. The value difference between LION and the established German brand is also 65 value points, or in price terms, DM 10,000. LION's value difference to the Japanese brand is 85 points; translated into price terms this would correspond to about DM 13,000. Reducing fuel consumption by 25% from 16 to 12 liters per 100 km adds 60 value points, corresponding to about DM 9,200.

These considerations show that the perceived value of each attribute

FIGURE 3-8

Values of Attribute Levels for LION Case

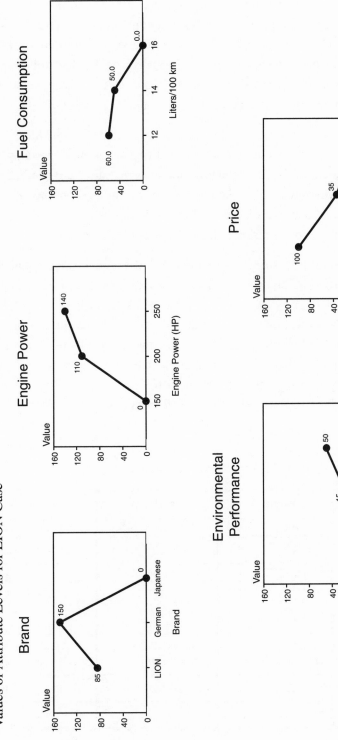

level can be measured in price terms. This information is extremely valuable both for setting prices and for designing products. If one knows these values and the costs associated with the various attribute levels, which level to offer and at what price can be decided. Product policy and pricing are simultaneously considered. Only levels whose value is greater than the costs should be offered for sale.

7. Given the information in Figure 3-8, we can predict which car the customer would choose in a given competitive situation. For example, suppose the cars available to the customer were cars A, B, and C in Table 3-3; which one would he choose? Given the descriptions of the cars according to their attributes in Table 3-3, we can calculate the total value of each car by referring to the value data of Figure 3-8.

As shown in the bottom row of Table 3-3, car model C, the Japanese brand, receives the highest total value with 290 points. This is mainly due to its high engine power and low price. Model A with the new LION brand has the lowest total value, with 230 points. The reason lies in the fact that LION's low fuel consumption and the technically excellent environmental performance do not matter much to the customers, while its low engine power strongly reduces the perceived value. To improve its total value, the LION model could increase its engine power to 200 HP.

TABLE 3-3

Calculation of Total Value for Three Car Models

Attributes	Model A		Model B		Model C	
	Level	Value	Level	Value	Level	Value
Brand	LION	85	German	150	Japanese	0
Engine Power	150	0	200	110	250	140
Fuel Consumption (liters/100km)	12	60	16	0	14	50
Environmental Performance	new standards	50	meets requirements	0	meets requirements	0
Price (DM)	DM 60,000	35	DM 70,000	0	DM 50,000	100
Total value		230		260		290

This would add 110 value points and bring it into the leading value position; or, it could reduce its price to DM 50,000, increasing its total value to 295. Marrying this demand data with technical and cost-constraint information shows this to be infeasible in this case.

To translate the values into market share and sales volume estimates, we need a rule for transforming the relative values shown in the last row of Table 3-3 to choices. The two common alternative rules are these.

A. Each consumer buys the car which offers him maximum value points; in this case, we say this consumer would buy car C in Table 3-3.

or

B. The likelihood that the customer will buy a given car is proportional to the value points of that car.

It depends on the specific situation which model is preferable (for further explanation we refer to Simon,[11] Green and Srinivasan,[12] and Elrod and Kumar[13]). For this "yes:no" situation (a customer either buys a specific car model or does not) we use the first rule. We can now derive the price response curve for car model A, the LION. Figure 3-9 shows this estimated curve together with the resulting profit curve.

The estimated price elasticity for LION is relatively high. A 16.7% reduction of the price from DM 60,000 to DM 50,000 would increase LION's market share in this segment from about 22.5% to 37.5%. This corresponds to a percentage volume change of 66%; related to the percentage price change of 16.7% the price elasticity is 66/16.7 = 3.95. The reason for this high price elasticity lies in the high value difference between the two prices (see Figure 3-8). This price response curve is valid if the competitors maintain their prices, but alternative reaction scenarios may be considered; we can assess the impact of any competitive actions considered feasible.

The profit curve in Figure 3-9 reveals that the optimal price for the LION model is not DM 60,000 as originally intended, but about DM 54,700. Setting the price at the originally anticipated level of DM 60,000 would imply a profit sacrifice of roughly 7% and a lower market share than when selling at DM 54,700. The low values customers place on the technically excellent environmental performance and fuel consumption surprised management and are responsible for this price position.

The LION conjoint measurement model was later employed to decide

FIGURE 3-9

Price Response and Profit Curve for LION Model

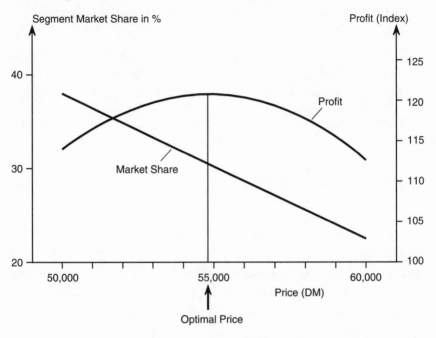

on future improvements of the car. R&D efforts were directed towards optimizing the relationship between perceived customer value and costs, no longer towards fulfilling the dreams of the engineers.

Detailed descriptions of other applications are available. Dolan describes Management Science America's use of the method to determine design, price, and time to market for a new material-requirements-planning system and Wind et al. describe its use by Marriott hotels to design its Courtyard chain.[14] It is worth reiterating that conjoint measurement can accommodate both "hard" and "soft" attributes. For example, one application evaluated key attributes of an electric motor used in various industries, including both product and service aspects: (a) reliability, (b) service interval, (c) energy consumption, (d) life duration, and (e) service quality. An important aspect—alluded to above—was using conjoint measurement to simultaneously price and design products. We expand on this key point below by describing a textile machine application.

A Textile Machine Application: Product Design and Target Pricing. As we will set out in detail in chapter 12 when we consider organizational and implementational issues surrounding pricing, good pricing does not start with a finished product just before its market introduction. Rather, price and features should be codetermined in the R&D phase. Only if R&D efforts are directed at creating the right customer-oriented values will a product be generated for which customers will pay a price that generates good margins. Conjoint measurement can be employed in the concept stage, before R&D starts, to target the right values for product attributes and prices. From these target prices, the engineers have to derive overall target costs. (One famous example of this target pricing approach is Canon's $1,000 copier.)

A textile machine was undergoing continual product improvement through successive generations. Five attributes seemed key to customers: (a) changeover time, (b) noise reduction, (c) end product quality, (d) maintenance downtime, and (e) threading speed. To give direction to R&D efforts, conjoint interviews were conducted with 150 customers worldwide. Parallel to the market study, the engineering department developed cost estimates for various improvements. Table 3-4 summarizes both the customer demand and the cost data.

For each attribute, the improvement which would increase the customers' willingness to pay by $100 was calibrated; it transpired that a 5-second reduction in changeover time from one textile design to the next was worth $100 per spindle for customers. The same amount would be paid for a noise reduction of 1 decibel (A) and so forth for the other variables. Cost data are summarized by a scale of 1 = small cost increase to 5 = large cost increase. Based on these value and cost data, optimal levels can be established for all attributes and optimal target prices can be derived. In developing the new machine generation, the engineers observed these targets and a value-cost-optimized system was conceived. Since the study revealed that customers in high-wage countries and developing countries differed strongly in their valuation of certain product attributes, a modular system was developed which allowed the firm to expand its production line, offering both more and less expensive machine versions than in the older generation. The price differentiation became more pronounced than before, and it is strictly value based.

TABLE 3-4

Target Pricing and Costing Based on Conjoint Measurement—Case of a Textile Machine

Attribute	Value of $100 per Spindle (Willingness to Pay More)	Cost (Scale)	Optimal Level
Changeover Time	−5 seconds	3	49 seconds
Noise Reduction	−1 decibel (A)	1	85 decibel (A)
End Product Quality	+0.3 technical coefficient	4	4.5 (scale from 1 to 5)
Downtime for Maintenance	−5 minutes	2	25 minutes
Threading Speed	−20 seconds	3	90 seconds

The target pricing approach unifies aspects of customer value, costs, and competitive positioning and deserves utmost attention. In Figure 3-10 we consider the problem under a more general perspective.

The horizontal axis describes the performance or technical level of an attribute. While the value to the customer increases with the performance, it does so at a decreasing rate, as shown, with the value curve becoming flatter as we go further to the right. The cost curve, however, becomes steeper as the technical performance level increases. It may eventually intersect the value curve.

The goal of target pricing and costing is to determine, and then to realize, the technical performance level for each attribute that maximizes the difference between value and cost. The goal is not to maximize performance—that costs too much—but to optimize it at the target cost. In Figure 3-10, if performance is at level B it should be increased, because the added cost is more than compensated for by the added customer value; however, if performance is at level A, it should be reduced. In quite a few of our projects we have found the latter to be true; companies were *over-*

performing in certain attributes (particularly in technical features), in that the marginal costs they incurred in so doing were higher than the marginal value realized by the customers. In short, the product was "over-spec'ed." In other areas, particularly in services, we often encounter underperformance as exemplified by level B. Aligning the value and cost aspects early on is the best foundation for power pricing.

The criticality of a profound understanding of the relative value of product features and price is underlined by the following examples. In the personal computer industry, Packard Bell had built its strategy on machines with slightly lower performance but lower prices than the competition. Until the mid 1990s this strategy proved very successful and made Packard Bell one of the leading PC manufacturers. But in 1995 the situation changed. According to the *Wall Street Journal Europe:* "Consumers appear willing to buy PCs with more power at slightly higher price points rather than settle for less-powerful, lower-priced models that are Packard Bell's specialty."[15] On the other hand, the added performance may not justify the price in the customer's mind. For example, a German maker of machining centers had a Dutch customer who told him: "Your price is DM 2.5 million; the price of an Italian competitor is DM 1.5 million. This is a price difference of 60%.

FIGURE 3-10

A Generalized Concept of Target Pricing and Costing

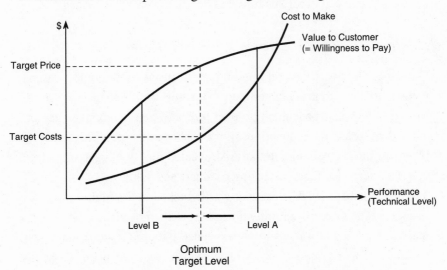

I acknowledge the higher value of your product and your service is better. But it is not 60% higher." (For details see Simon.[16]) The Dutch customer bought the Italian product.

Sometimes the value of new products and "having the latest" is overestimated and consequently the entrants are priced too high relative to older products. This was the case for video-game players in 1995. The old 16-bit players cost around $100, while newer 32-bit machines were sold for $300. At this price differential, consumers clearly preferred the older models, buying about four million of them compared to fewer than one million of the new players. The leading companies in this market, Nintendo and Sega, totally misjudged the perceived values of old and new games and set the price differentials wrong. Carlton comments: "The price tags of the new machines proved too high."[17] Nintendo could have sold double the stock of its old games but had supply problems due to misjudging demand. Substantial profits were sacrificed.

These cases underline the importance of understanding the perceived values and the costs of product features at an early stage in the new-product-development process. Misjudgment or ignorance in this regard is not forgiven by the market. Leading companies in the automotive sector like BMW or Mercedes systematically apply these new sophisticated techniques to set early price and cost targets. The same is true for many Japanese companies in information technology and other sectors. Power pricing starts with better information on R&D targets. Mistakes made at the R&D stage can hardly be repaired by pricing.

An Experience-Based Evaluation of Conjoint Measurement

Our experience with several hundred applications of conjoint measurement is that it often generated surprising results for managers. In the case of a new pharmaceutical product in France, company management wanted to price its innovation slightly above competition at FF 10 (French Francs). A conjoint analysis revealed that doctors assigned it a much higher value than competing products and suggested a price of FF 30 rather than FF 10. The product was launched at the higher price and in spite of the price being three times higher than originally planned by management, actual sales volume exceeded the prediction management had made for a price of FF 10. The reason was that doctors did not directly compare the new product with existing substitutes, but perceived it as creating a "value class" of its own. It would have been a major mistake to price position the innovation close to the incumbent products. In the meantime the price has been further increased to FF 36, and is extremely profitable.

In another case, management of a corrosion-protection firm was very hesitant to raise the price, which was at parity with major competitors, in spite of a clearly superior performance. A conjoint analysis revealed that customers actually saw the product's value to be about 40% higher than that of its main competitor. This led to management agreeing to implement a 20% price increase, which was accepted by the market without any loss in sales volume for the company. This is pure profit!

But we also observe the reverse. A service company was convinced that it offered superior performance and could charge a price premium. Conjoint revealed that the company was superior only in areas that had little or no value to the customers. In the core service areas it had no competitive advantages. It therefore reduced the price to competitive levels and substantially increased its market share.

Conjoint measurement is definitely the most important development of the last 20 years for gaining insight into customers in order to support product and pricing decisions. The method addresses critical but seemingly unanswerable questions, such as the following.

- What is the importance of product attributes such as quality, design, technical features, or price in the buying decision?
- What is the relative value of a brand in price terms?
- What is the price value of a service?
- What happens to our market share if we change the price or another attribute of our product?
- What is the effect of competitive price or product moves on our share?
- How do customers differ in their evaluation of product or service attributes and price?
- Is it better to use a given budget to fund a price cut or R&D to improve performance and provide additional value?
- On which value generators should R&D focus in order to create future value and support future prices?

Its ability to address these issues and its record of proven profit impact explains the increasing popularity of conjoint measurement. The method's usefulness has strongly gained from the advances in information technology. Computer interviewing has become a standard practice and offers options that are not available with the paper-and-pencil method. Multimedia computers allow us to show still and moving pictures to illustrate new product concepts or functioning: they bring the surveys closer to reality. Using prototypes or models of new products can help to improve the validity of conjoint results. It is, for instance, difficult to assess the weight or the size of a mobile telephone without actually holding it in your hand. Therefore prototypes should be used in such situations. The closer to reality the stimuli received by the respondent are, the more valid his or her answers will be.

The availability of easy-to-use and inexpensive conjoint software also introduces risks. Conjoint is a complex method. If this complexity is not fully understood by the people applying the method, the results can be highly misleading. Dozens of studies can be summed up as "Conjoint in—garbage out." It is a powerful technique but its complexity makes it relatively expensive, and expert assistance is required to use it well in practical applications.

Based on our own experience with several hundred conjoint studies we give the following recommendations.

- Only relevant attributes should be included.
- Only realistic levels of the attributes should be considered. "Realistic" does not mean that these levels currently exist, but they should not be too far from the respondents' experience. If the gasoline price is currently around $1 per gallon in the U.S. it makes no sense to ask U.S. consumers what they would do at a gasoline price of $5 per gallon. This is simply beyond their experience and imagination.
- For attributes which are difficult to describe in a few words (e.g., friendliness, atmosphere, environmental performance, positioning), a detailed verbal description should be communicated before the conjoint part of the interview. According to our experience, people can relatively well imagine such a situation if the description is complete and well worded.
- The selection and the instruction of the interviewers are critical. Since respondents frequently ask questions and require additional explana-

tions, the interviewer should understand the method and should be instructed on the specific case. Unlike in classical paper-and-pencil interviews, uneducated interviewers are unacceptable for conjoint interviewing.

- In-person administration of the survey is best, if practical. Interviews for a conjoint study for pricing purposes should not be done on the telephone. It is, however, possible to do it on a computer network where the respondent and the interviewer are connected.

Price Experiments

In price experiments, prices are varied and the effect on sales volumes or market shares is observed. This can take place in a laboratory with a simulated shopping situation or "in-market."[18] For an "in-market" test, different prices may be used and different stores within a market or prices may be varied across different geographic markets. Direct mail catalogs are particularly effective for price experiments. The advantage of experiments over surveys is that actual customer behavior is observed; i.e., one measures what people do rather than what they say they would do.

An example of an "in-market" test with price varied across regions is a study of a German mobile phone manufacturer. The regular price for its phone was DM 1,200. At this price, 24% of new car purchasers bought the phone. To test price response and whether a price cut made sense, the company tested three price levels in separate regions for three months. The regions were chosen to represent the market overall and to be comparable to one another. Figure 3-11 gives the results of the three-month experiment.

In region A of Figure 3-11 the price remained DM 1,200; even so, the adoption rate went up to 26%. Obviously this rise cannot be attributed to price but must be due to other factors. In region B a 25% price reduction produced a net sales gain of $41 - 26 = 15$ points over region A—a gain of 15 divided by 26 or 57.6%. Region C's low price of DM 600, 50% of the price of region A, produced a net gain of 45 minus 26 or 19 points—a gain of 26 divided by 19 or 73.1%. The price elasticity is 73.1% divided by 50% or 1.46. Many customers may have had a price threshold of DM 1,000, and so further reducing the price from DM 900 to DM 600 didn't attract many additional buyers. The telephone costs the company about DM 300; therefore, at DM 900, the company's unit margin is DM 600.

FIGURE 3-11

Price Experiment for a Mobile Phone

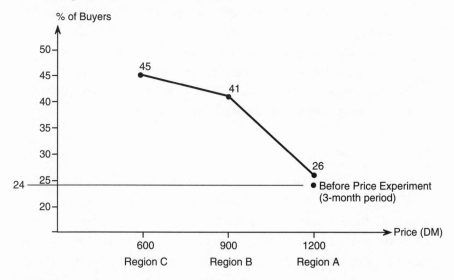

With 41% of potential buyers actually purchasing, the profit index for the DM 900 price is DM 600 × 41 = 246; at DM 1,200, the unit margin of DM 900 and buying rate of 26% translate to a profit index of 234. Thus, the profit is about 5% higher at a selling price of DM 900 than at DM 1,200. A further selling-price reduction to DM 600 would cut the profit index to DM 300 × .45 = 135, meaning a loss of almost half of the potential profit. The company decided to offer the mobile phone at DM 970, slightly below the buyer threshold of DM 1,000.

Experiments can be a very useful way to measure price response. Of course, unlike conjoint measurement, the product must already exist and reactions obtained apply to the product as a whole, not to individual attributes. While typically somewhat expensive to conduct, price experiments are popular with those who like the reality of observing actual purchase behavior.

Analysis of Historical Market Data

A fourth source of price response information is the day-to-day action in the marketplace, i.e., historical price and sales data. Supermarket scanners are a particularly efficient tool for providing this kind of data.

If prices have naturally varied over time, as they do in many markets, one can analyze how changes in absolute or relative prices affect sales volumes and market shares. Statistical methods provide price response and price elasticity estimates.

We illustrate the procedure for two frequently purchased consumer goods. One is the German market for ready-to-eat desserts. At the time of the analysis, the four main competitors—Gervais-Danone, Nestlé, Unilever, and Dr. Oetker—together had more than 80% of the market. Over three years, Dr. Oetker's prices varied between DM 0.60 and DM 0.70. Unit sales varied between 7 and 12 million for two-month periods. The data are shown in Figure 3-12 for 18 two-month periods. (Some points overlap on the graph, so one cannot make out 18 distinct points in Figure 3-12.) The points are actual observations of price and quantity sold during a two-month period. The linear curve in the figure was fitted by a regression procedure to show the line with the "best fit" to the data.

A price change of DM 0.01 at a level of DM 0.65 (1.5%) produces a sales volume change of 381,000 units or 3.8%. Thus, the price elasticity is 2.51 (3.8% divided by 1.5%). At the time of the analysis, the prices were hovering around DM 0.63–0.65 and had been on a downward trend. The analysis revealed that the optimal price was DM 0.69. The profit curve in Figure 3-12 shows that at a price of DM 0.63 almost 25% of the maximum profit is sacrificed. The conclusion was clear. Dr. Oetker had to halt further price declines by any means—in spite of the attractive volume expansion resulting from lower prices. Instead it should try to get the price up into the higher sixties. This move would result in lower share but increase the annual profit of the product by more than DM 1 million.

A second case concerns a special household cleansing product. This well-known brand had a market share of 85% when a new competitor entered the market with very aggressive pricing. Initially, the incumbent did not reduce price but instead increased advertising. In spite of this defense, the brand's market share had slipped to 55% by the end of 1993. An econometric analysis revealed that price elasticity was much higher and advertising elasticity was much lower than management had thought. A model was built that reproduced the actual development over 1992 and 1993 well, as Figure 3-13 shows.

FIGURE 3-12

Price Response Estimate Based on Historical Market Data

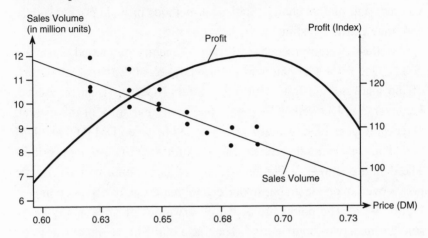

Based on the model, a new pricing and communication strategy was developed. It recommended to reduce the price by 15% and the advertising budget by 75% but to increase sales efforts by 15%. For the new strategy, a turn in the market share was predicted as shown by the heavy line in the exhibit. The actual development in 1994 confirmed the accuracy of the response estimates and the decline in market share could be halted. The profit situation improved markedly.

In using actual market data to estimate price response the following guidelines should be observed.

1. Start with a visual inspection of the data. It usually reveals a great deal.
2. Make sure that the historic conditions under which the data originated continue to prevail in the future. This is the major problem of the historic method in modern dynamic markets. The behavior of consumers and competitors is less stable than it used to be, making future price response estimation from historic data risky.
3. The power pricer should not rely on one hypothesis about price response but test alternative assumptions. Nonprice marketing instruments should be included (as in the cleanser case) since they may distort price effects.
4. Remember that economic plausibility is as important as statistics.

FIGURE 3-13

Response Estimates and Prediction Based on Historical Market Data

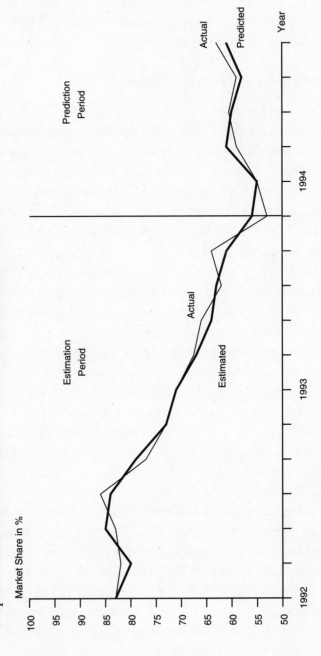

Analysis of actual market data can be a valuable method to estimate price response. It is, however, imperative to proceed with great care and not to believe naively in statistics. If possible, several methods should be used to cross-validate the price response estimates. Table 3-5 summarizes the relative strengths and weaknesses of the various methods.

Empirical Aspects of Price Elasticity

The degree of price elasticity is an empirical question that has to be investigated in each specific case. Price elasticities may range from close to zero for a life-saving drug to near infinite values for common commodities, where a slight price difference can induce the customer to switch.

Sometimes we can even observe positive price elasticities. If a higher price is perceived as an indicator of a better quality, a price increase may produce higher sales. Such an effect was experienced with an electric shaver from a little-known small company. It was styled similarly to the famous Braun shaver but sold at a much lower price. This price obviously made consumers suspicious about quality. After the company doubled the price, market share quadrupled—but still remained small relative to Braun's dominant share.

But these are exceptions. In typical markets price changes and sales volume changes move in opposite directions. In the literature we find numerous estimates of price elasticities. Tellis[19] has surveyed 367 price-elasticity estimates and found a mean absolute value of 1.76. This figure says that a 1% price reduction increases sales by 1.76%. He suspects that due to estimation biases the true absolute value is somewhat larger—around 2 to 2.5. According to our experience these are realistic average values.

It is interesting to compare these magnitudes to advertising elasticities. Across many studies, Assmus, Farley, and Lehmann[20] found an average advertising elasticity of 0.22; i.e., a 1% increase of the advertising budget increases sales by only 0.22%. In a study of many different products Lambin[21] found an average price elasticity of 1.81 and an average advertising elasticity of 0.1, i.e., a factor of 18 between the two elasticities. In a more recent analysis Sethuraman and Tellis[22] conclude that "on average the price elasticity is about 20 times the advertising elasticity." These estimates show how much more impactful price is than advertising.

TABLE 3-5

Evaluation of Methods of Collecting Price Response Data

Criterion \ Method	Expert Judgment	Customer Surveys		Price Experiments	Historical Market Data
		Direct	Conjoint Measurement		
Validity	medium	low	medium-high	medium-low	high
Reliability	medium-high	uncertain	medium-high	high	low
Costs	very low	low-medium	medium	medium-high	depends on availability and accessibility
Applicability to New Products	yes	questionable	yes	yes	no
Applicability to Established Products	yes	yes	yes	yes	yes
Overall Evaluation	useful for new products, new situations	questionable	very useful	useful	useful for established products

It is important to consider differences between markets and products. Table 3-6 provides a selection of elasticity estimates from the literature and our own experience (see Simon[23]).

The exhibit shows that even within industries large elasticity variations have been observed.

While typical price elasticities for consumer nondurables vary between 2 and 6, a price elasticity of about 100 was observed when the cigarette brand West cut its price from DM 3.80 to DM 3.30. Traditionally price elasticities for ethical pharmaceuticals were low, but managed care has changed this, so that elasticities have increased. An H2-blocker from Eli Lilly reduced its price by 40% and experienced a sales gain of 200%, a price elasticity of 5. For commodity industrial products, we sometimes observe price elasticities in the range of 100 or higher, i.e., a 1% price reduction can lead to a doubling of sales volume provided the competition does not react. With a great deal of caution, we can conclude that the following conditions generally tend to lead to high price elasticities (see also Dolan[24]):

• high similarity and substitutability of products, low differentiation
• high price transparency and price awareness, prices easy to compare
• high purchase frequency
• low risk perception
• good product knowledge, ability to judge products objectively (industrial products)
• decision maker pays for the product himself (as opposed to somebody else)
• low brand awareness and loyalty
• mass quality, mass distribution
• high absolute prices
• high share of the item in total costs for end product
• buyer/reseller compete on price in end-user market
• low importance of image and prestige
• heavy promotional activity in product category
• low market share. Both Guadagni and Little[25] and Kucher[26] found that products with lower shares have higher price elasticities.

These generalizations provide some guidelines to judge price elasticities but there are always exceptions. A careful estimate of this critical

TABLE 3-6

Empirical Estimates of Price Elasticities (Absolute Magnitudes)

Product Category	Literature	Our Experience
Consumer Nondurables	1.5 – 5	typically > 2
Consumer durables	1.5 – 3	high variation
Pharmaceuticals	ca. 0.5	innovative products: 0.2 – 0.7 me too products: 0.5 – 1.5 generics: 0.7 – 2.5 OTC-drugs: 0.5 – 1.5

Industrial Products
  Standard products
  Specialties
	n.a.	2 – 100
		
		0.3 – 2
		for some specialties extremely low values

Automobiles
  Luxury
  Normal
	n.a.	0.7 – 1.5
		> 1.5

Services
  Airlines
  Rail Transport
  Telecom
    Air Time
    Subscriptions (Mobile)
    Computer Services
	> 2
	1.5
	
	0.7 – 1.7
	n.a.
		1 – 5
		< 1
		
		0.3 – 1
		2 – 5
		0.5 – 1.5

determinant of pricing is recommended in each individual case using some combination of the four methods we have described.

SUMMARY

In this chapter we have outlined and discussed the problems and methods of price response estimation. Better information is at the heart of power pricing. In assessing price response a number of points should be observed.

- Price response depends on a complex system of causal and interrelated factors, on which information should be collected.
- There is no alternative to quantifying the sales effect of one's own price and of competitive prices. The sales response curve is a necessary, though difficult, ingredient of an informed price decision.
- In reality we observe a gap in price response information; most managers have no clear understanding of these effects.

- A battery of methods is available to estimate price response, namely expert judgement, customer surveys, price experiments, and the analysis of actual market data. All these methods have advantages and disadvantages.
- Expert judgment is best suited for new situations (product introduction, competitive entry). The method is simple and cost effective but also confined to the internal view.
- Customer surveys through direct questioning are simple and inexpensive but have questionable validity for price response estimation.
- Conjoint measurement addresses the core of price response in that it measures the value of the product and its attribute levels. It quantifies seemingly unmeasurable factors like the value of brands, technical features, or services in price terms. It provides an excellent foundation for value-oriented pricing.
- Value and price targets should already be set in the R&D phase of a product. The comparison of values and costs yields optimal attribute levels and allows for profitable pricing.
- Wherever possible conjoint measurement should be used to support price decisions. The method must, however, be applied with caution and thoroughness; it requires excellent knowhow and experience. An inadequate "black box" use can easily be misleading.
- Price experiments and market data look at actual behavior and can provide valuable information for price response estimation.
- Price elasticities in reality show a large degree of variation, even within the same product category. We recommend carefully estimating price response in each individual case. Generalizations from seemingly similar situations involve great risks of misjudgment.

The better the information on price response is, the more likely will the right price be found. Power pricing starts with superior information and ends with higher profits.

4

Pricing and Competitive Strategy

INTRODUCTION

A marketing manager for a specialty glass company described this perplexing situation to us:

> I have two product lines, GREENFLEX and RETRO. We make a ton of money on GREENFLEX and next to nothing on RETRO. They are used for very different applications—but the customers are pretty much the same kind of people and the glass plays the same type of role in their organizations. Maybe GREENFLEX is a little smaller part of the buyer's cost, but it isn't a big difference. We are the dominant supplier of each type of product, and we are equally good at making the two, and there is about the same small level of product differentiation in each market. I just could not figure out why we make 10 times as much with one product as the other. Then I looked at our competitors. In operations and technology, they are equally strong across the two products—but that's where the similarity ends. With GREENFLEX, we are part of a smart industry. With RETRO, we are in a dumb industry. Give me smart competitors any day. Every time these dumb competitors we face with RETRO have a little downtick in sales volume they cut the price to get it back. If we cut our price on an individual item to get rid of some inventory because we are discontinuing it, to them it's a major strategic move requiring immediate share defense via price cuts

across the board. If we take a price increase, all they do is emphasize to customers how they are cheaper. It's impossible to maintain any kind of reasonable industry price level with these just plain dumb competitors.

In part, this manager is right. Unless a firm has a very high level of product differentiation, its own profits are to some extent under the control of its competitors. For example, consider Delta Airlines, with its approved set of gates and runway times, operating a shuttle with hourly service between Boston and New York. Figure 4-1(a) shows Delta's pricing latitude if no other airline has Boston–New York shuttle rights. The reference products, i.e., the alternative ways to get from Boston to New York, are bus, car, and train. For many customers, Delta represents an option much preferred to these other modes. Hence, Delta has a high "perceived value." In principle, Delta's very low variable cost per passenger represents the pricing floor—resulting in a wide band of possible prices.

Figure 4-1(b) shows the early 1996 reality: USAir offers shuttle flights from New York to Boston as well, with Delta leaving every hour on the half-hour and USAir every hour on the hour. Some people have a slight preference for one airline or the other—due to a frequent-flyer program or past good or bad experience—but for most people the two products are highly substitutable. As shown in Figure 4-1(b), the upper

FIGURE 4-1
Pricing Latitude for Delta Boston–New York Shuttle With and Without USAir

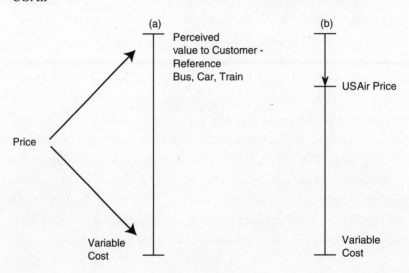

limit on Delta's price conceptually is still the "perceived value" a customer places on the Delta flight, but now it declines to the USAir price plus or minus a little bit for certain customers. Like our glassworks manager, Delta does not want a dumb competitor. It would be okay if the competitor were so dumb that it priced above the perceived value of Figure 4-1(a), but even if that happened, it would not happen for long. He would get little business and would soon figure out that a reduction was necessary. What Delta really does not want is USAir driving its price well below the perceived value of Figure 4-1(a) to build market share.

Thomas Bonoma, CEO at Renaissance Cosmetics, once vividly described this process as the "Veg-O-Matic Problem of Pricing," the Veg-O-Matic being a vegetable chopping and shredding device sold heavily on late night television. In the Veg-O-Matic model, shown in Figure 4-2, the firm's profits sit between variable cost and value-to-customer—but subject to "slicing, dicing, and shredding" by a quick downward movement in competitor prices. Veg-O-Matics rear their heads in many places.

Delta and USAir compete vigorously on the shuttle routes. But, as smart competitors, they do it not on the basis of price—which stand at identical $146 each way for both in March 1996—but with fringes such as free beverages (including beer and wine), discounts on local car transportation, and comfortable waiting areas furnished with free newspapers, magazines, orange juice, and coffee. Each realizes that a fare cut

FIGURE 4-2

Bonoma Veg-O-Matic Problem of Pricing

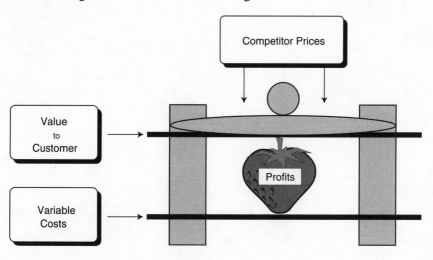

would almost certainly be matched by the competitor due to the volume swing that an unmet cut would engender. Gordon Bethune, the CEO behind Continental Airlines' remarkable turnaround, explained the source of profitability as competitors in airlines getting finally smarter: "The old testosterone-driven executives in this business have been replaced with people who want to make a profit, not make market share."[1]

In this situation, understanding likely *competitive* response is as critical as understanding customer response. Chapter 3 focused on methods for judging customer response. However, as shown in Figure 4-3, the power pricer is equally knowledgeable about competitive response and operates in the upper right portion of the graph. Chapter 3 was designed to help firms move to the right on this graph, and chapter 4 offers the complementary upward movement to achieve power pricer positioning.

The power pricer does not just bemoan how dumb competitors are in driving industry prices too low. He figures out whether he wants to raise the industry IQ and if so, he does something about it. Our specialty glass marketing manager was willing to accept responsibility for helping to establish favorable industry price levels for his GREENFLEX product—but he wanted to blame RETRO's poor margins solely on "dumb"

FIGURE 4-3

The Power Pricer's Knowledge Base

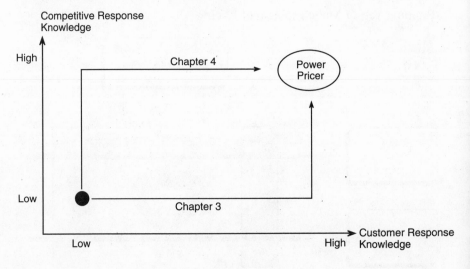

competitors. As the dominant player in both markets, he should recognize and accept the task of educating his "dumb" competitors, promoting a focus on industry profitability, and then maximizing his share of those profits.

WHAT THIS CHAPTER WILL DO

This chapter addresses the following questions.

1. What is the role of price in determining your product positioning?
2. How can a firm link pricing strategy to overall competitive strategy?
3. What is the significance of price tiers in the marketplace?
4. What type of competitive reaction can be anticipated to price moves in various situations? What industry supply and demand factors should be considered in judging competitive reaction?
5. How can price and other actions be used to manage competitors effectively and promote industry profitability rather than set off a price war?

Knowing this will help you to:

1. better link pricing and business strategy
2. assess the degree of price competition likely to characterize your industry
3. understand long-term as well as short-term implications of pricing actions as competitive reactions are considered
4. manage aspects of the pricing program so as to promote long-term profitability

PRICING'S IMPACT ON COMPETITIVE POSITIONING

Price helps to define a product's competitive position, i.e., how it is seen by consumers and the products it most directly competes with. For example, Table 4-1 shows the 10 top-selling beer brands in the U.S. market. In tier 1, seven brands from three suppliers compete within a ±2% range of the average tier price of $14.07 per 280-ounce case equivalents. Anheuser-Busch has its Busch brand in the middle-market position, 21% below tier 1; and its Natural Light brand competes against Philip

TABLE 4-1

Price Tiers for the 10 Top-Selling Beer Brands in the United States

Average Price and Index	Anheuser Busch	Philip Morris	Adolph Coors
Tier 1 $14.07 (100)	Budweiser Bud Light Bud Dry	Miller Lite Miller Genuine Draft Miller Genuine Draft—Light	Coors Light
Tier 2 $11.17 (79)	Busch		
Tier 3 $9.26 (66)	Natural Light	Milwaukee's Best	

Source: Derived from Marj Charlier, "Brewers' Price Cutting and Promotions Fail to Put Much of a Head on Beer Sales," *Wall Street Journal,* July 15, 1993, p. B1.

Morris' Milwaukee's Best in tier 3 at prices 34% below tier 1. Coors' pricing of Coors Light at $14.11 clearly positions it as a tier 1 brand competing against the Budweiser and Miller families.

Many markets have a structure in which brands or products are aligned on a "value-map" of perceived product value vs. price as shown in Figure 4-4. This particular map shows three market tiers: economy, middle market, and premium. Three-tier markets are common, e.g., the "good, better, best" strategy often associated with Sears and with the Green, Gold, and Platinum credit cards of American Express. The UK newspaper market has been described as having "popular, midmarket, and quality" segments.[2] Table 4-2 shows the "tiering" of the branded portion of the U.S. camera film market. A firm may have entries in one or in multiple tiers; e.g., Konica and Scotch (3M) are only in the Economy tier; Agfa only in Premium; Fuji in Superpremium and Economy. To stem market share losses, Kodak recently expanded its product line to offerings in each tier, introducing Kodak Funtime film "for casual picturing taking" into the Economy tier while also reorienting and renaming its superpremium brand positioning.[3] Mercedes-Benz had traditionally confined itself to the premier tier. In the late 1980s, it tried to

FIGURE 4-4

Three-Tier Value Map

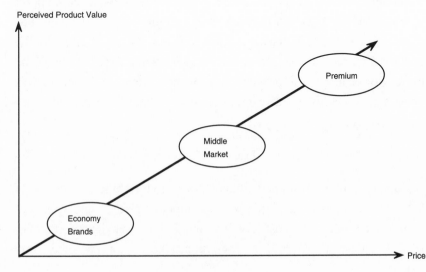

TABLE 4-2

Tiering of Camera Film in U.S. Market—Branded Products

	Average Retail Price Paid (24-Exposure Roll)
Superpremium Tier	
FujiColor Reala	$4.69
Kodak Ektar	$4.27
Premium Tier	
Kodak Gold Plus	$3.49
Agfa Color	$3.49
Economy Tier	
FujiColor Super G	$2.91
Konica Super SR	$2.91
ScotchColor	$2.69

move one tier down with the C-class. The 1997 introduction of the A-class will add participation in another tier.

The appropriate number of tiers to utilize is situation specific. A two-tier (branded vs. nonbranded) separation is sometimes useful; Ross[4] uses four tiers to describe the ice cream market and Kotler[5] uses seven for the automobile market. Regardless of the number of tiers, the essential point is the same: one's chosen position on the "value-map" effectively implies a strategy and defines a relevant competitive set. Consequently, early in the product design process, a target pricing decision should be made. For example, the project team for the Canon AE-1 camera was given a price target before design process even began.[6] Instead of a pattern moving from:

Product Design → Cost → Price → Market Position

Canon's thinking is flipped around, to run from right to left instead of left to right. The desired market position implies a price range, which determines the acceptable cost level—which, in turn, mandates certain design decisions. In short, price determines cost—not the other way around.

Extensive research in consumer packaged goods and our more general experience across industries show that:

- competition *within* a price-tier is typically more vigorous than *across* tiers.
- there is an asymmetry in competition across tiers. Price cuts by higher quality tiers are more powerful in pulling customers up from lower tiers, than lower tier price cuts are in pulling customers down from upper tiers; i.e., customers "trade up" more readily than they "trade down."

Pictorially, we show this in Figure 4-5 for a two-tier market, which for simplicity we show as having two premium brands P_1 and P_2 and two economy brands E_1 and E_2. In chapter 2, we introduced the notion of "price elasticity," defined as the percentage change in a brand's sales volume relative to the percentage change in its *own* price. Another useful concept is cross-price elasticity, which describes the impact of one brand's price change on another brand's sale volume.

Figure 4-5 shows a "fence" separating the premium and economy tiers. The "fence" denotes the fact that a price cut by any brand typically

FIGURE 4-5

Asymmetry in Price Tiers

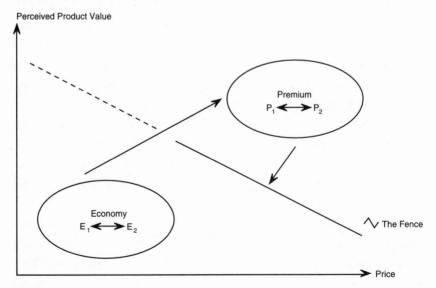

impacts its same-tier competitors more strongly. So, for example, relating to Table 4-1's beer data, a Budweiser price cut impacts its fellow tier 1 resident Miller more than it impacts tier 3's Milwaukee's Best; and a Natural Light price cut (tier 3) would impact Milwaukee's Best (tier 3) more than Miller (tier 1). This we show in Figure 4-5 with heavy arrows between E_1 and E_2 and between P_1 and P_2. The second important part of Figure 4-5 is the nature of the fence. A price cut by premium tier brand P_1 draws to it economy tier buyers—who are able to slip through the spacing in the "picket fence" portion at the upper left end of the fence. That is, P_1 has some clout in being able to induce customers from the economy tier to "trade up" to it. However, if E_2 cuts price, the premium brand buyers conceptually crash into the solid portion of the fence on the lower right, without trading down to the economy segment. E_2's price cut can increase its sales volume—by drawing E_1 customers or increasing the category consumption rate—but it will not draw many customers away from the premium brands. In terms of the beer data, this means that a Budweiser buyer, who usually pays $14.07 for a tier 1 brand—rejecting tier 3 brands selling at 34% less—is not going to be induced to switch to tier 3 if the tier 3 price drops by say 5%, from $9.26 to $8.80.

Figure 4-6 shows the structure we found in analyzing a five-brand consumer products market. The market has a rather tight price distribution. Three brands make up the middle market, flanked by a premium brand priced 7% above and an economy brand priced 9% below. Our hypothesis is that the middle-market brands would be in a more vulnerable position, in that they are able to steal share from one another due to being in the same price tier. The premium and economy brands, being somewhat separated from this tier and the three players in it, would be in a less competitive situation. This hypothesis was borne out in statistical testing; the average cross-price elasticity for middle market brands was over 5—meaning that a 1% decrease in a middle-market brand price resulted in a 5% drop in other brands' sales—while the premium and economy tier cross-elasticities averaged only 1.5.

Blattberg and Wisniewski[7] analyzed 28 brands in four frequently purchased consumer packaged-goods categories and found a similar result for the intensity of same-price-tier competition. Same-tier competitors are typically the ones hurt most by a price cut—and thus the ones most

FIGURE 4-6

Consumer Products Economy, Middle, and Premium Segments

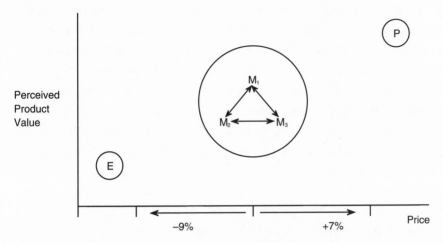

likely to react, if they can. Blattberg and Wisniewski extend their analysis into the nature of inter-tier price competition.

Their general conclusion is that "higher-priced, higher-quality brands steal share from other brands in the same quality tier *and* brands in the tier below. However, lower-price, lower-quality brands take share from their own tier and the tier-below brands, but do *not* steal significant share from the tiers above." An interesting phenomenon now taking place is the emergence of quality private-label products, which may break private labels out of their weak position due to the asymmetry found here.

Sivakumar and Raj[8] analyzed the asymmetry in inter-tier competition for four additional product categories and also considered the impact of price changes on the size of the market. They find the same asymmetry with more "trade-ups" than "trade-downs," thus favoring higher-priced/higher-quality brands. They also find that the high-quality brands have an advantage in their ability to induce otherwise nonpurchasers to enter the market through a price cut. For example, they find that a 10% cut in the price of a high-quality ketchup induces a 6% share point rise due to new customers coming into the market; whereas the low-quality ketchups do not have this power—pulling in only 0.3% share points from new customers with a 10% price decrease.

A first step for the power pricer in managing profitability is understanding the competitive set. We recommend explicit consideration of the notion of price tiers. Do they operate in your market? If so, the focus when considering a price change should be on same-tier competitors. Consideration should also be given to the asymmetry noted in the empirical studies. We recently found this useful in analyzing a car manufacturer's consideration of a sizable price cut at the low end of its product line. We found it would yield substantial sales volume benefit. And, consistent with the price tier ideas discussed here, business was drawn almost totally from competitors in the same price tier—rather than, as the company had feared, cannibalizing the company's own higher-priced, higher-margin cars.

In addition, individual competitors must be analyzed to assess their drawing power. Many large-market-share brands are powerful—but only in their ability to *retain* the customers they have (e.g., AT&T). This is passive power. They have less active power, i.e., their ability to take customers away from others is minimal. Other firms, perhaps small but new to the market, develop active power—the ability to attract other customers (e.g., MCI). Effective price management requires an appreciation of these two fundamentally different types of power. A reaction from an active power type can be more significant than a passive power reaction.

PRICE: COORDINATION, COMPETITION, OR WARFARE?

Figures 4-7 and 4-8 show decade-long price trends for cigarette and instant camera industries in the United States. Figure 4-7 shows that the average retail price of a package of cigarettes increased 139% (in nominal terms) from 72¢ per pack to $1.72 per pack over the decade 1982–1992. Annual price increases ranged from 7.3% to 12.8% and averaged 9.9% as compared to the average annual CPI change of 4.0%. In 1992, market leader Philip Morris made $5.2 billion in operating profit from U.S. tobacco operations—a 52% return on its $9.9 billion in revenues. This 10%-per-year steady improvement in price realization occurred even though the market size steadily declined—from 634 billion cigarettes consumed in 1982 to 500 billion in 1992—a 21% decrease.

Figure 4-8 shows the average retail price for a basic instant camera in real terms from 1976 to 1985. It declined 76%. There were only two

FIGURE 4-7

Average Retail Price of Cigarettes in U.S.A., 1982 to 1992

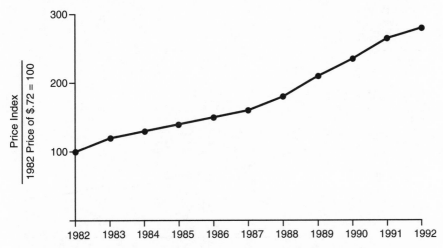

Source: Based on data in B. Issacson and A. Silk, "Philip Morris: Marlboro Friday (A)," Harvard Business School, Case #9-596-001.

players in the market: Kodak and Polaroid. Prior to Kodak's entry in 1976, Polaroid had obtained 40–50% gross margins on its cameras. By 1978, Kodak cut its price down to manufacturing cost.

From 1976 through 1979, Kodak lost $484 million on its instant-photography business. Prices continued to sink through the early 1980s, resulting in sales at prices below manufacturing cost—e.g., in 1982, Kodak's lowest-priced camera sold to dealers for $11.95 despite a $28 manufacturing cost. In the words of one industry participant, by 1985, the industry had taken on the "aroma of a fire sale." Kodak lost an additional $220 million from 1981 through 1984 before deciding to reduce its presence in the amateur instant market.

Here we have two industries evolving over about a decade: one with prices increasing like clockwork—139% over 10 years—making for a 74% industry gross margin in 1993; the other with prices declining 76%, costing both players in the market many millions of dollars. Why the dramatic difference in the price evolution of these markets?

A lot of the difference can be explained very simply: *price coordination* vs. a *price war.* In the cigarette business, the "Big 2" were Philip Morris and R. J. Reynolds at about 40% and 30% market shares respectively.

FIGURE 4-8

Average Retail Price for Self-contained Instant Camera of Basic Functionality in Real Terms (1980 $)

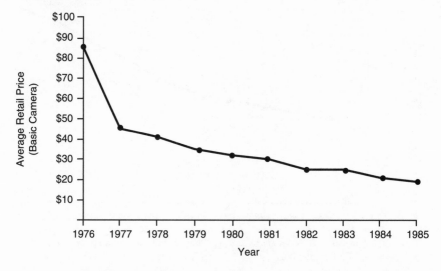

Prices for branded cigarettes from different manufacturers moved along in concert—although a discount-brand segment of the market did grow through the 1980s. Pricing behavior in the cigarette industry has been the subject of much academic investigation and commentators note that even as far back as the 1920s, the major players "clearly recognized their mutual interdependence."[9] In contrast, the prevailing attitude in the instant camera business was war. In the words of Polaroid's CEO, Kodak's move to lower pricing in 1977 was a "bombshell," which it would be "suicide" for Polaroid not to counter. The marketing executive responsible for defining Polaroid's competitive strategy referred to Kodak's price-cutting practices as being "wielded with a vengeance." It is clear that Polaroid's profits were caught in the Veg-O-Matic (see Figure 4-2) of Kodak's downward price movement and pursuit of market share over profitability.[10]

In competitive markets such as these two, and the majority of markets in the world, there is a natural tendency to price cutting, which left unchecked can destroy margins, choke off required capital for R&D investment, and end innovation. The natural tendency is well illuminated by the "Prisoner's Dilemma" concept. The dilemma goes like this:

> Fred and Ted are suspects in a crime committed by two individuals. Each is held in a separate examining room and encouraged to cooperate with the au-

thorities. Each knows that if neither of them confess to the crime, they will both get off with only having to pay a small fine. The authorities tell Fred, "If you cooperate, i.e., confess that the two of you did it, and Ted doesn't cooperate, you are free to go and Ted gets a long prison sentence. If you both confess, then it's a short prison sentence for each of you." Separately, the authorities tell Ted the same thing. What should Fred and Ted do?

The "dilemma" is that with this information, if Fred and Ted could get together they would be able to agree to hold out and thus would both walk away with only a small fine. However, they are held separately and cannot communicate, so what are their individual incentives? Figure 4-9 summarizes the situation.

Given this, Fred and Ted could come out not too badly. By neither confessing, they wind up in box 1 of Figure 4-9. But because they are held separately, they will never get there. Consider Fred's situation as he thinks this through logically.

Suppose Ted confesses (putting us in the right hand column of Figure 4-9). What should I do? If I confess, I get a short prison term (box 4); if I don't, I get a long one (box 2); so, if I think he is going to confess, I should confess. Suppose Ted doesn't confess (putting us in the left column of Figure 4-9). If

FIGURE 4-9

Fred and Ted Dilemma

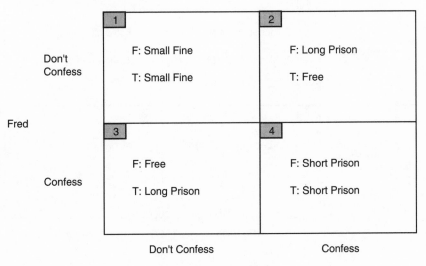

I confess, I get to go free (box 3); if I don't confess, I have to pay a small fine (box 1). So, if I think he isn't going to confess, I should confess.

Thus, Fred thinks it through and figures out that no matter what Ted does, he is better off confessing. Fred's thinking would be precisely the same. Thus, both confess and wind up in box 4—when *each* would be better off in box 1.

Now, instead of prisoners, suppose Fred and Ted are competitors in the marketplace and we change actions "don't confess" to "hold price level" and "confess" to "cut price"; and change "payoffs" as follows:

Go Free → Big Profits
Pay Fine → Moderate Profits
Moderate Jail Term → Tiny Profits
Long Jail Term → Make No Money

i.e., prisoners-turned-merchants Fred and Ted face the "payoff matrix" of Figure 4-10.

Fred obviously prefers box 3—just as he did in the prison example—where he cuts his price a bit but makes a big profit because he is below Ted and captures nearly the entire market. By the exact same logic as be-

FIGURE 4-10

Merchant Payoff Matrix

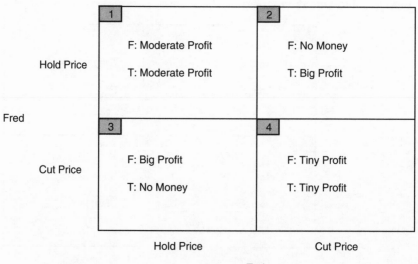

fore, noncommunicating Fred and Ted both wind up cutting price and the industry is in box 4—when each participant would be better off in box 1.

This is a highly simplified story; but it captures the crux of actual price competition in industries such as hotels, mutual funds ("Fidelity Joins Mutual Funds on Fee Cutting Bandwagon"),[11] and computer software and hardware ("Dell, Compaq continue to duel it out in price wars" and "Apple keeps price wars alive with Centris line").[12] In the short term, firms see individual gains in cutting price to improve market share—but these fail to materialize as competitors react. For example, Figure 4-11 shows the industry response to Procter and Gamble's price reduction on Pampers disposable diapers. The press referred to the P&G and Kimberly-Clark action as a "price fight," which Kimberly-Clark's chairman said "will reduce diaper revenues by about $50 million in 1993. . . . We expect diaper profitability to return to more traditional levels in 1994 . . ."[13]

FIGURE 4-11

Industry Price Reactions to P&G Price Moves

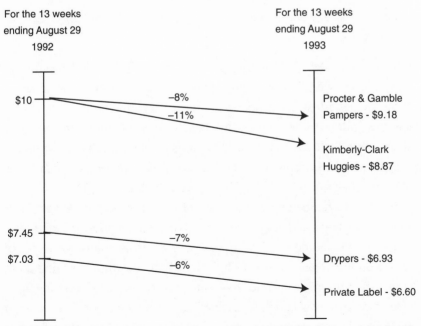

Data from Gabriella Stern, "P&G Gains Little From Diaper Cuts," *Wall Street Journal,* October 28, 1993.

An industry characterized by price coordination in one geographic region may find price competition rampant in another. For example, the German tobacco market has not enjoyed the steady price appreciation seen for the U.S. market in Figure 4-7. As mentioned in chapter 2, in January 1983, Reemtsma Cigarettenfabriken cut the price of its West brand from DM 3.80 to DM 3.30, the first such move in the West German cigarette market since World War II. Within four months West's market share increased from .6% to 10%. But then competitors feeling the share loss retaliated and the previously stable price structure collapsed. It took the industry four years to recover.

Recognition of the competitive aspects of pricing is becoming increasingly important. For example, Jack Welch, Chairman of General Electric, predicts the coming of "the Value Decade" marked by severe global price competition stemming from

- reduced core product differentiation
- global production overcapacity in many situations
- significantly diminished trade barriers
- efficient information and distribution systems that "give everybody access to everything"
- customers' attitude: "Don't tell me about your technology. Tell me your price."

In this "Value Decade," Welch contends: "If you can't sell a top-quality product at the world's lowest price, you're going to be out of the game."[14]

As suggested by the diaper and German cigarette examples above, however, allowing an industry to become focused solely on low price and market share typically has disastrous consequences. For example, consider the U.S. airline business and its disintegration into a situation of prices so low that all the major players call them "insane."

In early 1992, the pricing structure of the industry made no sense. A tenet of this book is that opportunities to customize price to individuals and situations should be pursued, but the U.S. airline industry was out of control in this regard. A given flight could find customers paying 25 or more different prices even for the same class of service depending upon when the ticket was bought, length of stay, and the personal situation of the customer, e.g., military personnel or bereaved and traveling due to a death in the family. The pricing structure was so illogical that customers on trips of short duration not involving a Saturday-night stay found it cheaper to buy two round-trip tickets fabricated to include Saturday night stays and then to use only the front half of each ticket to execute the desired itinerary.

On April 29, 1992, American Airlines made what it called "a major strategic announcement" in instituting "Value Pricing," claiming this new pricing structure would:

1. restore customers' faith in the airlines by giving customers a better deal
2. increase American's revenue
3. get both American and *the industry back to profitability.*[15]

Industry load factors were consistently around 62% of capacity from 1987–91 and U.S. suppliers' losses totaled $1.87 billion in 1991. American's new policy was to offer only four fares: First Class, Regular Coach, Discount Coach—7-Day Advance Purchase, and Discount Coach—21-Day Advance Purchase. Fares would vary in relation to mileage for the flight and were significantly below full-fare prices then published. American's price move was immediately matched by the other two "Big Three" U.S. carriers, Delta and United. Each of the Big Three had market shares in the 17–19% range; the "Medium Three" at approximately 9% shares at the time were Continental, Northwest, and USAir; the "Little Three" at approximately 4% shares were AmericaWest, Southwest, and TWA.

Three days later, TWA undercut American's price structure with fares 10–20% below American's, prompting downward price movements by USAir, Continental, and AmericaWest—and ultimately a response from American on selected routes, e.g., an additional 17% on Dallas–New York. On May 26, Northwest announced its "Grown-Ups Fly Free program—offering 2 for 1 pricing for the summer for families traveling. American responded by announcing 50% off some fares for the summer. Competitors, while calling the prices "insane," matched them. August 1992 saw record load factors for many and American and United both broke the record for highest number of revenue passenger miles ever flown by a U.S. carrier in a given month—but yielding a disastrous profit situation. The *Barron's*[16] article "Fare Wars are Hell—At Least for Airlines' Bottom Line," commented, "For travelers, it was the best of times. . . . For the airlines, however, it was among the worst of times." In 1992 each of the Big Three saw a 20% or more drop in the price of its shares between March and June.

In October, American dropped Value Pricing and Chairman Robert Crandall commented to the press that "We tried to provide some price leadership, but it didn't work, so we are back to death by a thousand cuts."[17] Crandall also lamented that: "We are more victims than villains—victims of our dumbest competitors . . . the business is driven entirely by the behavior of our competitors. Each airline decides what's best for it without regard to what is best for the industry."[18]

Using the terminology of our glass executive at the beginning of this chapter, this is a "dumb industry." The implications of this price-cutting battle are lasting. Consumers, having flown from Boston to Los Angeles for less than a hundred dollars, now regard anything above this as "unfair." This leads to competitors selling on price, not benefits, reinforcing the downward spiral.

Instead of just decrying the situation as our glass manager did with his RETRO line—"We are in a dumb industry!"—one must develop an understanding of competitors to anticipate their pricing moves and reactions and then, building upon this, begin to influence and manage competitors' pricing.

UNDERSTANDING AND MANAGING COMPETITORS

Empirical work by Lambin[19] has shown a high degree of pricing interdependence among firms. Specifically, for his sample, he found an average price reaction elasticity of .71—meaning that on average a 10% price decrease was met by a 7.1% decrease in competitor's price. By comparison, the average advertising reaction elasticity was only .38. While this shows that a price reaction is the norm, competitive response varies greatly by situation in systematic ways. For example, what would we expect from:

- Kodak—holding a 70% share of the $2 billion U.S. film market; if Fuji cut its price, would Kodak follow?
- Delta Airlines—if USAir cut its price on the Boston–New York shuttle route, would Delta follow?

Obviously in the first instance, Kodak, with high brand equity and high market share, will do almost anything it can to defend itself before resorting to a price cut. A 5% price cut while holding volume would cost Kodak approximately $50–$60 million in revenues. Obviously it will try to find another way as it did with Funtime film (see page 85 in this chapter). A firm with high market share is very adverse to price cutting.

Delta, on the other hand, sells a perishable good which has a low variable cost. It almost *has* to respond in price if USAir makes a significant move. It is clear that Delta is much more likely to respond via price than Kodak—unless Kodak's price response is in Fuji's home market of Japan, where Fuji holds a 70% share! Information about a firm's position can lead to sound judgments on the form of its likely response. Analyzing the contributors to the airline industry's dash to insane prices described above helps reveal those industry factors most important to consider in assessing a competitor's situation and ultimately its response.

Supply Factors

1. *Cost Structure:* The airline industry has a high fixed but low variable cost structure. Once the plane is headed down the runway from New York to Boston, it matters little to the cost if there is one more passenger on board. The price floor is thus close to zero. Hence, almost any incremental revenue that could be gained from pursuing those marginal customers would be worth it.
2. *Capacity Utilization:* With load factors averaging only 62% system-wide, there is substantial overcapacity on some routes. Hence, there is great opportunity to take on customers with their variable cost being the only cost impact.
3. *Product Perishability:* The product, i.e., the airline seat, cannot be inventoried for sale another day. Once the flight is gone, that opportunity to sell that seat is gone. In effect, the seat is "spoiled" and has no salvage value.
4. *Extent of Product Differentiation:* There is little differentiation in the core product of taking the traveler from point A to point B and competitors have not substantively pursued other means of differentiation.

5. *Number and Diversity of Competitors:* Competitors are a varied lot, with different route and cost structures, different objectives and financial positions. Delta and United, the other members of the Big Three, quickly followed American's new price structure, but others had different time horizons and different business models. TWA was in bankruptcy and focused on short-term cash flow. TWA's head claimed that American was trying to put it out of business. Southwest Airlines had an entirely different business model—setting its prices to compete with buses and trains—and took out ads crowing, "We'd like to match their new fares, but we'd have to raise ours."

Demand Factors

6. *Price Sensitivity of Selective Demand:* Partly because of the lack of product differentiation, customers buy largely on price.
7. *Efficiency of Price Shopping:* Through travel agents, competitive prices are easily known. Some computer programs are written to find cheapest routings; hence consumers are well informed and it is easy to "shop price."
8. *Degree of Brand Loyalty:* Although frequent-flier programs have tried to create "switching costs," for most fliers, with membership in every frequent-flier program of potential interest, there is no airline loyalty.
9. *Industry Growth Rate:* Industry demand is not growing relative to supply. Therefore, growing a firm's business significantly means taking share of market from others which increases the likelihood of their reaction.

All nine of these factors make it more difficult for the airline industry to be a "smart industry" with growing price realization as compared to an industry with low fixed costs, highly differentiated goods, and brand-loyal customers. An added factor in the airline situation was

10. *Lack of personal affinity of the participants:* for example, after American was sued for alleged predatory pricing, Crandall referred to Northwest's top management as "wheeler-dealers who loaded the balance sheet with debt."[20]

Apocryphal stories about these executives deciding the course of industry prices in the midst of a Saturday morning golf game are unlikely to surface.

In addition to these ten factors directly suggested by the airline industry analysis, our experience leads us to add five more factors to consider in assessing the industry and competitive intensity.

Added Supply Factors to Consider

11. *Impact of Sales Volume on Cost:* Increased price competitiveness occurs when sales volume impacts cost through economies of scale or experience-curve effects. One of the prescriptions of experience-curve price theorists is to anticipate cost declines and price in recognition of future cost levels, i.e., the cycle is:

Low Price → Sales Volume → Low Cost

12. *Barriers to Capacity Adjustment:* If capacity cannot be effectively adjusted downward due to exit barriers, low-capacity utilization persists and stimulates price competitiveness.

13. *Importance of the Market to Participants:* The greater the importance of the market to a firm, the more vigorously it will be defended. For example, Polaroid founder Edwin Land saw the instant photography business as "our soul, to them [Kodak] it's just another business."

Added Demand Factors to Consider

14. *Buyer Concentration:* A highly sophisticated, concentrated buyer base can create price competitiveness. These buyers adopt a procurement policy of aggregating purchases in large lots, e.g., by making multiyear commitments to increase their buying leverage and the amount of business an individual firm can attain via a price cut. For example, this was the case in the electrical industry and now in airplanes as Boeing and other suppliers sell to a handful of significant buyers worldwide.

15. *Complementary Product:* Price competition can increase if a purchase of the product has a secondary revenue impact. For example, one factor behind the Polaroid-Kodak low camera pricing was that

once a customer bought an instant camera from either manufacturer, he had to buy all his instant film from that manufacturer. The attitude of "invest in building the installed base," while not always unwise, can lead to strong price cut reactions.

Consideration of these 15 factors should give a good indication of the likelihood and nature of competitive response to price actions. One should also study competitors' pronouncements and policies on price reactions. For example, a number of firms have widely publicized policies guaranteeing that they will meet or beat the price of any competitor. Lechmere, a consumer electronics retailer, guarantees its prices and refunds the difference if a customer finds a lower price. Tweeter, a smaller retailer, goes one step further, promising to track competitors' ads in the future and refund the customer the difference for any lower prices found. Binhold, the world leader in anatomical training aids (e.g., skeletons) offers this guarantee worldwide and uses it as its worldwide competitive intelligence system.[21] Understanding the industry situation and any specific competitor policies is a prerequisite to managing competitors and industry profitability.

MANAGING COMPETITORS AND INDUSTRY PROFITABILITY: BOOSTING THE INDUSTRY IQ

As we have seen, some industries wind up being "dumb" as price cutting runs rampant; others wind being "smart" as major competitors enjoy high levels of profitability. As noted above in the 15 checks on the price competitiveness of an industry, some industries are inherently more prone to turn out to be "dumb" due to demand and supply characteristics. However, being "smart" or "dumb" is not driven totally by outside forces. An individual firm, skilled and determined, can impact the industry IQ. There are five key directions for a firm to undertake in order to boost its industry's IQ, keeping it from being one in which each participant's profit potential is "Veg-O-Matic'd" by the others' price cutting. These are:

1. adopting a profitability mentality
2. using a price war filter
3. shaping competitors' reactions

4. building your power base
5. maintaining flexibility

1. Adopting a Profitability Mentality

In the late 1970s, the most prominent strategic thinking of the day focused on the importance of market share. In the words of an extremely well-known *Harvard Business Review* article, "Market Share: A Key to Profitability,"[22] the route to long-term profitability was seen to be through building market share—forgoing short-term profit if necessary, and reaping profits from the business as the market matured. "Cash cows" for the firm were those businesses which had a high market share in low-growth industries.

The environment of the 1990s requires a shift in this thinking. In one industry after another, the aggressive pursuit of market share has led to overcapacity, price cutting, and profits for nobody. The focus must shift from market share to a broader conception incorporating industry profitability. Price impacts not only market share, but also the size of the market and the value of a market share point. McKinsey has articulated this point well in its "Marketers' Metamorphosis,"[23] describing the dimensions of the "fundamental transformation" required of marketers in the 1990s. First among the dimensions of change is redefinition of objectives from market share to market surplus:

> What matters is not share of market, but share of scarce market profits. . . . "market surplus" will replace market share as the measure of success. Companies—and their marketers will take a much wider view of their industry. . . . They will think not just about their own profits, but also about maximizing both the total profits in their industry—the market surplus—and their companies' share of these profits.

Industries are "smart" when participants all have an eye to enlarging the overall profit pie, which will be divided among players according to their competitive strength. This induces firms to keep "value" as the operant concept in customers' minds rather than "price."

Many firms are still stuck in the market-share mindset. For example, a California winemaker's strategic planners strongly advocate pushing down into lower quality/price segments to build share—ignoring the dilution of the value of a share point from these actions. The rush of computer manufacturers into the home market via mass-marketing channels stemmed from their desire to build volume at the low end of the market. Profits have been elusive there. The smart competitor defines his market advantageously. He respects the domain of others, avoiding collisions with competitors; he keeps an eye on industry profitability and through his actions encourages the competition to do the same.

2. Using a Price War Filter

As part of the implementation of direction No. 1, each anticipated price move has to be subjected to a simple test: if passed through a filter that trapped all actions likely to set off or exacerbate an existing price war, would it come out the other side? A downward adjustment in company price and in the industry price level overall is sometimes a desired action. However, the move must be accomplished in such a way that it does not spiral out of control. In the past, some firms undertook downward price action in the belief that it would hasten an industry shakeout and adjustment in capacity. The speed with which such adjustments happen—if they happen at all—has tended to be overestimated. In today's environment, capacity changes hands but does not often leave the industry.

3. Shaping Competitors' Reactions

Competitors' reactions will be a function of how closely they compete. The price-tier concept discussed above helps define the relevant customer set. For relevant competitors, their reaction relates to both the actions perceived by them and their inferences about the motives underlying those actions. Thus there are three elements here: the action, the perception of the action by competitors, and their interpretation of the action. Each is to some extent under the control of the firm.

The first step in this process is so obvious that it would hardly seem worth stating if our experience did not indicate it is sometimes passed over. Start the process by asking: what, within reason, would I want my competitors' response to be in both price and other elements of the marketing mix? For example, would I want them to:

- see my price increase, match it fully, and increase advertising budget to grow market size?
- see my price increase and go even higher?
- do nothing, because they did not know I did anything?
- see my price decrease as being only for select customers and therefore not respond; undertake advertising to stress product differentiation?
- see my price decrease and match it?

Each of these desired reactions, even the last, is plausible in different situations. For example, some contend that this is precisely what Philip Morris wanted R. J. Reynolds to do on "Marlboro Friday," April 21, 1993, when Philip Morris cut the price of Marlboros 20%. R. J. Reynolds' response would cut profitability and strain its ability to invest in emerging world markets such as China. In March 1996, when Compaq announced 20% price cuts at the high end of the personal-computer market, it had clearly thought through what it expected and wanted in terms of competitive response, the CFO commenting, "We believe these actions will accelerate our own momentum. To the extent, the competition will have to respond, that's certainly our intent."[24]

Once the desired reaction is envisioned, one can begin to see how to present the action, influencing the competitor's perception of it and of the motives underlying it. Power pricers prepare the market for price moves in a way that increases the likelihood of the desired competitive reaction. While staying within the bounds of the law that makes price fixing per se illegal, power pricers provide information that puts their actions in the proper context.[25]

Consider, for example, the half-page article in the trade magazine *Advertising Age,* entitled "Price War Bites at Pet Food Ad $."[26] This article featured statements from four major competitors in the market.

- *Ralston Purina:* identified in the article as "the pet food market leader in share and action"
  - Noted statements from a Purina shareholders' meeting in which the CEO of grocery products said that going forward Purina would respond to price discounting with "a more measured approach."
  - Noted public Purina statements saying it's trying to spend more on

advertising and focus on fewer and better new product introductions.

- *Alpo Pet Foods*—executives quoted:
  - "The whole category is being driven to commodity pricing."
  - "This year we hope there's a chance we'll see more normalcy in pricing."
  - "We don't want to compete at those [price] levels. That's just stripping out the profit for everyone."
- *Heinz Pet Foods*—executive quoted:
  - "Pricing for profit has been a problem for everyone."
- *Mars/Kal-Kan Foods*—executive quoted:
  - "These price wars are . . . running the risk of turning a very well-established branded category into a commodity."

What is the impact of these *public* statements on participants' expectations about reactions to individual firms' move to increase prices? Each player is indicating a concern for the category and dissatisfaction with the status quo on pricing. In short, this one article is filled with signals about competitive desires and intent and provides insight into likely reactions.

An extended example of signaling through the press is provided by the German cigarette market's price recovery from January 1985 to January 1990. Five price increases, boosting prices about 15% in total, were enacted throughout the market during this time, as shown in Figure 4-12. Each price increase was preceded by significant signaling. In three of the five cases, market leader Philip Morris began the process. The figure expands on the seven signaling events which took place over a 4-month period preceding the October 24, 1988 across-the-market price increase of 15 Pfennigs for premium brands.

The signaling started on June 15 with an announcement by BAT (British-American Tobacco) in a leading newspaper that a price increase is necessary due to a tobacco tax increase announced by the government. About ten days later this tax increase was criticized by the association of cigarette manufacturers. Philip Morris provided its first concrete price signal on July 22, using the leading newspaper and the tobacco trade press to announce a planned 15-Pfennig increase for "43rd week"—i.e., about the third week of October. Immediately thereafter,

FIGURE 4-12

A Case of Intense Signaling—The German Cigarette Market

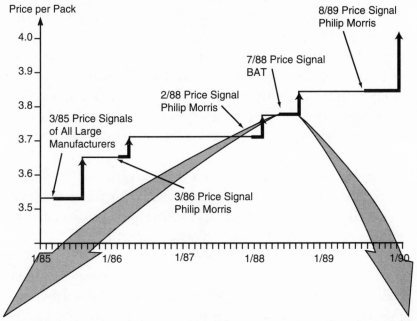

Date	Company	Medium	Announcement	
			Price increase	Planned date
June 15	BAT	FAZ	necessary due to tax increase	—
June 26	VdC	FAZ	criticism of tax increase	
July 22	Ph. Morris	DTZ/FAZ	15 Pfennigs	43rd week
July 22	Reemtsma Reynolds BAT	FAZ FAZ FAZ	15 Pfennigs no decision yet no decision yet	last week of October — —
July 29	BAT Brinkmann Reynolds	DTZ DTZ DTZ	15 Pfennigs 15 Pfennigs no decision yet	end of October end of October —
Sept. 23	Ph. Morris	NRZ	Further price increase necessary to compensate for tax increase	—
Oct. 14	Reemtsma	LZ	15 Pfennigs	in a few days
Oct. 24	Prices increase between 5 and 15 Pfennigs			

Faz: Frankfurter Allgemeine Zeitung (Leading national newspaper)
DTZ: Deutsche Tabak-Zeitung (German tobacco newspaper)
HB: Handelsblatt (Business newspaper)
LZ: Lebensmittels-Zeitung (Newspaper of the food industry)
NRZ: Neue Ruhr-Zeitung (Large regional newspaper)
VdC: Verband deutscher Cigarettenfabriken (Association of German cigarette manufacturers)

announcements of increases for other firms appeared, with Reemtsma endorsing the 15-Pfennig level and Reynolds and BAT endorsing a price increase but not yet decided on the level. Some of these signals came through press releases, while others originated with journalists who called the companies to inquire about their pricing plans. As shown in the figure, further signals appeared in the next months, essentially confirming the industry's need and determination to increase prices by the end of October. On October 24 the price increases were implemented. For most product categories, the increases were by 15 Pfennigs (e.g., in the premium category prices went up from DM 3.85 to DM 4.0); in a lower, more price-sensitive category prices were only increased by 5 Pfennigs.

There can be no doubt that the tax increase supported the price increase since it affected all manufacturers equally. But it also seems clear that the extended signaling process played an important role in the magnitude and the timing of this industry-wide price move.

Firms sometimes mistakenly believe that "the less competitors know about you the better." This attitude can lead to harmful misinterpretation of pricing actions. A power pricer thinks through what he wants competitors to know and what he wants kept secret. For example, it may be well worthwhile to make sure that a price cut on a discontinued item is understood to be just that, and not part of a continuing move. This would prevent competitors from interpreting it as an aggressive move requiring share-defending, margin-eroding action.

The early 1993 price war in the German television guide market was attributed to a lack of communication accompanying Gruner and Jahr's price cut of *TV Today* from DM 2.3 to DM 1.0. An industry consultant opined, "the industry would not have reacted half as fiercely if Gruner and Jahr had made it clear from the beginning that the price cut was only a temporary move."[27]

There are multiple ways to communicate with competitors: statements in the press, annual meetings and reports, published price lists and addenda to those lists. In the normal course of communicating with customers, one is communicating with the competition. Care must be taken to stay within the law; it is not true that as long as the information is made public, it is permissible to reveal it. For example, the Federal

Trade Commission (FTC) brought charges against Mead Johnson for ignoring states' statutory sealed-bid process on an infant-formula procurement. According to the FTC, the company sent its bid to the states in open letters, knowing that its competitors would see the information contained in the letters.[28]

Stating precommitments can also be a way to influence competitive actions; for example, price guarantees can be a mechanism that limits the extent of price response, since the firm knows that undercutting would trigger another price cut. Through patient application of the many mechanisms for shaping the context of price actions, one can shape ultimate competitive response as well.

4. Building Your Power Base

Exerting influence on the overall profit level of the industry and gaining effective control over your share of those industry profits is only possible if necessary actions to build the power base have been undertaken. The major dimensions of this are:

A. *Differentiated Product:* This can be either through technical performance, value-adding features or services or brand equity. Customers' perception of value and a preference for the goods of the firm are always the cornerstone of effective capturing of "market surplus."
B. *Cost Position:* Taco Bell was able to limit effective competitive reaction to its value pricing because it had invested in fundamentally changing its business model—facilities, management techniques, and relationships with suppliers. It is difficult to attain an influential position in the marketplace while working off a cost disadvantage at the given quality level.
C. *Competitive Information:* A power pricer knows what is going on in the marketplace—not just with list pricing, but with real transaction prices—and, beyond price, has an appreciation of the basic business model of the competition. What value do they try to provide? How? How does pricing line up with the value? Collection of competitive pricing information requires care. Customers are selective in what they disclose about prices they are offered or paid. Some competitive "offers" may be clouded by other terms or lost in the course of negotiations. Sales people should not be considered the sole reliable

source. Confirming one source with another is critical. Also, the power pricer understands the competitor's product offering well enough to adjust for size or performance differences.

D. *Broad Market Participation:* Presence in broad sectors and markets can help to control competitors in key markets. For example, Kodak's presence in the Japanese market—even at the limited scale at which it operates—gives it some power with respect to Fuji's actions in Kodak's home market. In 1995, Kodak sought ways to increase this presence by filing legal action regarding distribution blockages in Japan and also introducing private-label film in the Japanese market. The ability to respond to harmful acts in your key market by acting in key markets of the competitor—be they geographic or product type— helps control these competitive actions.

5. Maintaining Flexibility

A power pricer does not become inexorably committed to a significant market position or even presence in each market segment. On January 30, 1996, Digital Equipment Corporation said it had learned enough about the margins available and exited the home-computer sector of the market. As one industry analyst commented, "It's a very positive move to pull back to the business market, where at least the Digital brand name means something."[29] Withdrawing from a segment is sometimes inherently distasteful to management, but the ability to redeploy assets to more productive areas keeps one from being frozen to a market share goal which, given customer and competitor decision-making processes, can only be maintained by contributing to price erosion in the marketplace.

SUMMARY

The power pricer marries three types of underlying understandings: understanding his own competencies and costs, consumer behavior, and competitive reactions. He operates in the upper right part of the Figure 4-1 map. All these are inextricably linked in determining firm profitability. While the field of competitive strategy has burgeoned over the past decade, rigorous application of these ideas to the price response aspect has not been systematically pursued by many organizations.

We recommend that firms build their base for power pricing by:

1. recognizing that a firm can impact the industry IQ, making it smarter and more profitable overall. The firm should undertake efforts to educate industry participants in legal ways, such as through trade association seminars.
2. understanding the price tiers in the marketplace and the extent of competition between players. The price-tier concept has been useful in many situations and we recommend its applicability for the specific situation being considered.
3. employing the 15 supply and demand factors test on price competitiveness suggested in this chapter to improve their understanding of their industry.
4. understanding the useful and legal mechanisms for encouraging price coordination in an industry. There are a wide variety of signaling mechanisms that have proven useful.
5. analyzing individual industry participants—their market share, objectives, and cost position in particular—to assess what actions they will take in pursuit of those objectives.
6. subjecting all price actions to the "price war filter" test. Once started, price wars are hard to stop. One should not be overly confident about a "shakeout" occurring. These do happen at times, e.g., the departure of Anheuser-Busch from the salty-snack-food marketplace and the sale of its production facilities to its chief rival Frito-Lay, but they take a long time and true capacity reduction is infrequent.
7. envisioning what the desired competitive response is and recognizing that this may not be a price response at all; instead, it could be a product quality or advertising change.
8. having patience, not overreacting to every short-term erosion in sales volume.
9. maintaining flexibility by avoiding inexorable commitment to a share level. It is fine to say we must be Number One or Number Two in the industry—as long as "or we get out" is added.

PART II

Breakthrough Pricing Concepts

5

Price Customization

INTRODUCTION

The chapters to this point have made clear the central role of a product's value to the customer in pricing. Figure 1-2 showed the relationship of customer value to price; subsequently we described ways to estimate this value. As we have seen, all customers do not have the same value for a product, though; consequently, in a world of power pricing, they do not pay the same amount for it. Rather, customizing price to the customer's value is a breakthrough pricing opportunity. For example, on one day, sales of one-third-liter cans of Coca-Cola were brisk at each of the nine outlets within Bonn, Germany, listed in Table 5-1. The large supermarket customers paid DM .64; the median price of the nine was DM 1.20 at the gas station; the maximum price of DM 2.20 at the train station's newsstand was 3.44 times that paid at the large supermarket. Subsequently, we even observed that the price at an outlet on the way into the train station was higher than at an outlet on the way out! These prices were set independently by the individual operators but the underlying logic is clear: low prices for those buying for "take-home" in a non-time-pressured environment and high prices for those "on the move" with little time to seek alternatives, looking for something for immediate consumption.

TABLE 5-1

Prices of One-Third-Liter-Can of Coca-Cola at Nine Outlets within the
City of Bonn, Germany

Point of Sale	Price (DM)	Index
1. Large Supermarket	0.64	100
2. Grocery Store	0.69	108
3. Bakery	0.80	125
4. Vending Machine—University	0.90	141
5. Gas Station	1.20	188
6. Vending Machine—Street	1.50	243
7. Newsstand—Street	1.60	250
8. Newsstand—Airport	2.00	312
9. Newsstand—Train Station	2.20	344

Even when the price is set by an individual firm rather than a series
of retailers, price customization can be quite significant. For example,
Microsoft's pricing scheme for the "Office 95" suite of products
(Word, Excel, PowerPoint, and Schedule Plus) customized the standard price of $499 in three ways. Upgraders, who have the option of
sticking with their old system, receive a $200 discount. Time is the sec-
ond customizing dimension—a $50 discount to those who act by year's
end. Third, current Microsoft customers receive an additional $40 re-
bate, bringing the price for a particular customer, i.e., a current Microsoft customer upgrading by year's end, down to $209—42% of the
standard price.

A power pricer recognizes the profit-enhancing possibilities of price
customization. Different customers have different levels of willingness
and ability to pay. A common failing in pricing practice is not to adapt
prices to these realities, thereby forgoing significant profit opportunities.
Sir Colin Marshall, British Airways chairman, cited the significance of
even "slight" customization to his bottom line:

> ... the great majority of the traveling public will buy on price. ... [but]
> some people will pay a slight premium. I want to stress that when I say

'slight' I mean precisely that. In our case, we're talking on average 5%. . . . However, that 5% translates into an extra £250 million or $440 million a year.[1]

Price customization is frequently the best means to improve overall price realization. As the case of British Airways shows, the payoff to 5% price customization can be large. The information requirements for any type of price customization are more extensive than if a uniform price policy across the market is pursued. Customization necessitates the understanding of product value at a more disaggregate level. For example, Microsoft had to understand how their product's perceived value differed for upgraders vs. new users, and for those who might buy now vs. those who would wait until the product became better established. But recall the leverage of pricing discussed in chapter 1; on average, a 1% improvement in price realization leads to over 10% improvement in profits. Thus, finding those 10% of customers to take a 10% customization premium—or 20% to take a 5% premium—or 50% to take a 2% premium—any way to get a 1% price realization improvement is worth a lot of effort.

WHAT THIS CHAPTER WILL DO

This chapter addresses the following questions.

1. What makes price customization profitable?
2. What information is required to design a customized schedule?
3. When is price customization feasible?
4. What are the best ways to implement price customization?
5. What are the risks in price customization and how can they be managed?

Knowing the answers to these questions will help you:

1. identify pricing customization opportunities
2. develop the needed data
3. assess the best methods of separating market, i.e., keeping your low-price customers from reselling your product to higher-priced ones
4. choose an implementation plan

This chapter is actually an introduction to the price customization concept. Specific bases for customization are presented in subsequent chapters:

- geographic location in chapter 6, "International Pricing"
- quantity purchased in chapter 7, "Nonlinear Pricing"
- quality level sought in chapter 8, "Product-Line Pricing"
- other products purchased in chapter 9, "Price Bundling"
- time of purchase in chapters 10 and 11, "Time Customization of Prices: The Short Term" and "The Long Term"

THE RATIONALE BEHIND CUSTOMIZED PRICES

Sir Colin Marshall refers to a particular kind of customization in his "slight" example above, namely finding customers within the economy segment who are willing to pay a little more. Airlines also customize in a more significant way, with pricing for first class, business class, and economy-class seats on the same plane. On some international flights, the price difference between first class and coach can be a factor of 10. The basic rationale for this is obvious: the family going on vacation is more price sensitive than the CEO off to a key business meeting. But to really understand the power of price customization, we have to analyze the situation more carefully.

Chapter 2 introduced the sales response curve, i.e., the relationship between price and quantity sold. Figure 2-6 showed the sales response curve for the electric power tool POWERSTAR. Consider the sales response curve for an airline. For business executives, air travel may be the only real option; thus they place a high value on the flight. Potential vacationers have more options: just stay home, take a bus, pick a different vacation spot, or perhaps drive themselves. Figure 5-1 depicts such a situation, with a 380-seat plane and the airline's cost to serve a customer equal to $100. There are 380 potential customers for the flight, where we define "potential" as the number willing to pay at least the airline's $100 variable cost. If the airline charged only $100, all 380 would buy tickets, completely filling up the plane—but the airline would lose money, since it is just covering its variable cost. As price is increased above $100 sales volume declines linearly; it dwindles to zero when the price is raised to $3,900—this being the maximum anyone is willing to pay. The

FIGURE 5-1

Airline Sales Response Curve

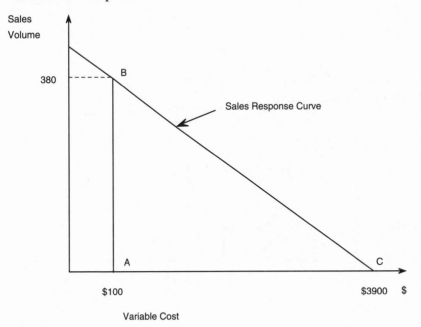

area of triangle ABC in Figure 5-1 has an important interpretation: it is the amount by which the potential value created by the flight exceeds the airline's cost. Points along the line from B to C show the value for various customers, e.g., there are 380 who value at $100 or more, 280 who value at $1100 or more, and so forth. The "potential profit" for this situation is thus:

1/2 × 380 (height of triangle) × $3,800 (width of triangle) = $722,000

This $722,000 is distributed in different ways depending upon the price charged. If the airline charged $100 all 380 would fly, the airline would just cover costs, and all the "value" would be enjoyed by the customers. If the airline charged $4,000 nobody would fly, so the $722,000 in "potential" value would disappear. Obviously, optimal pricing means maximizing the airline's share of the $722,000 and is achieved by a price somewhere in between these two.

If the airline was constrained to set just one price for a seat on the plane, as POWERSTAR's supplier was constrained in chapter 2, it

FIGURE 5-2

Airline Pricing with a Single Price

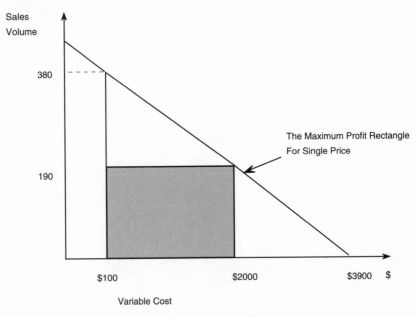

would pick the price that carves out the largest profit rectangle from under the sales response curve. As we know from chapter 2, for a linear demand curve like that shown in Figure 5-1 this is easy to find, being simply the mid-point between the firm's variable cost and the maximum willingness to pay, i.e., here $100 + $3,900 = $4,000/2 = $2,000. The implications of this are shown in Figure 5-2. At a $2,000 price 190 customers buy, yielding a contribution to the airline of $2,000 – $100 = $1,900 × 190 = $361,000. The "load factor," i.e., the percentage of capacity utilized, is 50% and the airline gets 50% of the $722,000 value potential for itself.

Why was the firm only able to reap 50% of the potential value? As explained in the discussion of POWERSTAR'S pricing in Figures 2-6 and 2-7, any single price carves out from the "potential profit triangle" a profit rectangle, with the width denoting the unit contribution (price minus variable cost) and the height the sales volume. The equivalence of picking a price and choosing a rectangle from the "potential profit" triangle underneath the sales response curve shows the limitations of a single price policy. Any rectangle leaves behind two associated triangles, such as the X and Y triangles in Figure 5-3.

Triangle X is "passed-up profit" due to *not* making a sale. Its height is the number of customers who value the product above its cost to the supplier, but who do not buy because the chosen price exceeds their value. Its width is the difference between price and firm's cost. On average, for these excluded customers, their valuation of the product over and above its cost to the supplier is half of this. Thus, triangle X represents the total potential profit not realized because sales did not take place with these customers. Because the firm wanted to get the customers who did buy to pay a higher price, it had to pass up an opportunity to serve these customers even though their value exceeded cost. Thus, we term triangle X "passed-up profit."

Triangle Y is simply "Money left on the table." Some people were willing to pay more than the price charged. In Figure 5-3, there are QP of them. Adding up the money left with each, we get triangle Y. Now we can see what happened to the $722,000 profit potential for the *optimal* pricing shown in Figure 5-2. It is split up among the three possible "buckets" profit potential can go into as follows:

FIGURE 5-3

The Profit Rectangle and Associated Triangles

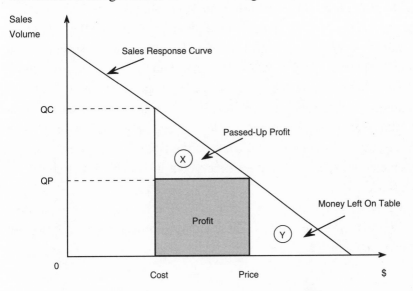

- Firm's Contribution = $361,000 (= 50%)
- "Passed Up Profit" = 190 × ($2,000 – $100) ÷ 2 = $180,500 (= 25%)
- "Money Left On Table" = 190 × ($3,900 – $2,000) ÷ 2 = $180,500 (= 25%)

For a linear price response curve, restriction to a single price always creates a situation where even at the best price of the firm, it captures only 50% of profit potential—the other 50% being equally split between the other two buckets. Twenty-five percent of the created profit potential is "left on the table," or more precisely in the pockets of the customers (triangle Y), and 25% disappears into thin air (triangle X): the role of price customization is to transfer some of the dollars in the "buckets" of triangles X and Y to the profit bucket of the firm.

HOW PRICE CUSTOMIZATION WORKS: INTRODUCING FIRST CLASS

Suppose the airline could set two prices rather than one and it figured out how to build a little fence to corral high valuation customers into paying the high price and let the lower valuation customers pay the lower price. (How to build these fences is taken up in the next section.) What would the airline do then?

Figure 5-4 shows the impact of implementing customized prices to the high and low valuation customers and having a fence—like a Saturday-night stay or advance booking requirement—to keep the high value customers from getting to the low price. Panel (a) shows the single price situation and the 50%—25%—25% distribution of the profit potential triangle. With customized prices, we have two prices P_L and P_H and $P_L <$ single optimal price $P < P_H$. Since $P_L < P$, triangle X_1 in panel (b) is smaller than X in (a), i.e., there is less passed up profit. Having P_L and P_H creates two smaller "money left on the table" triangles. Effectively, we increase the amount in the airline's contribution bucket as shown by the shaded area.

Given the data of our example shown in Figure 5-1, we can determine the optimal two-class prices. These and the optimal one-class price are shown in Table 5-2.

FIGURE 5-4A

Single Price

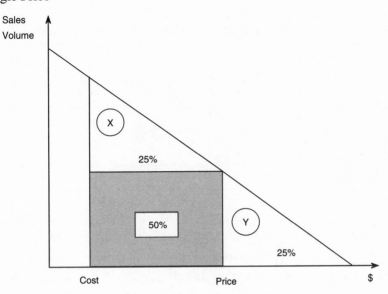

FIGURE 5-4B

Customized Pricing

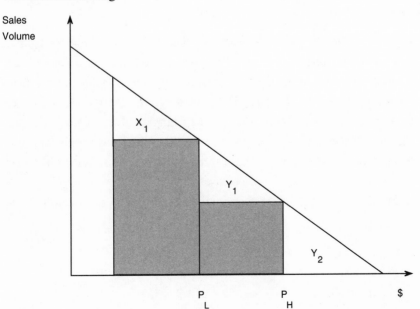

TABLE 5-2

Comparison of Two-Class and One-Class Pricing

	Single Class	**First and Economy Class**
Price	$2,000	First Class = $2,633 Economy = $1,367
Sales Volume	190	First Class Customers = 127 Economy Customers = <u>127</u> 254 (+34%)
Contribution	$361,000	$482,600 (+34%)

The airline's contribution increases by $121,600 or 34% to $482,600; 67% of the "profit potential" is now in the firm contribution bucket, up from 50%. The average price paid remains $2,000 but now one group pays a $633 premium and the other gets an equivalent discount. This airline's contribution increase comes from decreasing both the "money left on the table" and "passed-up profit," and the "load factor" increases from 50% to 67%.

Business Class

If two classes are better than one for the airline, are three better than two? Yes—as long as you can effectively build fences to separate high, middle, and low customers. It is easy to envision what three prices means in terms of a Figure 5-4 type diagram: triangle X gets even smaller and there are three little Y-type triangles of the same size representing "money left on the table" with first-class, business-class, and economy-class customers. These three Y triangles sum up to less than two Y triangles of the two-price case.

For this example, the three optimal class prices and sales volumes are:

	Price	*Number of* *Passengers*
First Class	$2,950	95
Business Class	$2,000	95
Economy Class	$1,050	<u>95</u>
Total		285

Contribution is $541,500—a 12.2% improvement over a two-class system and a 50% improvement over the single-class system. This 50% improvement is due to a 50% increase in sales volume from 190 to 285, while maintaining the average price paid per seat at $2,000. Now 75% of the $722,000 in profit potential is in the airline's contribution bucket. The equal number of people in each class is a result of the initial assumption that the sales volume curve was linear. In reality, there are typically more customers in the lower end than the higher end; but the principle is clear. The key is to be able to build the fences between the segments. Airlines, of course, do this with advance purchase requirements, Saturday-night stays, different seat sizes, and various amenities. The different mechanisms for building fences generally are set out in the following section. A key point is that even if the fence is not perfect, price customization offers substantial profit opportunity.[2]

The optimal number of classes and the optimal ratio of the prices between them depends on how different potential customers are from one another. Very heterogeneous customers warrant the cost of administering multiple classes and high relative price ratios. In the case of linear demand, it is always true that increasing from one optimal price to the optimal set of two prices increases the percentage of profit potential reaped by the company from 50% to 67%; adding a third increases it to 75%. The general relationship is as shown in Figure 5-5. The important point here is that a good deal of the potential gain is captured quickly. The cost side should not be ignored, however. More complex schedules increase communication costs to the customer and the cost of "fence building" and required monitoring. American Airlines' decision to begin three-class service was a major strategic move with cost implications throughout the system. The potential profit demonstrated here shows why these costs may well be justified. Figure 5-6 shows the evolution of the number of classes and relative prices for the German national railroad since 1907, when there were four classes of cars on the railroad with:

First Class:	7 Pfennigs per kilometer
Second Class:	4.5 Pfennigs per kilometer
Third Class:	3 Pfennigs per kilometer
Fourth Class:	2 Pfennigs per kilometer

FIGURE 5-5

Value of Price Customization

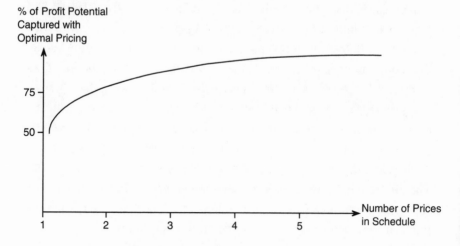

In 1923, first-class passengers paid 9 times the fourth-class rate. But then a move to fewer classes and less variability began. In 1928, there were only three classes and in 1951 the system was cut to two classes, where it remains, with a price differential of 50% between classes.

Implementation: Achieving Price Customization Through Fence Building

The four primary ways in which to build fences to sort customers and permit customized pricing are:

1. *Product-line sort:* develop a product line and have customers sort themselves among the various offerings based on their preferences.
2. *Controlled availability:* selectively present products and their prices only to the groups for which they are intended, e.g., by choosing channels that distribute and price in different ways.
3. *Sort on buyer characteristics:* observe the characteristics of buyers, e.g., their age or type of business institution, and customize the price to the key characteristic driving the perceived value variation across customers.
4. *Sort on transaction characteristics:* observe the characteristics of the

Number of Classes and Relative Price of Classes

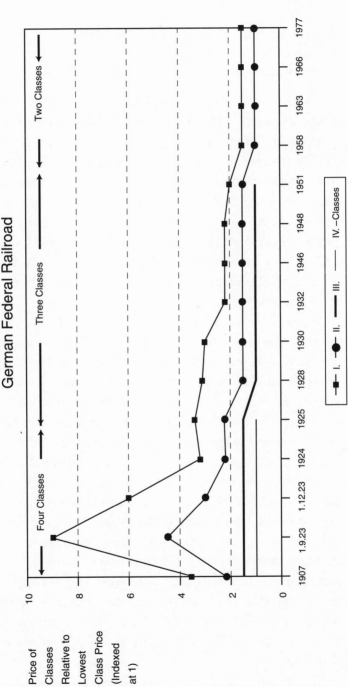

Ratio: Best Class Price/Lowest Class Price

German Federal Railroad

transaction, e.g., the timing or quantity involved, and use this as a basis to customize prices.

We now show how each of these can be used.

1. Product-Line Sort

Proctor-Silex sells its top-of-the line iron for $54.95 while its next best is priced at $49.95. The manufacturing-cost difference between the two is less than a $1.00, as the top model adds only a small light to signal that the iron is ready for use.[3] According to Proctor-Silex's marketing manager, this product-line extension allows the company to improve its margins because "there is a segment of the market that wants to buy the best despite the cost." How does Proctor-Silex find these people? Simple; just observe who picks up the $54.95 model. Proctor-Silex does not build a price customization fence; the high-valuation customers who want the best choose to fence *themselves* in, paying $5 for a feature costing the firm only $1.

Whereas Proctor-Silex was concerned about sorting on the high end of the product range, low-end sorting can also be a useful strategy. In 1995, Ford's newly redesigned Taurus was introduced in two models, the basic GL and the more upscale LX. Some customers and dealers complained that the $19,150 price of the GL was too high an entry-level price for Taurus' traditional customers. In early February 1996, Ford responded to the price-sensitive customers—not by dropping the GL price, but by announcing the April introduction of a new G version at $18,545 as an addition to the product line.[4] The new G buyer would be identifying himself as someone who preferred keeping $600 to paying for cruise control, floor mats, cassette player, power door locks, and a GL brand designation—these being the features stripped out of the GL to make a G. The G would also be available only in a more limited color selection. As opined in the press, "Some popular options will not be offered on the Taurus G, as a way to limit the number of buyers who choose the less expensive vehicle."[5] Ford's vice president for marketing and sales estimated that only 5–10% of Tauruses sold would be G models.

This decision came amid press reports of Taurus' sales being a big disappointment after the R&D investment and spending on the re-design and product launch. A January 24, 1996 *New York Times* piece headed "Ford Tests the Price Barrier" described Ford's strategy as based on the belief that "the only way to both satisfy customers in today's car market and make money is to offer even better vehicles at premium prices."[6] Expanding the line at the lower end—with a clearly-thought-out feature deletion and customized pricing strategy—allowed Ford to keep its overall pricing structure and strategy in place. The intent is clearly an outcome as described in chapter 4: as GL customers consider trading down, they bump into a mental fence. The design decision on the G model helps to construct the fence, while the lower-entry-point pricing helps deal with a price-sensitive segment of the market.

This product-line strategy is followed by *Encyclopaedia Britannica*, which offers identical content in four different coverings, ranging from utilitarian hardcover to a beautiful leather cover. At London's Heathrow Airport, the utilitarian model at the low price point was £999. Other coverings were £1,295, £3,200, and up to £4,000 for the top-of-the-line leather cover. An interesting example of the same type is Sotheby's catalogue for the April 1996 auction of Jacqueline Kennedy Onassis' estate. The "special edition catalogue of over 500 pages" was priced at $90 for a hardcover edition and $45 for softcover. Presumably, the $45 version is for those who are buying the book as a guide to the auction, while the $90 version is for addition to the buyer's library.

For nondurables, product lines can sort an individual across different purchase occasions. For example, as mentioned in chapter 1, Kodak markets three grades of film, with Royal Gold being the top of the line at a 20% premium over the flagship brand, Gold Plus. The packaging declares Royal Gold to be the smart buyer's choice "for extra special moments." On appropriate occasions, the customer self-selects into the higher-priced offering; typically, the higher-priced offering carries higher margins to the firm as cost differentials are small relative to price differentials.

In many cases, the product-line differentiation has a vertical dimension to it—the "good, better, best" idea. However, horizontal differentiation to fit a particular situation and permit price customization to that situation can be useful. For example, for one chemical product used in production processes for various segments, we identified the contribution of the chemical's cost to the final product cost as follows.

Segment	Contribution to Final Cost
Heat insulation	50%
Silicon rubber	33%
Adhesives and sealants	10%
Polyesters	5%
Paint and coatings	3%

Due to these vast differences in contribution to total costs, the five segments exhibited very different price sensitivities. Customizing the chemical to segments by packaging and services permitted profitable price customization.

The "product-line sort" fence has one advantage over other methods: it is viewed as "fair" by everyone. All products are fully available and a customer can choose whatever model/price combination he wishes. The key to making this approach work is the design decision to differentiate products in such a way that customers' preferences sort themselves among the options in the desired fashion. This concept is developed more fully in chapter 8, "Product-Line Pricing."

Another "product-sort" mechanism is through the timing of product releases and price reductions. Doubleday, publisher of John Grisham's novels *Time to Kill, The Firm, The Pelican Brief, The Client, The Chamber,* and *The Rainmaker,* knows that some people value Grisham's novels more highly than others do. Obviously, the publisher would like diehard fans to pay more than others. This is accomplished by publishing the hardcover version first at about $26; diehards buy it even though they know that the paperback version will eventually be available at about $7.00. Less enthusiastic, more price-sensitive fans can wait; thus customers identify themselves by their behavior. The same phenomenon is seen in movies: first-run theaters at $7.25 a ticket, neighborhood theaters weeks later at $5.00 a ticket, and eventually home rental at $3.00 for the whole family. This is the logic generally in offering more stripped-down, lower-priced versions of a product over time. The principle here is that anyone is free to buy whatever they want at any time, but consumers self-select in a way that supports customized pricing.

2. Controlled Availability

A woman brought suit against Victoria's Secret on the basis that her catalogue included only a $10-off coupon while an "adult male with a higher income" received the same catalogue with a $25-off coupon. The woman's lawyer proclaimed, "It's just not fair. Every company should advertise equally and give every consumer the same opportunity to get the same good deal."[7] Whatever the particulars of the Victoria's Secret case, the lawyer's proclamation is not a good general rule. Prices can effectively be customized by limiting their availability in time or place or controlling customers' awareness of them. As one-to-one marketing becomes more prevalent and highly targetable media become the norm, limiting the scope of price presentations is now more practical and advisable. Specific methods for this are:

Coupons. In their book *Sales Promotion,* Blattberg and Neslin note that one specific purpose of coupons is "to deliver a price decrease to a selected targeted group . . . The potential efficiency of using coupons to deliver a price decrease to the appropriate target group is compelling."[8] While coupons have historically been thought of as "cents-off" for some frequently purchased consumer packaged good, more innovative uses are being implemented. For example, General Motors sent a $1,500 coupon incentive on a new Oldsmobile only to those who had expressed unhappiness with their present Oldsmobile in a customer survey.[9] The logic of this is that these potential buyers assign a lower value to a new Oldsmobile than do those expressing delight with their present Oldsmobile. The coupon can be made nontransferable so as to limit its use only to those intended.

Direct-Mail Catalogues. Particularly with information about past purchasing available, price customization through catalogues is a potentially profitable tactic. A shoe manufacturer has a series of seven catalogues to send out to "new names," with the level of price incentive becoming successively greater with each mailing. If the customer does not order shoes at the "regular price" in the first catalogue, he receives a second catalogue offering $15 off; if he does not buy from the second catalogue, he receives a third with an even greater "dollars off" offer, and so forth. Victoria's Secret's customization of discount level to particular customers makes good sense as long as the discount level is tied to the customer's perceived valuation of the products in the catalogue.

Geographic Pricing. In our research, we have found very different sales response curves in different geographic markets. As long as a price difference between markets will not induce mass transshipments from one market to another, customizing the price to the location of the buyer is good practice. We discuss this in detail in chapter 6. For example, certain camera models are 50% higher in price in the UK than in the U.S. Price differences between Japan and the United States have been significant in many instances. Cosmetics are one particular area wherein prices differ by a factor of 3 to 4 in some cases. In clothing, Eddie Bauer and The Gap price in Japan at 1.5 times the U.S. level, under the name of "fair pricing."[10] This puts pressure on J. Crew with its pricing at:

	U.S.	Japan
rollneck sweater	$48.00	$130
polartec cap	$14.00	$39

Pharmaceuticals are a product category for which we find extreme differences in sales response across geographic markets; the product may be highly valued in all markets, but sheer ability-to-pay constraints operate. Some view the tailoring of price to the economic status of the country as "fair," while others to not. Wyeth-Ayerst Labs was viewed negatively by some for its pricing of its long-acting contraceptive Norplant, which U.S. critics maintained sold at a 1500% premium in the United States ($350) vs. developing countries ($24).[11] While pricing a socially sensitive product such as contraceptive devices requires careful consideration of a host of factors, geographic customization can be quite profitable. While sustaining price differentials across geographic markets has become more difficult with recent changes, we do not recommend automatically adopting a single worldwide price. Rather, firms should consider the permissible price differentials, and balance price customization and harmonization forces as discussed in the next chapter.

Restriction on Place of Purchase. Some prices are available only at certain locations, such as a rail pass for travel in Europe that must be purchased in the United States. This restricts its use to international travelers planning well ahead and keeps the low prices away from those using the routes regularly.

Negotiations. A January 1996 article in the *Wall Street Journal Europe* was entitled "Phone Firms Offer Shoppers Discount Deals"[12] and offered the advice that to become a "savvy shopper" entailed "simply calling up your present telephone company and asking what sorts of discounts are available." The article noted that France Telecom "hasn't seen fit" to advertise its 15% discount for any three numbers called for 15 francs per month and "has been relatively quiet" about a discount program for large-volume discount callers. The strategy here is to customize price to shoppers, who by asking for a discount reveal their price sensitivity and willingness to look for competitive offers. Similarly, large national accounts or bulk buyers may not buy off the published price list, but can have prices individually negotiated. This face-to-face price setting, while perhaps somewhat costly to administer, can be an effective forum for price customization.

Each of these methods effectively restricts the availability of certain prices. The direct involvement of the firm places the customer on one side of the price fence or the other. Salespeople regularly do this via the information they provide about product and price availability. In some cases, following France Telecom and being "relatively quiet" or, better put, "selectively quiet" about available lower prices is good strategy.

3. Sort on Buyer Characteristics

There are many situations of significant price customization which are fully presented to all, as was the Microsoft "Office" example presented in the introduction to this chapter, for example:

• Eurodisney	"Kinder Gratis— vom 01.01.96 bis zum 04.04.96"	or	"Kids Free— from January 1 to April 4, 1996"
• Movie Theater	Adults: $7.25 Children Under 12: $4.50		

- Quattro Pros   Borland charged:
  Spreadsheet Software   • $325 for first time spreadsheet buyers
                           • $99 for "upgrades" for current spreadsheet
                             owners; such as Lotus 1-2-3 users

- Harvard Business   Academic Institutions: $28.00
  School Publishing   Corporate Customers: $50.00
                           for a Custom Casebook with 15 items

- Landing Fees at   747-200: DM 18,600
  Munich Airport   747-400: DM 10,100

In each case, the different prices are published for all to see. However, the customer does not have a choice. Based on an observable characteristic of the buyer, the firm determines whether the customer qualifies for a lower price or not. The Disneyland employees and the ticket seller at the movies look at the patron to assess age. Borland asks that a $99 price order be accompanied by some proof of current spreadsheet ownership, such as a page from the instruction manual. HBS checks the "ship to" address to assess "academic" status. The airport knows the type of plane that landed. None of these methods is perfect—some 13-year-olds do slip past the ticket seller and pay only $4.50—but even without perfect fencing ability, price customization prevails over uniform pricing.

The principle here is to select a characteristic which (a) is observable without great expense and (b) separates the market into groups with different ability, or willingness, to pay for the product. For example, a spreadsheet user with Lotus 1-2-3 already up and running on his machine, who is familiar with Lotus 1-2-3's mode of operation, gives less value to a new spreadsheet from a Lotus competitor than a similar person without a familiar spreadsheet available. Hence, Borland customized its pricing to these two groups—charging the Lotus "upgraders" 30% of the new user price. Lotus itself has also offered "upgrade" pricing from one version of 1-2-3 to the next. The past activities of the prospective buyers have created a customer base quite different in terms of their familiarity with and possession of a durable good which functions as a substitute. Or, as in the airline landing-fee case, there can be a longer-term motive. The tariff is less for the 747-400, even though it is heavier than the 747-200, because it is a low-noise aircraft that the airport wishes to encourage.

Availability of alternatives is also the driver behind one of the more controversial price customizations of the recent past. In the United States pharmaceutical drug manufacturers came to charge lower prices to HMOs and mail-order pharmacies than to independent pharmacies. As HMOs and mail-order operations grew in size and power, they were able to influence the sales rate of products. These added discounts average about 15%. While this practice is controversial, as is much about drug pricing, the underlying logic of it is clear and compelling. A pharmacy stocks all the leading drugs. It has no choice. It is in business to fill the prescriptions that customers bring in, *as written*. HMOs, on the other hand, do not stock every drug but might select the two or three leaders within the category who offer the best deal. Reportedly, Kaiser-Permanente will not even see a salesperson who is not willing to grant it added discounts. Since small pharmacies are unable to influence the sales level of the drug, whereas the HMOs and big mail-order operations have demonstrated their power over brand choice, the logic is to customize price with lower prices to the powerful, whose power stems from the availability of alternatives created by their ability to constrain end-user choice.[13]

Common attributes used in sorting by buyer characteristic are:

- Age—both children and "senior citizen" discounts
- Institution type—e.g., end user vs. reseller
- User status—new buyer vs. old customer
- Ability to pay—colleges effectively practice price customization under the name of scholarships and financial aid. In this case, ability to pay is closely examined and extensive data on income and resources must be provided. It was recently estimated that 20% of the payment by full-tuition payers is used to subsidize others.

4. Sort on Transaction Characteristics

Customization can be effected by tying it to particular features of the transaction. Eurodisney's "Kids Free" policy applies only to transactions at a given space in time. In the airline industry, a ticket that is booked well beforehand and includes a Saturday-night stay is a signal of a price-sensitive pleasure traveler. These features are thus used as a fence around low fares.

A seat on the Eurostar train between Paris and London costs DM 435 round-trip first class if prebooked and DM 517 if the ticket is bought just before departure. A CD player purchased at an automobile dealership at the time of a new-car purchase signals a convenience-oriented person to whom adding this option impacts his total outlay about 1%. This person is probably less price sensitive than the one considering adding a CD player to the car he already drives, who has multiple equally convenient outlets to choose from. The CD player in the first instance will almost certainly cost more than the second one will. The Coca-Cola example in Table 5-1 at the beginning of this chapter is this type of price customization to location.

By ascertaining those characteristics of the transaction that correlate with willingness to pay, one can effectively construct fences based on these characteristics to enable price customization.

The transaction characteristic most widely used for price customization is the quantity sold—either at one time or over some time period. This is seen with products ranging from a season's pass at a ski slope to bottles of wine (e.g., 20% off for case purchases) to time on the Internet to computers. For example, Club Med's Winter 1995–96 rates for ski vacations in Europe include an "11th person in a group is free" feature. A variant of this is software pricing to an organization based on the number of users. For example, Novell priced Netware 4.1 as shown in Table 5-3, with a large site paying only 20% per user of what a small site pays.

The underlying rationale here is that bigger-quantity buyers value the product less—perhaps due to their capacity to find alternatives. This type of customization is addressed in chapter 7, "Nonlinear Pricing."

In quantity discounts, the transaction characteristic is the number of units of the same good purchased. Another form is to use the bundle of different goods as the characteristic. Car options are often bundled, e.g., a "cold weather" package consisting of traction control, heated seats, and heated side-view mirrors. Service contracts can be bundled in with the product. Chapter 9 on "Price Bundling" addresses this form of price customization.

There are a wide variety of procedures available to implement price customization, resulting in buyers with higher product valuations paying higher prices. As we showed at the outset of this chapter, the potential profit impact of price customization is great. To start the price customization process, one must first identify the driver of the value varia-

TABLE 5-3

Netware Pricing and Number of Users

No. of Users	Site License Fee	Price Per User
5	$396	$79.20
10	$796	$79.60
25	$1196	$37.84
50	$1596	$31.92
100	$2236	$22.36
250	$3996	$15.98

Source: L. DiDio, "Novel dangles bargain bait before Netware users," *Computerworld*, July 10, 1995, p. 1ff.

tion and then construct a fence based on it to separate the high- and low-value customers. These, then, are the first two questions to ask in considering a price customization scheme.

1.   Can the variation in perceived value across customers be identified and understood, i.e., what are its key drivers?

2.   Can an adequate fence be constructed using one of the methods described above? A fence does not have to be perfect—but it should accomplish two needed elements: (a) divide customers according to value and (b) in concert with the nature of the good, prevent resale of the good from a low-price customer to a higher-price customer. This second condition is typically more easily met for services where purchase and consumption events coincide. The arbitrage issue needs to be considered carefully in the case of goods—especially nonperishables with high value-to-transport-cost ratios.

———

We recommend that three additional areas be addressed when considering any type of a price customization plan.

1. Customer Perception of "Fairness"

While most of the airline pricing mess described in chapter 4 stemmed from competitive battles, a contributing factor was that customers perceived airline pricing to be basically unfair. If they will fly me from Boston to Minneapolis for $400 round trip to see the Red Sox play the Minnesota Twins on Saturday evening, coming home on Sunday, why do I have to spend three times that to see Boston play Minnesota on a Tuesday night returning on Wednesday? In the short term, customers may well buy according to economic rationales: if the price is below my perceived value I buy it, if not I don't. But in the long term, customers are motivated to find their way out of what they perceive to be unfair situations. Airline customers expended great amounts of time and showed great creativity in devising routes and travel patterns that "beat" the system. If it were not for this "fairness" consideration, restaurants would all raise the prices on Saturday nights when they are busy. In reality, of course, a "Saturday-night surcharge" could well be the beginning of the end for a restaurant. Note, however, that a "Tuesday-night discount" would not. The general point here is that the particular manner in which the price customization is stated can impact the perceived fairness—and that perceived fairness is critical.

2. Legality

Two of the price customization plans discussed above—Victoria's Secret and pharmaceuticals' price discounts to HMOs—have been the subject of legal proceedings, with the latter a large-scale affair involving hundreds of millions of dollars and some of the best talent in the legal profession. So legal issues must be considered. Price customization based on product-line design such as the Taurus and *Encyclopaedia Britannica* examples above are not at issue. Products and prices are freely available and the customer chooses the specific item based on his preferences.

The other methods of effecting price customization need to be screened for legal considerations. It is difficult to summarize adequately the governing law on price customization, or "price discrimination" as it is called in the legal world, because the pertinent law, the Robinson-Patman Act, has been called "one of the most confusing, complicated, and questionable pieces [of legislation] ever passed by the U.S. Congress."[14] However, the key point is that according to Section 2(a) of the Robinson-Patman Act, it is unlawful to "discriminate in price between different purchasers of commodities of like grade and quality. . . . where the effect of such discrimination may be to substantially lessen competition. . . ." The focus is thus on whether the price customization has a negative impact on competition. That is, does selling to party A at a lower price than to party B preclude B from effectively competing? Many price-customization schemes do not involve such anticompetitive effects. As a first step, consulting more detailed descriptions of the relevant laws[15] is useful; but a legal opinion should be sought if the possibility of anticompetitive effects exists.

3. Impact on Customer Contact Person's Job

A focus on price customization through selectively offering price concessions in a personal selling situation can change the basic nature of the salesperson's activities from selling product benefits and value to focusing on price. In the United States, this has been most notably associated with the retail automobile market historically; breaking this tradition, GM's Saturn division has gained a great deal of attention with its "no price customization" policy. Unlike the vast majority of dealers, a Saturn dealer does not negotiate price, having instead a "one-price, no-haggling policy." The objective is to make the buying experience a pleasant one and to focus the Saturn sales associate on matching the customer to the right Saturn model and communicating its benefits, rather than trying to separate the customer from his or her last possible dollar. Saturn has been so successful with this policy on its new cars that in January 1996 it extended the policy: introducing used cars, advertising the same no-haggle policy. The Hotel Elysée in Hamburg has a similar policy—a nonnegotiable DM 270 rate regardless of how many of its rooms are occupied or empty.

The effect of price customization has to be analyzed both internally and externally. Chapter 12, "Organizing for Power Pricing," addresses the issue of location of pricing authority in the organization and proper incentive mechanisms for customer-contact people. These incentives and the form of price customization should be tailored to create the necessary context for effective delivery of the benefit message, rather than having the price negotiations dominate. A packaging-material supplier moved to a system of "flexible pricing" in the field where sales people were allowed to negotiate price within a range. This so dramatically changed the nature of the discussion with companies that the packaging supplier found its customer contact point change from engineers to the customer's purchasing department.

SUMMARY

As we have seen, a "single price" policy can have severe limitations in capturing for the firm the profit potential which its product or service creates. Price customization can boost firm profitability sharply. There are a number of creative ways to implement price customization. But effective use of the concept can come only through deep understanding of the drivers of customer value.

In designing and implementing price customization programs, the power pricer:

- understands the drivers of value valuation across customers
- seeks to adapt price paid to the value perceived
- identifies the basis for customization that best suits his situation (Customizing via geographic location is detailed in chapter 6; by size of the transaction in chapter 7; by product line in chapter 8; by other products purchased in chapter 9; and by timing of the sale in chapter 10.)
- is creative in mixing and matching the various methods for customization (The Microsoft example mixes customization by customer type and time, as does the Eurodisney "Kids Free" program.)
- considers both the cost and benefit side of customization (Care must be taken to not try to implement too complex a schedule. We recommend moving to customization incrementally, i.e., switching to a two-price policy first, then adding discounts as perceived beneficial and implementable. Our experience is that much of the gain comes from the first steps in customization. "Overcustomization" can cause high administrative costs and loss of customer goodwill.)
- understands the legal environment and screens any customization plans for legal issues

In general, we believe that not near enough attention is paid to the opportunities of customization. How to customize requires as much rigorous thinking as any aspect of the pricing program—and has as much potential payoff.

6

International Pricing

INTRODUCTION

The globalization of markets is progressing rapidly. From 1970 to 1993 global exports rose from $314 billion to $3,645 billion, an average annual growth rate of 11.2%. No single national economy has sustained this rate of growth over such a long period. As noted in chapter 1, the increased geographic scope of business and the "interrelatedness" of markets greatly increase the complexity of pricing. Prices have to be determined for many different national markets. These markets have traditionally been separated and heterogeneous. Geographic boundaries and companies' tendency to customize products to local markets provided a national "fence," and price customization on a geographic basis was practiced without much thought. Now, however, worldwide geographic markets are becoming increasingly interrelated and similar.

International pricing has thus become a big headache and problem for many companies. Globalization forces require fundamental rethinking of international pricing strategies. Long-proven price structures are collapsing across the world. This is particularly true within new trade areas like the European Union or the North American Free Trade Agreement (NAFTA). Gone are the days when country markets were neatly separable, and gray imports (the shipment of a good from one geographic market to another by a third party) were solely a problem of exotic high-priced products such as French perfumes or Swiss watches. Today almost every product and service is affected by the pressures for international price coordination and alignment.

At the same time, we continue to observe large price differentials between countries for some products. Consumer habits, competitive positions, and distribution channels vary from country to country and offer opportunities to customize prices in order to exploit profit potentials. The response to the forces of globalization should not be automatic adoption of a policy of one worldwide price. International pricing is and will remain one of the main areas of price customization. The art of international pricing lies in finding the best compromise between customization opportunities and harmonization pressures.

Table 6-1 provides an overview of global price differences for selected products. It proves that prices show amazing variations across countries. These examples are by no means extreme but rather very typical.

Prices for identical products often differ by a factor of 2 or 3 even between neighboring countries. Extreme differences often persist in pharmaceuticals. For example, for one of the more advanced Parkinsonism therapies, one tablet costs $0.50 in Italy and $2.50 in Germany. On average credit-card fees are 1% in France, 2.2% in England, and 3.4% in Germany. If the index for a life-insurance policy in the UK is set at 100, the corresponding value for Italy is 262. Large price differentials even extend to industrial products. A standard chemical product that is sold to repair shops has a price in the United States of about half its price in Europe. Products like industrial batteries, trucks, or tools show price variations between 30% and 50% across countries.

These prevailing price differences reflect variations in customers' price sensitivity, the firms' use of price as a competitive weapon, and the role of distributors. Many of the existing pricing structures have developed over time and show a certain inertia.

But the market forces are working towards a global alignment of prices, as the following cases clearly show. LOGO, a leading manufacturer of nondurable consumer goods, distributes its products through large retailers, some of whom have Europe-wide operations. LOGO sold the same products throughout Europe and had negotiated a set of prices with the country-level managers of its retailers. In 1995, LOGO's

TABLE 6-1

International Comparisons of Highest, Median, and Lowest Prices for Selected Products

Product	Highest Price	Median Price	Lowest Price (Index = 100)
Hertz Car Rental 1 week July 1995	Greece DM 504 Index 224	Spain DM 339 Index 151	Florida DM 225 ($139) Index 100
Aspirin 100 tablets June 1994	Paris $7.07 Index 714	Mexico City $1.78 Index 179	New York $0.99 Index 100
Compact disc June 1994	Tokyo $22.09 Index 170	London $14.99 Index 115	New York $12.99 Index 100
10-minute call to New York September 1995	Mexico City $20.45 Index 138	Tokyo $18.64 Index 126	Paris $14.83 Index 100
Coca Cola (Sixpack) 1992	Tokyo $5.01 Index 242	Sydney $2.47 Index 123	London $2.07 Index 100
Nikon Camera 1994	Mexico City $1,054 Index 167	Tokyo $768 Index 122	New York $630 Index 100
Windows Word 1994	France $185 Index 148	Japan $152 Index 122	UK $125 Index 100
Domestic Telephone Private Services 1995	Portugal Index 295	New Zealand Index 190	Iceland Index 100
Business	Turkey Index 600	Canada Index 300	Iceland Index 100

biggest retailing customer requested that all products be supplied at the lowest European price, which happened to be the price in Portugal. LOGO had to comply. The ensuing 20% price decline across Europe resulted in a profit disaster.

A second case is BETA, a manufacturer of durables in the upper price segment. Parallel imports of BETA's products from all over the world into several high-price markets have been increasing for years. These gray imports are undermining BETA's price policy and creating much annoyance in its distribution channels. The management has had to reconsider its global pricing strategy and has made radical adjustments. Among other actions a second, less expensive brand was introduced in low-price countries.

In Germany, more than a million cars are gray imports. In 1996 gray importers offer an Italian car like the Fiat Punto at 28% below its official list price in Germany, the Spanish Seat Ibiza at 26% discount, a Swedish Volvo and a Japanese Suzuki at 22% below list. Even gray reimports of Mercedes models can be bought at 15% below list.[1]

Gray imports can also create havoc within organizations. For example, the European operation of the leading manufacturer of a data storage product finds its main competitor to be its own U.S. subsidiary. The U.S. price is about 40% lower than the average European price. The products flow into Europe in large container loads, and the European managers suspect that their colleagues from the American sister company secretly support this flow since it adds to their profits. Under such circumstances it is necessary to reorganize international pricing towards a higher degree of coordination and centralization.

Increasingly, the central coordination of pricing is forced upon suppliers by globally sourcing customers. In the household appliances industry Whirlpool, as one of the large players, demands that its European suppliers not exceed the U.S. prices, which previously have been much lower. This, in turn, leads other appliance manufacturers that only manufacture in Europe to demand the same prices in order to avoid a position of cost disadvantage relative to Whirlpool.

Fluctuations in currency-exchange rates are also a serious issue in international pricing. They can suddenly change competitive price positions and create price chaos. The devaluation in 1993–94 of the U.S. dollar and some European currencies like the Italian lira or the Spanish peseta against the French Franc, the German mark, and the Japanese yen induced a major reshuffling of prices and market shares. Kärcher, the German world market leader in high-pressure cleaners, lost about 8% of world market share against Italian products, which all of a sudden got a price advantage of 20% to 25% from the devaluation. Only a radical cost-cutting program and an international reallocation of manufacturing restored Kärcher's ability to compete on price and recapture lost market share points.[2] The failure in 1996 of Fokker, the Dutch world leader in regional airplanes, was mainly attributed to the devaluation of the U.S. dollar, in which practically all of Fokker's sales were invoiced, whereas 70% of Fokker's costs were in harder currencies like the Dutch guilder or the German mark. Pricing has to deal with such very serious threats in the international arena, but it cannot cope with them all alone. In addition to price adjustments, global manufacturing and sourcing approaches are required. Some auto companies have learned this lesson the hard way. In early 1996 Hiroshi Okuda, CEO of Toyota, announced that "Toyota's goal is to reach within five years the point where we are not influenced by currency-exchange fluctuations."[3]

International pricing is also becoming increasingly critical for services. Traditionally, service markets were effectively separated and large price differentials could prevail. This is no longer true, especially in service sectors that transcend national borders. International callback systems (you call a number, a computer provides a line, you pay the rate of the callback service provider) are undermining the pricing of national telecommunications monopolies. Callback systems exploit the fact that in many countries it costs more to make one international telephone call than it does to make two from the United States, where competition keeps long-distance rates low. Global callback volume increased by 63% in 1995, and by 1996 more than 100 American companies will be providing this service. Some countries (e.g., Thailand) try to prohibit it, but the call-back firms say they are beyond the reach of local laws; they operate in a transnational, truly global market and set global prices.[4]

Within regions we observe strong price alignments in the service sector. While international call charges between Italy and the UK differed by a factor of 2.5 until the mid 1980s, the factor has come down to about 1.5 by the mid 1990s. The airports in London and Amsterdam are attracting substantial numbers of passengers from surrounding countries, where the prices for long-distance travel are considerably higher. English hospitals try to get patients from continental Europe, for whom the additional cost of travel is more than offset by the lower price of hospital service in the UK.

Underlying these anecdotal observations are two countervailing forces that operate in the environment simultaneously: price customization factors and price harmonization factors. As shown in Figure 6-1, we have identified five underlying drivers for each. Price customization is made profitable by geographic regions' differences in such market factors as customer behavior, competition, and the company's costs of doing business. This customization force is enhanced by the external factors of inflation and exchange rates and the regulatory situation. On the other hand, the forces behind price harmonization are growing stronger. Environmental factors impacting all markets to some degree are falling trade barriers, lower transport costs, sophisticated third parties, and technology providing information and information flow. In many cases, these environmental factors are exacerbated by a company policy of increasing pursuit of global brands and standardized products. We dare say that the differentiation factors are strongly influenced by the past, while the harmonization factors are primarily future related. But

FIGURE 6-1

Countervailing Forces in International Pricing—Customization and Harmonization

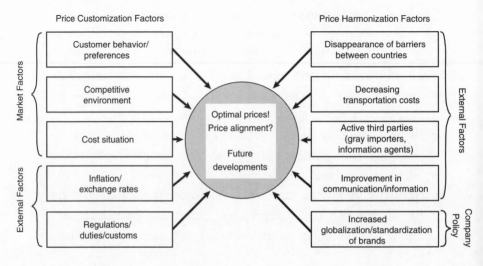

differences will prevail between countries. In most cases a uniform price is not the best answer to the international pricing challenge. The harmonization factors gain in importance and their development has to be carefully monitored. The extreme price differentials of the past will disappear, and proactive behavior is required from the power pricer. Excellent information on the various factors in Figure 6-1 is necessary to draw the right conclusions. The worst case—that all prices decline to the lowest level found today, as was true for LOGO—should be avoided by all available means.

WHAT THIS CHAPTER WILL DO

This chapter addresses the following questions.

1. How should international prices be set?
2. How should the power pricer react to changes in currency exchange rates?
3. How can the differentiation and harmonization factors be integrated into the pricing decision?
4. What is the interaction between the requirements of international pricing and the organization of a company?
5. Which external aspects have to be taken into account in international pricing?

Knowing the answers to these questions will help you to:

1. understand the complexities of international pricing better and set international prices optimally
2. respond in an optimal way to currency-exchange-rate fluctuations
3. reunify the countervailing forces of differentiation and harmonization through a system which we call the "international pricing corridor"
4. implement organizational changes to cope with pricing in a global market

SETTING INTERNATIONAL PRICES

By definition, international pricing implies that prices in several countries have to be determined. In principle, this is not different from setting prices for different market segments, the problem discussed in chapter 5,

"Price Customization." If the countries can be neatly separated we simply set the optimal price for each individual country. This is likely to lead to differentiated prices depending on how strongly price elasticities, values, and competitive positions vary across countries. Companies differentiate prices more strongly *across countries* than *within countries*. Studying the pricing behavior of more than 400 companies, Wied-Nebbeling reports that 34.9% differentiate their prices between domestic and foreign markets, whereas only 17.0% applied regional price customization within their home market.[5]

We rarely find, however, that international price customization is based on well-founded information concerning customers' and competitors' behavior. Rather, international price differentials are even more cost-plus driven than price determination for the domestic market. A camera manufacturer set its domestic price to maximize home market profits, and then just added costs for international markets and mechanically converted the local-currency price through prevailing exchange rates to set prices in each country throughout the world. In an in-depth analysis of a large German automotive supplier we found that the list prices were fixed in German marks through such a cost-plus approach and the German-mark price was used as a base in all other countries, simply adding a further markup. By contrast, the main competitor—and market leader—differentiated prices strongly across countries based on market factors. Thus, in some countries the German supplier's prices of our client were 10% higher, in others 30% lower than the competitor's—total chaos. Most international marketing books present cost-based calculation schemes focusing on the issue of whether international prices should be based on full or marginal costs.[6] A study of U.S. exporters reports that 70% of the firms determine their international prices on a cost-plus basis.[7] Since the costs of export sales tend to be higher than those of domestic sales, this results in higher export prices. But we also observe lower export prices. They are typical for companies that export only a small share of their total production (the "excess capacity") and calculate their prices based on marginal costs. They are satisfied with getting a positive contribution from their international business.

These cost-based approaches break our fundamental pricing rule and should not be used. As argued in earlier chapters, prices should reflect the perceived values of our product and of competitive products. The basics of pricing do not change because the arena is international. Thus, the power pricer acquires comparable information on the behavior of customers, competitors, and distributors across countries. The better this global knowledge is the more likely that prices will be optimally customized for the individual countries. Figure 6-2 provides an illustration for the perceived values of a premium household-appliance brand in different countries. The brand value is measured in percentage of the average market price. The product itself is identical in all four countries, but the perceived brand premiums are very different. These value differences should be reflected in the prices for the countries (of course, adjusted for strategic considerations) and the forces of harmonization.

In order to exploit such differences between countries we must precisely know the price elasticities in those countries. We find little professionalism in this area. Even large multinationals rarely estimate values and price response across countries in a rigorous and truly comparable way.

On the other hand, we acknowledge the difficulties and the costs of achieving this ideal. A company that sells its products in dozens of countries is unlikely to provide such detailed information for all countries. A reasonable compromise is to focus on the larger countries and to infer from them to smaller neighboring ones. Thus, common practice

FIGURE 6-2

The Perceived Value of a Brand in Different Countries—
These Differences Should Be Reflected in the Prices

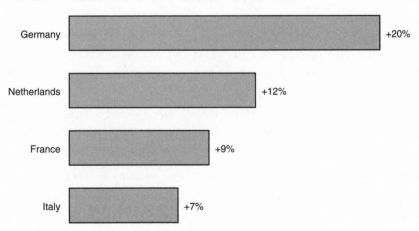

Germany   +20%

Netherlands   +12%

France   +9%

Italy   +7%

among the global power pricers is to do formal studies that include the U.S., Japan, and one or two European countries. For European pricing strategy development the focus is typically on the big four: France, Germany, Italy, and the UK.

Country markets tend to be separable under much the same conditions that foster a low price elasticity—that is, low price awareness, high differentiation of products, etc. (see the end of chapter 3 for a detailed discussion). Brioni, a famous Italian maker of expensive suits, did not change its prices in the target market currencies after the devaluation of the Italian lira. As a consequence Brioni's prices now differ strongly across countries without grave problems, as customers either do not perceive the price differences or are not inclined to take the time to exploit them. Brioni is free to pursue an independent pricing policy in the countries where it sells.

INTERNATIONAL PRICES AND CHANGES IN CURRENCY EXCHANGE RATES

The Brioni case leads us to an important and specific aspect of international pricing. Unlike in a domestic business, where costs and prices are denominated in the same currency, two currencies are involved if a product is exported from country-of-origin A to target country B.

Consider an American company selling into Germany. The situation is as follows:

- marginal cost of production = $60
- price in Germany = DM 150.

At an exchange rate of \$/DM = .67, i.e., 1 DM converts to 67 cents (the actual rate in the fall of 1996), DM 150 convert to $100, meaning a $40 per-unit contribution for the U.S. firm. The firm sells 100 units and thus has a contribution of $4,000.

In the decade 1985 to 1995, the dollars-to-marks exchange rate ranged between .74 and .29. Now, consider the implication of variation within this range. Suppose the U.S. dollar appreciates to 0.50, i.e., 1 mark converts to only 50 cents. The price in Germany is still DM 150— but now these DM 150 convert to $75, dropping the per-unit contribution to $15—a 62.5% reduction in per-unit profit!

Consider movement the other way: the U.S. dollar goes to the top of the range at DM 1 = $0.74. Now DM 150 becomes $111, so per-unit contribution increases to $51—a 27.5% increase over the $40 per-unit contribution.

Figure 6-3 illustrates these effects graphically. The lightly shaded rectangle to the left shows the profit if the exchange rate is .50; the dotted rectangle in the middle shows the incremental profit with the rate at .67 rather than .50; and the darkly shaded rectangle on the right shows the incremental profit with the rate at .74 rather than .67. Thus, at .74 the American firm gets all three rectangles in profit; at .67 it gets the two on the left; and at .50 only the leftmost one. This shows how dramatically exchange-rate variation within that range—actually observed in the past decade—can drive profit.

How should the American firm react in its German pricing if the U.S. dollar appreciates and the exchange rate goes from .67 to .50? The U.S. firm is now less competitive in the German market, since its costs calculated in DM go up from DM 90 ($60 divided by .67) to DM 120 ($60 divided by .50). The firm has essentially three options:

FIGURE 6-3

Profit Effects of Changes in Currency-Exchange Rate $/DM

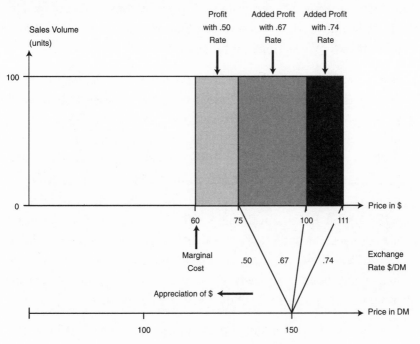

Option 1: to keep the price to the German customer constant at DM 150. We have seen the disastrous consequences of this; it will result in a profit decline to $1,500.

Option 2: to keep its contribution margin in U.S. dollars constant at $40, the firm continues to ask a price of $100 from its German customers, raising the local market price from DM 150 to DM 200. If we assume that a price increase of DM 1 reduces sales volume linearly by 1.67 units (which corresponds to a price elasticity of 2.5), a sales decline of 83 units (DM 50 times 1.67) would result in driving units sold from 100 to 17. Profit would decline to $680 ($40 times 17 units), which is even worse than Option 1.

Both options are extreme reactions to the change in the rates, in that in Option 1 the supplier carries the full burden, while in Option 2 the burden is fully shifted to the customer. In practice, Option 2 is very popular with exporters since it is equivalent to billing in the exporter's currency. Many exporting firms are proud that they can impose this billing method on their customers (Americans in dollars, Germans in marks, etc.), because they think that they get rid of the currency problem in this way. This is, however, an illusion, since the customer thinks and decides in his own currency; i.e., the customer's price response is determined by the price he has to pay in his own currency. Neither of the two extreme options, therefore, is optimal for the supplier.

Option 3: to implement a moderate DM-price increase. The German customers have to pay more, but the U.S. firm also sacrifices some of its unit contribution margin. The burden is shared between both partners. In the current case, with a price elasticity of 2.5, an increase in the DM price of 10% to DM 165 would be roughly optimal. This gives the U.S. firm $82.50 (DM 165 times 0.50) or a unit contribution margin of $22.50 ($82.50 minus $60). Due to the higher DM price the sales volume declines by 25 units to 75 units. The resulting profit for the American firm is $1,687.50 ($22.50 times 75 units). While this is considerably less than the original profit of $4,000 (which is no longer attainable in the new situation), it is clearly better than the profit situation with either of the two extreme options.

If the value of the U.S. dollar declines, say from 0.67 to 0.74, analogous considerations in the opposite direction apply. Again a "moderate" response of "sharing" the price decrease in Germany would be preferable to the two extreme options (Option 1: keeping the DM price constant, Option 2: keeping the dollar margin constant).

It is illustrative to consider practical cases of price adjustments following changes in currency exchange rates. Let us look at Table 6-2, which shows a selection of Japanese and German products exported into the U.S. market. (Thus the perspective is now reversed.) The time interval is January 1986–January 1987. In this period the value of the U.S. dollar declined strongly against the Japanese yen and German mark. According to our considerations Japanese and German exporters should raise their dollar prices in the American market. Table 6-2 shows the actual price developments.

All companies have essentially followed the pattern derived above. The price changes are in the expected direction. It is, however, interesting to note that the percentage of the price changes is mostly "moderate" relative to the percentage of the exchange-rate changes. Differences may be explained by variations in the competitive situation or in the goals of the firms. We can assume that the firms in this sample are rather professional in their international pricing, since the lion's share of their revenues comes from foreign markets. But exchange-rate changes can produce strange consequences. In the first half of 1993 the Japanese yen's value increased by 20% against the U.S. dollar. Eastman Kodak

TABLE 6-2

Changes in Exchange Rates and Price Changes (January 1986–January 1987)

Product	Change in Exchange Rate ($/DM, $/Yen)	Change in $-Price
Seiko Watch	–0.24	+13.5%
Sony Walkman	–0.24	+20.0%
Canon Camera	–0.24	+14.6%
BMW 528	–0.25	+ 7.8%
Mercedes-Benz 190E	–0.25	+11.5%

accused its Japanese rival Fuji Photo Film of dumping because Fuji did not raise its U.S. prices after this appreciation of the yen.

Based on these considerations and observations, we conclude with the following recommendations regarding currency fluctuations.

- If the exchange-rate changes, it is not optimal to keep the price in the customer's currency constant.
- Neither is it optimal under these circumstances to maintain the unit contribution margin in the supplier's currency.
- Rather, both parameters should be adjusted so that both partners share the burden or reap the fruits of a change in the exchange rate.
- If the supplier's currency appreciates (in the example, the dollar goes from 0.67 to 0.50) the price in the customer's currency should be "moderately" increased—and vice versa for a currency depreciation. "Moderately" means that both extreme options are to be avoided.
- In addition to the customers' response, the competitive situation must be taken into account when deciding on price changes in the aftermath of currency-rate changes. Competitors with different home currencies can be very differently affected by currency fluctuations, so they are likely to act and react differently. Currency changes can radically alter price positions and price competitiveness.

INTERNATIONAL PRICE ALIGNMENT

If the price harmonization forces described in the introductory part of this chapter are at work, a company has to be alert. An international price time bomb may be ticking. The harmonization factors shown in Figure 6-1 are likely to become stronger and to put pressure on price alignment. What can a company do in this situation? Several solutions are available. The worst, yet easiest, one is to let all prices slide to the lowest common denominator. An alternative is to align prices towards the highest level. This option is usually not realistic since it could lead to extreme market share losses in the countries with currently low prices. One situation where this strategy is advisable is when a low price in a small country endangers a high price level in a larger country. In this case the best alignment may be to just raise the price in the small country and sacrifice market share there—or even pull out of the small country totally.

A third option is to raise some prices and to lower others so that an overall acceptable price range is established. To achieve this we suggest a so-called "price corridor" into which the prices of all countries have to fall. The two realistic options are illustrated in Figure 6-4.

The international price corridor takes into account both the differences between countries and the mounting pressures for alignment. The corridor has to consider the market sizes and price elasticities of the individual countries, gray imports resulting from price differentials, currency-exchange rates, costs within countries, and arbitrage costs between them, as well as data on competition and distribution (such as differences in distribution margins). According to our experience the power pricer's application of the corridor concept typically improves profits by 15% to 25% compared to uniform pricing and the corridor largely eliminates gray markets, whose damage is difficult to quantify. Relative to these improvements the costs of establishing such a system are insignificant.

We illustrate the determination of a price corridor for a pharmaceutical product which we call SYNOP here. SYNOP is marketed by one of the leading pharmaceutical companies in the world. In order to establish the optimal international pricing strategy for this innovative product a study was carried out in five countries: United States, Britain, France,

FIGURE 6-4

Possible Developments of International Prices

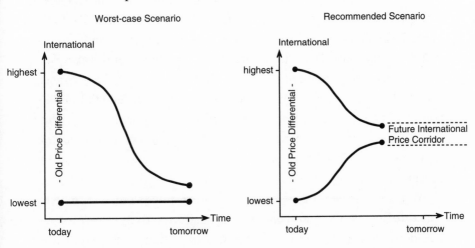

Italy, and Germany. Based on the results, the optimal country-specific prices given in the left part of Figure 6-5 were derived. These prices do not take interrelations among the countries into account; i.e., these are the optimal prices if we could effectively build a fence to isolate each country market.

These optimal prices show considerable differences. The optimal price in the United States undercuts the German price by 57% and the British price by 48%. At these price differentials our fences would be jumped over or run around or run through, i.e., strong gray-import activities would be expected. The goal was to maximize profits and not to suppress all gray imports as such; some people could still get through the fence if this was consistent with optimal pricing. Based on expert judgment a set of gray-import curves was developed in a one-day workshop with managers. Such a curve estimates what percentage of a market will be served through gray imports if the price differential between two countries reaches a certain level. The gray import curve between the United States and Germany is shown in Figure 6-6. It tells us that if the country-specific optimal prices were implemented and the differential between the German and the U.S. price would be 57%, then about 32% of the sales volume in Germany would be served through gray imports from the United States. By contrast, for a price differential of less than 20% gray imports into Germany were expected to virtually disappear.

We employed the INTERPRICE (for INTERnational PRICE) system developed by Simon, Kucher & Partners to optimize the price corridor. The right-hand panel of Figure 6-5 shows the result. The optimal international pricing corridor is set between $1.90 and $2.50; relative to the upper limit the width of the corridor is 24%. All prices have to fall within this corridor. Thus, the separately optimal prices of Germany and the UK have to be reduced to $2.50, while the prices in Italy, France, and the U.S.A. must be raised to $1.90. At a price differential of 24% there will be some gray imports from France and the United States into Germany and the UK, but based on the gray-import curves they are expected to remain below 5% of the market volume. This was considered acceptable by the company.

We also considered a policy of a uniform price across all markets which (of course) would mean no gray market activity. However, the corridor of prices ($1.90 and $2.50) and tolerating some gray market

FIGURE 6-5

Optimal Prices for Individual Countries and Optimal Price Corridor for SYNOP

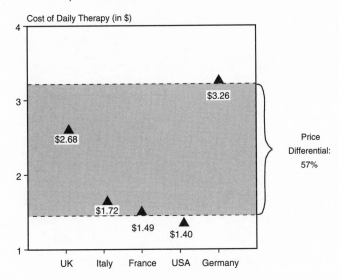

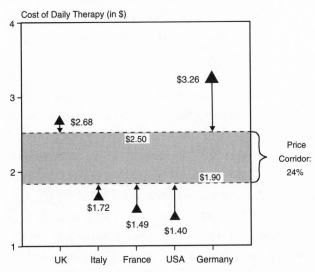

FIGURE 6-6

Estimated Gray Import Function for SYNOP

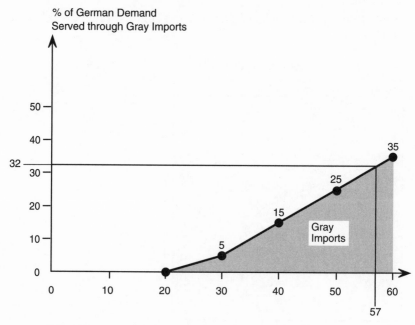

Price Difference between Germany and USA (in % of German Price)

activity led to a much higher profit than imposing a uniform price policy would yield. Compared to the individual optimal prices which were not implementable the (theoretical) profit sacrifice was not too large from the price corridor and the annoyance of gray imports would be largely avoided.

The price corridor attempts to find a compromise between warranted price customization and necessary price uniformity. It implements in a systematic, quantified way the principle "as much customization as possible, as much uniformity as necessary." The corridor is, of course, affected by changes in currency-exchange rates, arbitrage costs, or other factors. The INTERPRICE system allows us to insert new parameters and provides recommendations on the adjustment of the corridor and the prices.[8]

In establishing a price corridor it should be observed that international arbitrage costs are not given but can be influenced through branding, package design, distribution, or similar measures. However, building such barriers between countries usually sacrifices economies of scale.

The advantages and disadvantages of these actions meant to support international price customization should be carefully weighed against each other. We summarize our recommendations on international price alignment below.

- The pressure for international price alignment should not lead to a uniform price across countries, since customization potential is sacrificed. Great care should be taken to avoid the decline of all prices to the lowest common level.

- It is increasingly unrealistic and dangerous to implement country-specific optimal prices. Frequently the price differences resulting from this approach are large enough to induce gray markets. These create trouble with customers, who increasingly are moving to worldwide procurement and distributors, etc.

- We recommend setting up an international pricing corridor which on the one hand allows for a certain customization of prices and on the other hand avoids the danger of too much differentiation. In order to determine the optimal corridor, reliable information on price elasticities, arbitrage costs, and gray-import effects is required. Considering the profits at stake in international markets, the additional costs for information collection and analysis typically pay off within weeks or months. Determining optimal international prices is one of the biggest challenges for the power pricer.

IMPLEMENTATIONAL ASPECTS OF INTERNATIONAL PRICING

International pricing is fraught with implementational difficulties. While the necessary responses to sudden changes in exchange rates may be evident it is often extremely problematic to put them into practice. It is not always clear whether such a change is temporary or permanent. Short-term ups and downs in currency rates may collide with the desire for continuity in pricing. The market position in a country has to be judged both strategically and under aspects of short-term profit maximization. In some countries lower prices may be reasonable in order to keep competitors at bay. For example, an American manufacturer of special glass is attacking a Japanese competitor in its home market with aggressive prices because it wants to prevent the Japanese company from generating enough cash flow to invade the European market. Such considerations have to be observed when international prices are determined.

International price alignment may collide with the organizational structure and the incentive system of a company. In most companies, country managers are responsible for pricing in their markets and are compensated and evaluated at least partly on their country's profit. Any international coordination reduces their pricing latitude and thus the opportunity to maximize their country-specific profits. Assmus and Wiese suggest four possible coordination methods, namely economic measures/incentives, centralization, formalization (country prices are determined by a formula), and informal coordination. They show that all methods have strengths and weaknesses.[9] Our corridor concept includes three of the approaches proposed by Assmus and Wiese. It takes into account the need for international coordination but, at the same time, leaves the individual units with some freedom in price setting. The fundamental conflict between the interests of headquarters and the decentralized units cannot be fully resolved in practice. If the interrelatedness of country markets increases, it is necessary to have price decision making more strongly centralized. The more homogeneous the markets, the more uniform the pricing policy has to become. The resulting conflicts between national subsidiaries are unavoidable. A particularly difficult and often emotional conflict is that between larger and smaller countries. The dumbest thing a company can do is to allow a low price in a small country to destroy a high price in a large country (as happened in the case of LOGO). Even if movement of the product from the low price market is impractical, the low price can become a reference price for the whole international pricing structure. It may be wiser to abandon a small market completely than to accept a 10% price drop in a large market.

International pricing is closely related to the international coordination of other marketing aspects. We already mentioned that it can make sense to erect barriers between markets through branding, design, packaging, etc. In the same vein it should be clear that a global brand and localized pricing are incompatible. Kodak had to learn this the hard way. After years of trouble with its global brands, which were massively gray-imported, it introduced a second brand and a private label in Japan in 1995.

A further need for centralization exists in research on pricing issues.

Only if price-relevant facts in various countries are measured comparably can a coordinated pricing strategy be achieved. Therefore, a central organizational unit should at least set the standards for estimating price response and other facts. The same applies to international competitive price information, where we usually encounter big information gaps. This information can be easy to obtain, as the previously mentioned case of Paul Binhold shows. Binhold, the world market leader in anatomical teaching aids, has a worldwide price guarantee. If somebody finds a comparable product anywhere at a lower price Binhold will deliver at the same price. According to Otto H. Gies, Binhold's managing director, this is a perfect global price-information system. Whenever anybody undercuts Binhold anywhere in the world Gies is likely to learn it within hours.

Most companies we know are far from such global information ideals. The same applies to price decision processes and the capability to implement price changes, particularly price increases on an international basis. We recommend educating and informing everyone involved about the consequences of confining one's price considerations to one country. A better understanding of the complex intricacies of international pricing facilitates implementation of power pricing.

Restrictions on Country Pricing

Legal and other government restrictions play a much larger role in international than in domestic pricing. The crossing of borders has implications for taxes and duties. Quotas may have to be observed and antidumping rules may limit the pricing latitude of a company. Almost all of these aspects have an effect on prices. Transfer pricing between units of a company in different countries is strongly influenced by tax considerations. Import duties hamper the competitiveness of foreign firms. Antidumping legislation can make market entry through aggressive penetration pricing infeasible—or it can help an incumbent to fend off foreign competitors. And international authorities like the Commission of the European Union (EU) can observe and influence the pricing behavior of firms across countries. The EU essentially prohibits all attempts to separate country markets in Europe from each other.

But such restrictions may even offer pricing opportunities—for an example, see the import restrictions for Japanese cars in the U.S. market.

If the number of cars to be imported is limited, the pricing problem is to set the price at exactly the level that will lead to selling the number of cars imported. To achieve this, the sales response curve must be known (see chapter 3). Historically, the Japanese manufacturers have managed this exercise well in the U.S. market. At the same time, there were two important side effects. First, import quotas induced a cartel-like situation among the incumbent Japanese competitors in the U.S. market because their market shares were fixed by the agreement. Second, smaller and potentially price-aggressive Japanese car companies were kept small or kept out. In the same sense, antidumping duties may protect not only domestic firms but also foreign competitors who are not interested in pricing aggressively. Sometimes we have observed (e.g., in the Brazilian market) that foreign investors, once they have a manufacturing operation going, become strong supporters of import restrictions in order to protect themselves from price-aggressive foreign competitors.

It is evident that such implications must be well understood in order to implement a power pricing policy in a complex international environment. This may be difficult to achieve—but declining barriers, the introduction of common currencies (like the Euro in the European Union), better information technology, and more international experience foster progress towards this goal. The better-informed and more responsive pricer can exploit opportunities to his advantage and avoid pitfalls in international pricing.

SUMMARY

Adapting to the rapidly advancing globalization of markets is a distinguishing characteristic of power pricers' pricing. It creates new opportunities for price customization but it is also fraught with dangers for existing price structures and levels. In international pricing the following aspects and recommendations should be observed.

- Two countervailing forces must be taken into account: customization factors and harmonization factors; both are dynamic.
- Traditionally markets, customers, competitors, distributors, and regulations have differed from country to country. These differentiation factors call for customized country prices.

- It is not optimal to calculate international prices on a cost-plus base. Rather the perceived value of a product in each country should determine the price in that country.
- Currency-exchange rates play a crucial role in international pricing. Changes in these rates should lead to moderate price adjustments. It is not optimal to keep either the price or the margin constant after such changes.
- In many markets an alignment of international prices is required because harmonization factors increasingly gain the upper hand. Disappearance of barriers, better information technology, decreasing transportation and arbitrage costs, global sourcing, etc., are the drivers of this development.
- A uniform price across countries is usually not the optimal answer to these trends since the sacrifice in profit potential is too great. Neither can the historic price differentials be retained, since they induce gray imports and similar problems. We recommend the implementation of an international price corridor that strives for a compromise between differentiation and harmonization. While it may seem the thing to do, driving gray-market activity to zero is rarely the best solution.
- Setting the corridor requires well-founded information on country-specific prices and their interrelations. A coordination of pricing research across countries is strongly recommended.
- The more homogeneous and interrelated country markets become the greater is the need for central price coordination. International pricing involves a substantial conflict potential between subsidiaries and headquarters. Several methods to deal with this conflict are available, but none is without disadvantages. The more managers understand the intricacies of international pricing the more likely it is that the conflicts will be resolved in a reasonable way.

We expect that the dynamics of international pricing will even accelerate in the future. This suggests that every company that is internationally active should pay great attention to this area. The power pricer can reap big profits by mastering the challenges.

7

Nonlinear Pricing

INTRODUCTION

The preceding chapters have shown that prices can be customized profitably along different dimensions, across customers, regions, product variants, and so on in order to better match prices to customers' willingness to pay. Another important possibility for the "variable quantity case" (where customers buy fewer or more units of a product depending on the price) is the customization of price. Nonlinear pricing, as this practice is known, usually involves a discount in the price with increase in number of units.

Nonlinear pricing abounds, in practice, and can take many different forms, as the following examples illustrate:

- Most industrial firms offer so-called quantity discounts for larger volumes. In a study we did in the chemical industry, 63% of the respondents said that they frequently give quantity discounts, with an average discount of 19% off the highest price. The quantity-discount schedule of Sealed Air Corporation is typical. Due to transportation efficiencies, the prices for one of Sealed Air's packing materials vary with the size of an individual order: $50.00 per 1,000 square feet for quantities below 5,000 square feet, $45.40 per unit for a total quantity between 5,000 and 10,000 square feet, down to $33.50 per unit for a whole truckload of 200,000 square feet.[1]

- Software companies typically set nonlinear prices for licenses. As discussed in chapter 5, Novell's NetWare costs $1,196 for 25 users (= $38 per user) and $3,996 for 250 users (= $16 per user). The base model of the statistical package SPSS for Windows is sold at DM 2,500 for one user, at DM 12,250 for ten users (= DM 1,225 per user), and at DM 23,450 for 50 users (= DM 469 per user).

- The American Club in Bonn prices exercise sessions at $6 for one session, $50 for ten sessions ($5 per session), and $90 for 20 sessions ($4.50 per session). Many theaters have similar schedules for subscribers. A photographer in the same city promotes passport photos at DM 4.00 for one photo, DM 14.00 for six photos (= DM 2.33 per photo), and DM 21.00 for 12 photos (= DM 1.75 per photo).

- The Atlantis Sheraton Hotel in Zurich has this schedule for telephone calls.

Number of Units	Charge per Call
First 10 seconds	SFr 0.40 each
Second 10 seconds	SFr 0.30 each
Over 21 seconds	SFr 0.20 each

- Newspapers and television stations offer quantity discounts for advertising space and time respectively. A quantity discount of the *Los Angeles Times* involved 32 price breaks and a maximum discount of 40% for buyers of more than five million lines in a year.[2]

- Bank charges for portfolio management depend on the size of the portfolio. Deutsche Bank charges 0.05% for portfolios up to DM 50,000, 0.04% between DM 50,000 and DM 100,000, and 0.03% for more than DM 100,000.

- Fortune magazine offers a one-year subscription in Germany at DM 5.25 per issue, a two-year subscription at DM 4.73 per issue, and a three-year subscription at DM 4.20 per issue.

- Telephone companies and utilities usually have price schemes consisting of a fixed monthly charge and a variable usage price. A higher quantity leads to a lower share of the fixed monthly charge per unit.

The average price decreases with the number of units. A similar structure typically applies for rental car rates.

- Deutsche Bahn, the German railroad corporation, offers a so-called BahnCard at prices of DM 220 for the second class and DM 440 for the first class. The BahnCard entitles the owner to buy tickets at a 50% discount off the normal price for one year.

- Frequent-flier programs offer discounts for people who fly a lot with the same airline. Sales or loyalty bonuses have similar effects, particularly when the discounts increase progressively with purchasing volume.

- A specific form of nonlinear pricing is multiperson pricing, in which price discounts are awarded to a second or an additional person buying the same product or service as the first (or "main") person. Many airlines periodically offer programs where the spouse or the companion of a full-paying passenger can fly at half price (e.g., Lufthansa, Air New Zealand) or even for free (e.g., Southwest Airlines' "Friends Fly Free" Program). Similar schemes are popular in the hotel industry. A German waste-disposal firm has a scheme where the price for its services decreases inversely proportionally with the number of persons in a household. The annual prices are DM 208 for a one-person household, DM 256 for a two-person household (= DM 126 per person), and DM 350 for a five-person household (= DM 70 per person). Programs of the "Friends & Family" type, pioneered by MCI in the U.S. telecommunications industry, can be seen as a variant of multiperson pricing with additional network effects.

As these examples suggest, the typical case is that price declines with increasing quantity. In some situations a supplier wishes to discourage high-volume users rather than encourage them. For example, in Boston, water and sewer charges for a household follow an increasing schedule: the first 10 units in a six-month period cost $2.63 per unit, increasing through eight break points to $9.53 per unit for any units over 200 used by the household in a six-month period. However, in most real-world situations one finds decreasing rates.

These numerous examples show that nonlinear schedules are common in practice and can have important profit implications. Our experience is that few firms have really thought through the rationale for—and the implications of—their discount schedules.

WHAT THIS CHAPTER WILL DO

This chapter addresses the following questions.

1. What forms of nonlinear pricing exist?
2. Why is nonlinear pricing optimal and under which conditions?
3. Which information is required to develop nonlinear pricing schedules?
4. How should prices for multiple persons be set?
5. Which aspects should be observed in the implementation of nonlinear pricing?

Knowing the answers to these questions will help you to:

1. understand the reasons for and intricacies of nonlinear pricing
2. decide whether to apply a uniform or a nonlinear price schedule in your specific situation
3. organize the collection of the information you need and to design an optimal schedule
4. avoid the implementational pitfalls associated with complex structures

FORMS OF NONLINEAR PRICING

Figure 7-1 presents the forms of nonlinear pricing graphically. Graph (a) shows a uniform price schedule with a linear through-the-origin relationship between quantity and the total paid by the customer ("Total to Customer"). The price per unit is constant, as shown by the horizontal line in the graph.

Graph (b) shows an all-units quantity discount wherein, if a certain quantity level is exceeded, the lower price applies to all units. The Sealed Air example above exemplifies this schedule. If the quantity purchased is between 5,000 and 10,000 square feet, the customer pays $45.40 for all units, not $50 for the first 5,000 and then dropping down to $45.50 for the remainder. This form leads to an inefficient set of purchase quantities. For example, the cost to a customer buying 4,700 square feet at $50 per 1,000 square feet would be $235. However, 5,000 square feet purchased at the discounted price of $45.40 per 1,000 square feet costs $227. The inefficient purchase quantities are between 4,540

FIGURE 7-1

Forms of Nonlinear Pricing

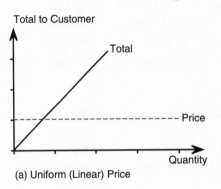

(a) Uniform (Linear) Price

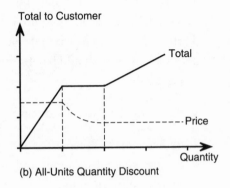

(b) All-Units Quantity Discount

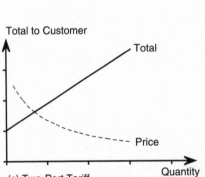

(c) Two-Part Tariff

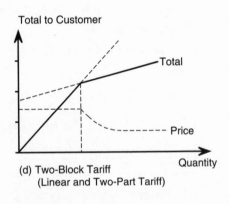

(d) Two-Block Tariff
(Linear and Two-Part Tariff)

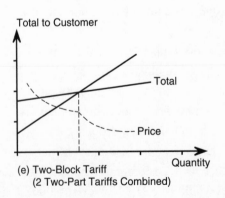

(e) Two-Block Tariff
(2 Two-Part Tariffs Combined)

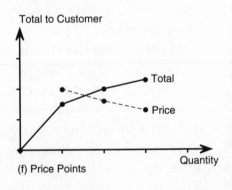

(f) Price Points

and 5,000 square feet, because 5,000 × $0.0454 = $227 is equal to 4,450 × $0.05 = $227. In all-units discount pricing the quantity breakpoints of the discounts and the prices for each interval have to be determined. In the simplest case, with two price intervals, these are three parameters: the breakpoint and the two prices. With three intervals we have five parameters, three prices, two break points, and so on. This shows that non-linear pricing can become quite complex.

Graph (c) shows the two-part tariff, which consists of a fixed charge and an additional marginal price per unit. Essentially the customer pays for the right to buy the goods at a fixed charge and then has to pay the marginal price for each unit actually bought. This is the nonlinear price schedule typical for telephone companies with a monthly fixed charge and a charge per service unit. Rental cars have the same price structure; typically a fixed charge per day plus a fee per mile are levied. The "un-limited mileage" version is a special case of a two-part tariff where the marginal price is set to zero. Purchasing clubs where members pay an annual membership fee and then can buy goods or services at lower prices are two-part tariffs. With increasing quantity the fixed charge is distributed over a larger number of units so that the average price per unit decreases as shown in the figure. Two price parameters, the fixed charge and the marginal price, have to be determined in a two-part tariff.

Graph (d) shows a two-block tariff in which a price per unit is charged up to a certain quantity, then the price per unit changes to a smaller number for all units. This is also called an "incremental units quantity discount" as opposed to an all-units quantity discount. The At-lantis Sheraton telephone schedule exemplifies this. When a linear tariff and a two-part tariff are offered, the structure is analogous to the Bahn-Card case described later in this chapter.

Graph (e) shows a variant of the two-block tariff where each of the two blocks has both a fixed and a variable price component. This form is typical for utilities. Rhenag, a German natural-gas supplier, offers two options. Tariff A has a fixed monthly charge of DM 4.00 and a variable price of DM 10.90 per 100 kilowatt-hours (kwh). Tariff B has a fixed charge of DM 14.00 and a variable price of DM 6.10 per 100 kwh. Tele-phone companies offer choices between combinations of fixed and vari-able price components. This strategy is very popular in the cellular sector. E-plus, the third entrant into the German market, innovated with a two-part tariff, the "Partner-Tarif" consisting of a monthly charge of DM 44, plus a variable price per minute of DM 1.64 aimed at light users, and a "Profi-Tarif" with a monthly charge of DM 59 plus a variable price per minute of DM 1.19 for heavy users. Analogous structures exist in the product sector. Compare traditional light bulbs and compact fluorescent lights (CFLs): the light bulb costs around DM 1 (the "fixed" price component) and consumes energy costing DM 1.88 per 100 hours (the "variable" price component), while the CFL has a purchase price of DM 30 but costs only DM 0.38 per 100 hours and has a much longer life. Thus, "fixed" and "variable" price components are structurally similar to those in the service examples.

Graph (f) of Figure 7-1 shows the form of price points. Like in the case of the American Club in Bonn or the Bonn photographer described above, prices are set for specific units, but in each case the pattern is nonlinear. Multiperson pricing can also be subsumed under the price point form.

The different forms require different types and numbers of price parameters to be determined. Table 7-1 summarizes what has to be determined to use nonlinear pricing. We see that—unlike in uniform (linear) pricing—in all forms of nonlinear pricing several price parameters have to be set. In the case of the *Los Angeles Times'* quantity discount schedule, with 32 price breaks, a decision had to be made on 32 prices and 31 break points. Nonlinear price decisions are considerably more complex and require more information than decisions on uniform prices. But the power pricer meets the analysis needed to make these decisions pay dividends.

RATIONALES FOR NONLINEAR PRICING

Why and under which conditions is nonlinear pricing optimal? The prevalence of this practice suggests that the answer to this question is well understood. But our experience has been that when asking why quantity discounts are offered or why the particular form is used, one usually receives an unconvincing answer. Many managers justify the quantity discounts by cost savings. Larger order quantities induced by the discounts reduce logistics and the inventory costs of the seller. Others argue that big buyers simply demand discounts and, given the importance of keeping

TABLE 7-1

Parameters to be Determined under Different Forms of Nonlinear Pricing

Forms of Nonlinear Pricing	Parameters to be Determined	
	Type	Number
Uniform (linear) pricing	Price	1
All-units quantity discount	Price Break points	2 or more 1 or more
Two-part tariff	Fixed charge Marginal price	1 1
Two-block tariff	Fixed charges Marginal prices	2 or more 2 or more
Price points	Prices	2 or more
Multiperson pricing	Prices	2 or more

large customers, price concessions have to be made. Others cite competition; Tom Johnson, publisher of the *Los Angeles Times,* was quoted as stating that "Our rates have been established in response to our costs and to competition from both newspapers and other media."[3] American Airlines considers its invention of the frequent-flier program as "the single most successful marketing tool we've ever had."[4] Its success induced all major competitors to clone this program. In 1994 the nonlinear price policy of E-Plus mentioned above was immediately copied by the two incumbent cellular networks, D_1 and D_2. Thus, competitive interdependencies seem to be strong drivers of the diffusion of nonlinear price schemes. A further argument often heard from service companies is that the fixed charge reflects the fact that an infrastructure with high fixed costs has to be maintained. The high-fixed-cost share of the supplier is translated into a fixed charge the customer has to pay—a specific form of cost-plus thinking.

All these arguments have some truth in them. But there are further rationales for nonlinear pricing. Nonlinear pricing should not be looked upon as a defensive strategy—against either big buyers or competitors—but as a way for a power pricer to customize prices and enhance profit. Profitable nonlinear pricing can be instituted due to demand, cost, or competitive reasons. We will first consider the demand aspect.

Demand

The basic demand driver is the simple fact that often a consumer's willingness to pay decreases for additional units; that is, he is willing to pay more for the first than for the second unit, more for the second than for the third, and so on. In this case, the seller increases his profit by charging more for the first unit than for the second unit, to mirror the consumer's values. The average price per unit decreases with a higher purchase quantity. This applies to an individual consumer or a set of consumers with identical maximum prices. If we know the consumer's values, we can just step down the prices with the values until our costs are reached. We fully exploit customer value by our nonlinear pricing.

If customers differ from one another, the rationale for nonlinear pricing still applies but is not as efficient for the firm. We will illustrate this by considering a simple case for a cinema in Bonn. This cinema offers discounts for a second, third, etc., visit within one month. The number of visits is monitored by means of a card that is issued at the first visit and is valid for one month. We consider three consumers—A, B, and C—who are representative and whose willingnesses to pay for a first, second, etc., visit to the cinema are given in Table 7-2. All prices are in marks.

One option for the cinema operator is to set a uniform price per visit (linear pricing). Since marginal costs per visit are essentially zero, we will assume that the operator wishes to maximize ticket sales revenue. Given the values in Table 7-2, at a price of DM 12 there would only be one visit per month (by consumer C) yielding DM 12 revenue. At DM 10 consumer C would visit twice and consumer B once, and the revenue would be DM 30 (3 × DM 10). Considering all alternative prices, we find that DM 5.50 is the optimal uniform price, yielding 9 visits (4 by C, 3 by B, and 2 by A) and DM 49 revenue (= profit).

In nonlinear pricing we proceed differently and set the profit-maximiz-

TABLE 7-2

Nonlinear Pricing with Three Heterogeneous Consumers—A Case of Cinema Visits

Visits (Unit)	Maximum Prices per Consumer and Visit			Optimal Price for n-th visit	Visits	Profit
	A	B	C			
First	9.0	10.0	12.0	9.0	3	27.0
Second	6.0	7.5	10.0	6.0	3	18.0
Third	3.5	5.5	8.0	5.5	2	11.0
Fourth	2.0	4.0	6.0	4.0	2	8.0
Fifth	1.1	1.5	3.5	3.5	1	3.5
Total with Non-linear pricing					11	67.5
Total with Uniform Price				5.5	9	49.0

ing price for each visit. This is the technique of "price points." For the first visit we could ask DM 12, only consumer C buys, and revenue is DM 12; at DM 10 both C and B buy, yielding DM 20; at a price of DM 9 all three consumers would visit, yielding DM 27. Thus, DM 9 is the optimal price for the first visit. Analogously the optimal prices for each consecutive visit can be derived; we find DM 6 for the second, DM 5.50 for the third, etc. Table 7-2 provides the numbers and shows that 11 visits and a total profit of DM 67.50 are obtained through optimal nonlinear pricing. This figure exceeds the optimal uniform pricing profit of DM 49 by 37.8%! The reason for this huge improvement is explained in Figure 7-2.

In Figure 7-2 the price is on the total horizontal axis and the total number of visits for the three customers on the vertical axis. The surface of the "triangle" below the outer step curve (the price response curve) denotes the profit potential. Through uniform pricing we cut the darkest-shaded rectangle, with sides equal to DM 5.50 and number of visits equal to 9, out of this triangle. We sacrifice substantial profits and consumer surplus on both sides. Through nonlinear pricing we step down

FIGURE 7-2

Comparison of Nonlinear and Uniform Pricing—From Rectangle to Triangle

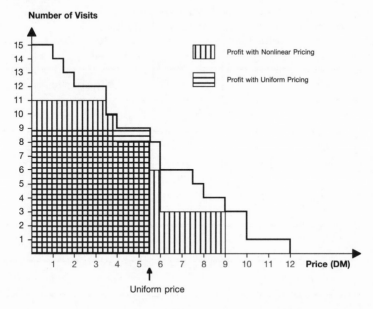

the value curve and come much closer to exploiting the triangle, leaving less "money on the table." Since the customers are heterogeneous it is not possible to harvest the full triangle, even through nonlinear pricing.

It is obvious from this case that the better we can fine-tune the nonlinear prices the closer we come to exploiting the full profit potential. Thus, implementation costs aside, more complex schedules are better: two-block tariffs are better than two-part tariffs, multiblock tariffs are better than two-block tariffs, and so on. But implementation costs, such as for gathering the necessary customer data, and possible customer confusion set a practical limit to this. But the important point here is that the simple and prevalent phenomenon of willingness to pay declining over successive units means a big profit potential from customizing prices through a nonlinear schedule.

A second demand driver of quantity discounts is the higher price elasticity of large customers. Figure 7-3 shows a result from a conjoint measurement study of industrial air-pollution test equipment. These devices are bought by manufacturing companies; depending on its size, the customer may need fewer than 100 or several thousand of these items per year.

The large customers (over 1,000 units) have a price elasticity of 2.20, while the small buyers (less than 100 units) are considerably less price sensitive, with an elasticity of 1.54. This difference in elasticities led to the optimal price for medium-sized customers being 24% less and for large customers being 36% less than for small customers.

There are good reasons for large customers to be more price sensitive. Their larger purchasing volumes make it worth their while to shop around and compare prices because their savings potentials are higher. They may also have procurement alternatives that are not practical for small buyers. In selling ad space, a newspaper like the *Los Angeles Times* faces competition from newspapers, billboards, and perhaps local TV in the case of small buyers, but large customers have the added option of advertising on national television. Large firms have the knowledge and systems to purchase globally, thus expanding the competitive set. Large buyers' higher price elasticities make offering them quantity discounts the profit-maximizing thing to do. It is not just a simple matter of "the big guys always beat me up."

In specific cases nonlinear pricing schemes can effect a transfer of values from the business to the private sphere. The phenomenon is well known for frequent-flier programs, where miles earned on business trips are privately used. Because of the potential for abuse, some companies prohibit such transfers to their employees.

FIGURE 7-3

Price Elasticities and Purchase Quantities—A Case of Air Testing Devices

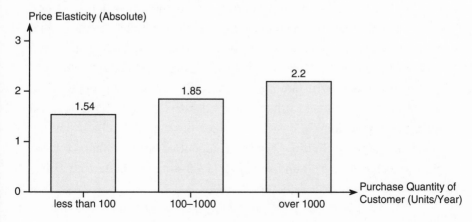

Costs

Cost savings can also drive nonlinear pricing. If quantity discounts generate larger individual order sizes, production and transportation efficiencies may result. If the discounts increase overall demand, economies of scale and learning effects can induce lower unit costs. Quantity discounts may be an effective way to minimize the system cost in the supplier-customer value chain. They imply a sharing of the transportation cost savings, and they shift the inventorying responsibility for a bulky item down the distribution channel, as in the case of Sealed Air. For the same reason we observe heavy discounting in industries like tires or fertilizers. An additional effect is that competition is kept out if the inventories of the retailers are full. Jeuland and Shugan show that manufacturers' quantity discounts can improve channel coordination.[5]

Competition

Nonlinear pricing is also highly interesting under competitive aspects. Oren, Smith, and Wilson have shown that, if quantity discounts are optimal in monopoly, they are also optimal under competition.[6] Dolan has shown that nonlinear pricing can be optimal in a competitive bidding situation in which the buyer has a preference for a multisourced environment.[7] Quantity discounts, sales bonuses, etc., can build barriers to entry, since a customer has to go through the stage of high initial prices to get the big discounts. That is why antitrust authorities have frequently investigated these practices and prohibited some of them. Two-part and multiblock tariffs can be a particularly effective way to lock competitors out. If a customer has bought the right to a certain discount or service through an up-front payment (as in the cases of the BahnCard or mobile phone services) he is unlikely to switch to a competitor, where he would have to pay the initial fixed charge again. In many industries where two-part or two-block tariffs are not yet used this offers a great opportunity for an innovator. Hotels, airlines, or similar service providers could use such systems to lock in customers, since they are unlikely to pay the fixed charge twice. In order to keep competitors out it is important that the fixed charge be paid up front. This is a distinguishing feature of frequent-flier or similar loyalty programs.

Nonlinear pricing allows a firm to target particular market segments.

A case in point is that of Sprint up against AT&T. Sprint offered two-part tariffs with high fixed charges but low marginal prices. This schedule was aimed at the heavy users and turned out to be very successful. Orange, a new cellular entrant in the UK, attacked the incumbents in the same way in 1995.

This overview reveals that there are many situations in which nonlinear pricing can boost profit substantially. The great potential of this method has only been touched so far. In order to take full advantage of this strategy, difficult measurement problems have to be solved. Information on aggregate price response is totally insufficient for nonlinear pricing. Optimizing nonlinear prices requires knowledge of the marginal values that individual customers attribute to each additional unit of a product. We illustrate some of these problems and some solutions to them in the following discussion of application.

APPLICATIONS OF NONLINEAR PRICING

Tacke addressed nonlinear pricing of chocolate bars, developing a conjoint-measurement approach to assess potential customers' marginal values of additional units.[8] Since the conjoint method has been described in chapter 3, we present only his results here. He derived optimal pricing for the uniform price and six alternative nonlinear schemes.

Table 7-3 shows the optimal prices for these seven price structures. The optimal uniform price was DM 1.12 and each nonlinear method yields significant sales volume and profit increases. The maximum profit, achieved through a three-block tariff, is 70.3% higher than the uniform-pricing profit. This test application is not meant to imply that all listed forms are implementable in this case, but to point out the enormous potential of nonlinear pricing with regard to increasing sales volume and profit. It should be kept in mind that this test application took place in one supermarket and did not take competitive reactions into account. Such reactions could moderate the volume and profit increases, but still leave nonlinear pricing superior to uniform pricing.

Tacke also shows that nonlinear prices involve substantial risks. If the optimal values of the nonlinear price components are missed by relatively small margins, strongly negative profit effects can occur. The reason is

TABLE 7-3

Results of a Test Application of Nonlinear Pricing for Chocolate Bars

Form of Nonlinear Pricing	Optimal Prices (DM)	Differences to Uniform Pricing	
		Sales Volume	Profit
Uniform price	1.12	0	0
Two-part tariff	Fixed charge 0.57 Marginal price 1.03	+46.3 %	+58.1 %
All-units discount	1.27 1 to 7 units 1.10 8 or more	+52.8 %	+49.8 %
Incremental quantity discount	1.31 for first unit 1.03 as of second unit	+50.0 %	+61.3 %
Two-block tariff	Block 1: 1.37 per unit Block 2: Fixed charge 0.57 Marginal price 1.03	+50.0 %	+63.7 %

Three-block tariff	Block 1: 1.37 per unit
	Block 2: Fixed charge 0.41
	              Marginal price 1.08
	Block 3: Fixed charge 0.65
	              Marginal price 1.03
		+46.0 %	+70.3 %

Price-points (3 Points)	1.37 for 1 unit
	3.66 for 3 units
	           (= 1.22 per unit)
	8.80 for 8 units
	           (= 1.10 per unit)
		+64.9 %	+66.6 %

that the prices charged are shifted very close to the maximum prices that the consumers are willing to pay. If these maximum prices are exceeded the respective consumer does not buy. The attempt to almost fully exploit the consumer surplus leaves very little margin for error. These findings underline the extreme importance of valid and reliable measurements for nonlinear pricing.

In the chocolate case, "price points" would be the best form for implementation. The profit is the second highest and price points are relatively easy to implement. Either the chocolate bars could be offered in packs of one, three, and eight, or the scanner system of the store could be programmed to select the right price points if a consumer buys three or eight bars. The three price points should be communicated to the buyer at the shelf or in promotional advertisements. In a second test application, for yogurt desserts, Tacke achieved similar results: profit improvements were between 50.45% (all-units discount) and 73.55% (three-block tariff).

The BahnCard Case

Our experience from these test applications was used to develop a large-scale nonlinear pricing project for Deutsche Bahn AG, the German railroad corporation. Their policy was to charge DM 0.24 per kilometer for second class and DM 0.36 per km for first class. While the system did customize price somewhat through having first- and second-class train cars, it did not permit segment-specific pricing for heavy and light users. Also, many perceived the prices to be too high compared to the costs of using a car. This was mainly due to the fact that when most consumers use their cars they only consider as costs their out-of-pocket costs for gasoline.

This led to consideration of the concept of the BahnCard, envisaged as a personal card that has to be bought once a year, giving the owner the right to buy tickets at a substantial discount. The customer has to invest first and can then harvest the benefits of this investment for a whole year. Conceptually the BahnCard is a two-part tariff. Given that the customer can choose not to buy the card and just pay regular rates, the system constitutes a two-block tariff (see Figure 7-1).

The following questions were raised by the management of Deutsche Bahn.

- What percentage discount should be granted to BahnCard buyers?
- What should the price of the BahnCard be?
- How should the price of the BahnCard vary by class and for special groups (e.g., students, elderly)?

The effects on the magnitude and the structure of sales volume and revenue had to be quantified, particularly with regard to cannibalization of regular rate business by the discounted rate payers. The card concept involved a substantial risk if the price parameters were set incorrectly. If, at one extreme, the cards were given away for free and awarded a discount of 50%, revenue would be halved. If, at the other extreme, the card's price were too high, it would not have an effect since too few customers would buy the card. The status quo would be maintained but a significant profit opportunity would continue to be missed. Finding the optimal midpoint between these two extremes was the challenge. Since the marginal cost of an additional traveler is close to zero, revenue was to be maximized. Revenue and profit maximization are effectively equivalent in the case of the German National Railway.

In order to address these complex issues more than 8,000 customers and potential customers of the railroad system were computer-interviewed. A special conjoint measurement design was used to measure values and willingnesses to pay for various variants of the card. We found that the perceived value of a 50% discount was 2.7 times (and not 2.0 times!) higher than the value of a 25% discount—maybe because it is much easier to calculate a 50% than a 25% price reduction. This clearly suggested that the only effective discount was 50%. A complex model was developed to simulate the effects of the new pricing structure and to optimize the card's price for the different groups.

The discount was set at 50%. Figure 7-4 shows the predicted sales volume of the card and the total sales revenue for alternative prices of the BahnCard for second-class service. At a card price of DM 100, a very large volume of the cards would be sold but the effects on overall sales revenue would be negative because too much revenue would be lost from otherwise full-paying heavy travelers. At a high card price of, for example, DM 400, only a few people would buy the card and, thus, no new customers would be attracted and existing customers would not intensify their use of trains. The optimal price lay in the range of DM 200 to DM 250 and was eventually set at DM 220.

In a similar way the optimal price for the BahnCard First Class was found to be DM 440, twice the price of the second-class card, whereas the normal per-kilometer price surcharge for first class is only 50% (DM 0.36 versus DM 0.24). The bigger differential in the card prices is due to greater perceived value differences found in the market. For special groups, such as the elderly and students, each card was offered at half the above prices, the second-class card at DM 110 and the BahnCard First at DM 220.

FIGURE 7-4

Sales Volume and Revenue Effects of Alternative BahnCard Prices

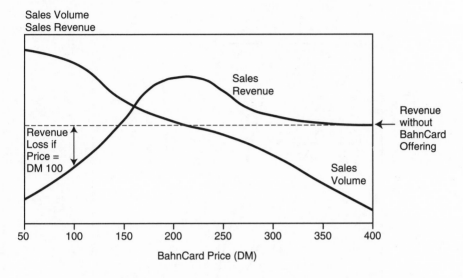

Figure 7-5 shows the resulting nonlinear pricing system for the second class. The BahnCard customer incurs a relatively high up-front investment cost of DM 220, but this gives him the right for a year to buy train tickets at DM 0.12 per kilometer instead of the full price of DM 0.24. Thus the average price per kilometer at the start of using the card is very high: for the first 100 kilometers it is DM 220 + DM 12 = DM 232 divided by 100 kilometers, or DM 2.32. The break-even point between paying DM 0.24 per kilometer and buying the card and paying DM 0.12 per kilometer lies at a distance traveled of 1,833 kilometers. If a passenger travels more than this distance of the card year she saves DM 0.12 per kilometer off the normal price. At 3,000 kilometers, the total cost for a card owner is DM 580, at an average price of DM 0.193 per kilometer, compared to the total cost of DM 720 at the full price, a saving of DM 140 or 19.4%.

The BahnCard has several interesting effects. Once a person has bought the card, the DM 220 is a sunk cost and the decision to take the train depends only on willingness to pay the marginal price of DM 0.12 per kilometer. This induces increased customer loyalty and additional traffic, since the competitive position of train and car is reversed for a BahnCard owner. Even considering gasoline costs alone, it is now

FIGURE 7-5

The BahnCard Nonlinear Pricing System

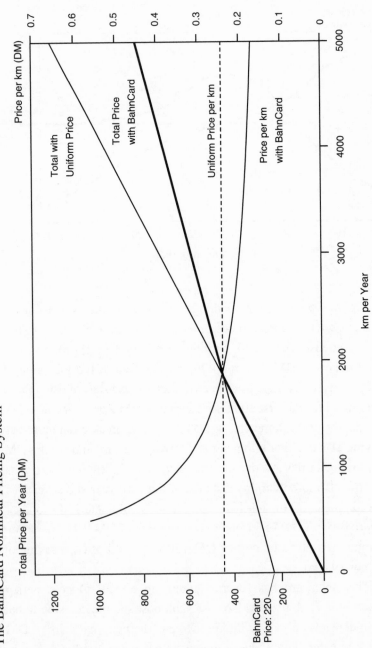

cheaper to take the train. Typically, gasoline in Germany costs about DM 0.15 per kilometer. Before the BahnCard, it was cheaper for everyone to drive. But a BahnCard owner is in a totally different situation. For him the marginal price of a train ride is DM 0.12 per kilometer, 20% less than if he drives. For a 300-kilometer trip, he saves DM 9 by taking the train. Thus, a nonlinear price schedule can serve to reverse a competitive position. By adding a fixed component, the BahnCard brings the structure of paying for train travel closer to the cost structure of a car. Before, the train had a totally variable price based on the distance traveled. Now, with the BahnCard, it has both a fixed and a variable component just like the car, where the purchase price (or depreciation), insurance, taxes, etc., are up-front "fixed" (or sunk) expenses and only gasoline is variable.

The first full year of the BahnCard was 1993. Today 3.1 million cards are sold per year and generate a revenue of DM 2 billion. The BahnCard is by far the best-known product of Deutsche Bahn. It is not only a pricing instrument but also a tool to improve customer retention. The BahnCard comes complete with a photo for identification and an optional credit-card function to ease payment at the ticket counter and on the train.

MULTIPERSON PRICING

A special form of nonlinear pricing is multiperson pricing, in which a second person pays less than a first, "full-price" customer. The rationale for the discount is that the second person's willingness to pay is less than the first person's. Consider the case of a couple, one going on a business trip and the other considering tagging along. The business traveler's willingness to pay (maximum price) is $1,000 and the potentially accompanying spouse has a maximum price of only $600. With uniform pricing, the airline can charge either $1,000 and get only the business traveler, yielding a profit of $1,000. Or it can improve profit by pricing at $600 from each person; both will travel and a higher profit of $1,200 is obtained. However, a nonlinear price schedule with $1,000 for the first and $600 for the second person is even better. Both would buy and a 30% profit improvement, to $1600, would be achieved.

The rationale can be extended to include a transfer of consumer surplus from one person to another. This situation is structurally identical to price bundling, which we discuss in chapter 9. Applied to the present example, let us assume that the business traveler's maximum price is $1,200 and the spouse's is only $400. We also assume that—due to overall customer and competitive considerations—it is optimal for the airline to set the first-person price at $1,000. At the given schedule of $1,000 for the first and $600 for the second person, the couple would still be willing to fly since their combined willingness to pay is $1,600.

Situations where one person's fare is paid by the business and the other person's fare is privately paid offer interesting opportunities for the transfer of consumer surplus from the business to the private sphere. We often observe multiperson price schemes that allow a second person to stay or fly for free provided the first person pays the full price. American Express tries to induce customers to use its Platinum Card by mentioning a program offering free companion travel with a full-fare first- or business-class ticket on certain airlines at certain times. The French hotel chain Ibis and Southwest Airlines in the United States offer such programs. These offers can make sense. In the hotel case such a program can generate additional revenue from the second person for meals and other services. Similar considerations apply to "kids are free" programs.

Multiperson pricing is also used for larger groups. As mentioned in chapter 5, in its 1995–96 winter catalogue Club Med offers a free stay for one person for each ten persons who pay full price. Deutsche Bahn AG has various discount schemes depending on group size. In this context competitive considerations can be important. For the potential customer choosing a mode of transportation, adding another passenger to a car has essentially no impact on cost. But if a train has a uniform pricing plan, an additional passenger has a proportionate impact on total cost. Multiperson pricing can mitigate the cost disadvantage of the train.

IMPLEMENTATION AND LEGAL ASPECTS OF NONLINEAR PRICING

There are powerful theoretical arguments for nonlinear pricing and there are some outstanding examples of power pricers using nonlinear pricing to boost profits in practice. However, it is not for everyone or for all situations. The method typically involves costs of information and implementation, and legal and antitrust restrictions must be carefully considered. And under certain market conditions it is not workable.

For nonlinear pricing to work, resale by the buyer must be preventable. In the same vein, buyers should be restrained from combining their demand. If one person (a buyer or reseller) can combine the demand quantities of several buyers, he gets the attractive quantity discounts and passes them on to the other buyers who do not have to pay high initial prices for the first units. This happens on both the small and the large scale. In procuring heating oil it is customary in Europe for several neighboring households to form a "purchasing alliance" in order to get bigger quantity discounts. Instead of buying 4,000 liters each, three households can combine to buy 12,000 liters. They then ask the truck driver to deliver the oil unofficially to their individual filling points, which he is not supposed to do. In Bonn on January 4, 1996, they would have saved DM 444 ($310) or 8.7% through this simple trick. Even after deducting a tip for the trucker this "purchasing alliance" is attractive. A similar problem occurs with frequent-flier miles where "coupon banks" are buying and reselling these bonuses. This was definitely not intended by the airlines.

The risk of resale and the opportunities to prevent it have to be judged in each individual case. Contracts may be effective, but they involve control costs. The risk of resale or bundling is reduced if the product is perishable. In a famous European case, United Brands prohibited its resellers from dealing in green bananas, which could easily be resold. They were only allowed to resell yellow bananas, which are highly perishable. This case also points to a variant of aggregating purchase quantities, namely forward buying. Excessive forward buying combined with low inventory-holding costs can make nonlinear pricing unprofitable.

Personal services offer ideal conditions for the implementation of nonlinear pricing. Services are the ultimate perishable goods and therefore optimally suited for nonlinear pricing. This is particularly true for services where the person receiving the service has to be present and can be identified, as with airlines, hotels, or trains. To prevent fraud Deutsche Bahn has put an ID photo on the BahnCard as of July 1995.

Each firm must assess its ability to detect and its costs to prevent violations of the conditions that make nonlinear pricing profitable. If resale and bundling of purchases or excessive forward buying cannot be prevented effectively, uniform pricing may be preferable.

A further very important implementation aspect concerns time. How long should the time interval be to which the nonlinear price schedule applies? And what prices should be charged at what time? In the case of quantity discounts, should the buyer pay high prices for the initial purchase units or the price for which he ultimately plans to qualify? The answers depend on how easily charge-back and similar procedures can be implemented. Typically the supplier would prefer to charge high prices initially and grant discounts as the required quantity levels are reached. However, the power of large buyers typically makes this infeasible.

If the duration of a time-related quantity discount scheme is too long, most buyers may eventually qualify for the highest discount. If the period is too short, few may enjoy this attractive situation. A longer duration interval induces stronger customer retention since more of them fall into the highest discount bracket. The retention effect is particularly strong if discounts or sales bonuses are progressive, as in the case of Effem, the pet-food market leader in Germany.

For specific forms of nonlinear pricing like the cinema card, the Bahn-Card, or membership fees the value and the customer-retention effects are directly related to the duration period. Nevertheless it makes little sense to maximize the duration period, since this increases the up-front amount to be paid and the perceived uncertainty of the customer.

Particular attention should be paid to the communication of the nonlinear price scheme in order give customers a clear understanding of the implications. If even sellers and managers have difficulties in understanding these complex schemes in all their ramifications, how can the customer grasp the complexities? But if the customers do not understand what is going on they are unlikely to respond in the expected way. Therefore, effective communication can be crucial for the success of a nonlinear pricing schedule. On the other hand, the complexity also provides the opportunity to use nonlinear pricing as a "smoke screen" to obfuscate one's true price position. High-price sellers may have an interest in such obfuscation. Price comparisons definitely become more difficult if several price parameters instead of only one have to be included. Does one ever know whether one is getting the best deal in cellular phone service?

———————

In highly competitive situations, nonlinear pricing schemes should be applied only after competitive reactions have been thought over carefully. While the method offers interesting competitive opportunities, it also involves dangers. While operating with several price parameters instead of one uniform price is smart in a competitive environment, the competition can retaliate quickly and strongly, as we have seen in the cases of frequent-flier programs and mobile phone multi-block tariffs. Because of their complexity, it is easy for a competitor to make a big mistake—offering too-generous discounts, for example. Used as an aggressive price weapon nonlinear schedules may, however, initiate the same downward spiral as normal price cuts. The whole area of competition is not well-researched in connection with nonlinear pricing. Therefore, nonlinear pricing activities must be judged and applied judiciously by the power pricer.

In nonlinear pricing, the same price schedule is offered to everyone. Different customers do pay different average prices due to the different quantities which they buy. This, of course, is the source of much of the added profit from nonlinear pricing. However, this does also create the possibility that it may be considered price discrimination. In the United States, the Robinson-Patman Act prohibits price discrimination where its effect "may be to lessen competition substantially." In the *FTC v. Morton Salt Co.* case, the court decided against the firm because its total discount levels based on cumulative volumes over a period were, in effect, reachable by only a few firms. In addition to the price schedule being the same for all, the discounts had to be "functionally available."

Similarly, in Germany, authorities forced Effem to change the basis of its sales bonus system from annual to quarterly. The annual period was seen to create too great a hold on customers and to lessen competition severely. The key is that legality is typically related to the issue of competition; sales to end users rather than resellers typically do not have competitive aspects. Stern and Eovaldi and others provide more extended discussion of legal issues;[9] but the permissible practices need to be assessed on a case-by-case and country-by-country basis.

SUMMARY

Nonlinear pricing is one of the most interesting and effective methods of price customization in the variable quantity case. Its optimal application requires a high level of sophistication. The following aspects should be observed:

- Nonlinear pricing can work whether customers are the same or different. It is more efficient, though, in extracting full value from the customer in the "same" case.
- Cost and competitive aspects affect the advantages of nonlinear over uniform pricing and should be well understood in this regard.
- Nonlinear pricing can take on many different forms. A careful selection is necessary. The more complex forms allow for a better fine-tuning of the customization but require setting up more parameters and are more difficult to implement.
- The information requirements for effective nonlinear pricing are high. Ideally individual price response curves would be known. Imprecise information on individual maximum price involves substantial risks of overextending the exploitation of consumer surplus and losing the customer altogether.
- With regard to its implementation, nonlinear pricing has the great advantage of self-selection by the customers; i.e., the same schedule is offered to everyone and the actions determine the average price.
- Great attention should be paid to the communication of nonlinear price schemes. Only if the customers understand the schemes will they respond in the intended way.
- The application requires certain conditions, such as the prevention of reselling by customers or the identification of individuals. These conditions generally seem most easily met in the service sector but the potential for nonlinear pricing is not restricted to services.
- Multiperson pricing is a specific form of nonlinear pricing that can attract additional buyers and alter the competitive position of a service.
- Information, implementation, and monitoring costs have to be con-

sidered in the decision on whether to use uniform or nonlinear pricing. Sometimes the simplicity of uniform pricing is superior in practice.

- Whenever discounts are offered, one must carefully analyze the impact on margins. The discount structure has a tremendous impact on margins and should be examined as closely as the base prices themselves.

The huge profit potential of nonlinear pricing suggests that each company should carefully examine the adoption of this strategy. The information needs and the degree of sophistication are high, but the rewards for the power pricer are even higher.

8

Product-Line Pricing

INTRODUCTION

As noted in chapter 1, this is the age of product variety. We have observed the fragmentation of the mass market and its breakup into segments of customers wanting and demanding "customized" products. Coca-Cola used to be the "anywhere, anytime" drink but now it is Coke, Diet Coke, Caffeine-Free Coke, Cherry Coke, etc. This demand phenomenon, combined with advances in flexible manufacturing techniques, has created what Pine calls "Mass Customization: The New Frontier in Business Competition."[1] In this new frontier, individual firms offer multiple products attuned to the needs of particular segments, even extending to the "hypervariety" of Sony having 200 models of the Walkman on the market at a given time.[2]

Few firms have just a single offering anymore. This multiple-product strategy presents new pricing issues and opportunities. How it affects pricing decisions hinges on the nature of interdependencies between the products. If the products are totally independent with regard to both manufacturing and selling, their pricing can obviously be considered independently. If, however, interdependencies on the demand or the production side exist, they must be recognized in designing and pricing the product line. Our focus in this chapter is on demand interrelationships.

WHAT THIS CHAPTER WILL DO

This chapter addresses the following questions:

1. Which interdependencies are relevant for product-line pricing?
2. How do complementary and substitutional relationships between products impact optimal prices?
3. Which considerations are required in introducing and positioning additional products in a product line? How should prices of existing products be adjusted?
4. How does the expected revenue stream from services affect the selling price of a product?
5. What implementation considerations arise from product-line pricing—as opposed to individual-product pricing?

Knowing the answers to these questions will help you to:

1. assess the importance of considering product line interdependencies in your pricing decisions
2. structure and collect the information required for effective product-line pricing
3. set prices right given product line effects
4. design the pricing organization and processes consistent with the requirements of the product line

PRODUCT-LINE INTERDEPENDENCIES

Figure 8-1 shows the four key possible demand interrelationships in product-line pricing.

Linkages 1 and 2 in Figure 8-1 show that demand for product A can directly affect demand for another product, B. If this interrelation is positive (arrow 1), i.e., if an increase in demand for A leads to higher demand for B, we deem A and B to be *complements*. If the interrelation is negative (arrow 2), we refer to A and B as *substitutes*. A classical case of complements is Polaroid camera and film. A customer who buys a Polaroid instant camera has to buy Polaroid film. The famous Rockefeller saying that you can give the oil lamps away free because people will buy oil fits into the same pattern. Machinery makers count on service revenues when they price their machines. In many cases, over the life of a product, the service revenue is higher than the revenue from the product sale. A large manufacturer of diesel engines sells his products at very low, sometimes even negative margins, because of the profitability of the ensuing maintenance and spare parts business.

Add-ons and special features are another category of complements. In the automotive market, companies offer a "base model" and a large assortment of add-on features at prices which are usually high relative to the costs of these features. The margins on the features are thus more attractive than the margins of the base car. In most companies an inordinate share of the total profit comes from add-ons. The sellers take advantage of the fact that the price elasticities for the base car and the features are different.

Banks try to achieve some "cross-selling" between their products, for instance using the banking relationship as a way to sell insurance products.

Substitutes, shown by arrow 2 in Figure 8-1, are equally abundant in the real world. Auto companies have differing models that are in a substitutive relationship. The differing models, classes, or variants allow

FIGURE 8-1

Possible Product-Line Linkages—Impact of Lower Price on Product A

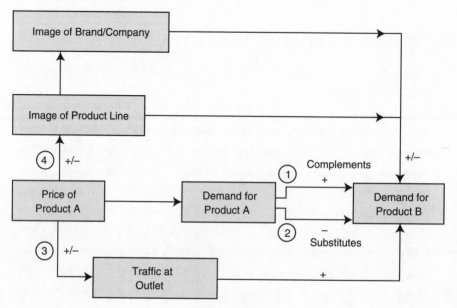

them to segment the market along the price dimension and to customize prices. Manufacturers like Mercedes-Benz and BMW, which have traditionally confined themselves to the premium segment, are introducing less expensive models to cover a wider range of the price and purchasing-power scale. In the 1980s, Mercedes-Benz made its first step of this kind by adding the C-class, the so-called "Baby Benz" to its line. In 1997 an even less expensive category, the A-Class, will follow. And in 1998 it plans to introduce a totally new kind of inexpensive city car, the so-called "Smart" car—though not under the Mercedes umbrella. On the other hand, companies like Toyota or Nissan have moved their product line up, adding luxury models like Lexus and Infiniti.

Many auto companies are using different brands to position their cars along the price and performance dimensions. A key issue is that these different cars provide the same basic transportation function and hence substitute for one another. A buyer of a Mercedes C-class car will not also look to buy a larger Mercedes model. The pricing of such complex product lines has to be handled very carefully. For example, in 1995–96 Volkswagen's new Polo reported large sales gains, but these took largely from Volkswagen's flagship, the Golf, the best-selling car in Europe. Was the Polo priced and positioned too closely to the Golf? Did Volkswagen sacrifice profits because the Polo largely substituted for the Golf?

The substitution issue is particularly key as additions are made to the lower end of the product line. Second brands, "less expensive alternatives," "fighting brands" are considered by more and more companies. For example, in addition to its premium product "Gore-Tex," a semipermeable fabric used for outdoor wear, medical and industrial purposes, W. L. Gore & Associates have introduced a whole range of less expensive brands like Gore Light, Windstopper, and Gore XCR to fend off price-aggressive competitors like Sympatex. BSHG, Europe's No. 2 in household appliances, has two premium brands, Bosch and Siemens, and offers several lines of less expensive products like Constructa, Neff, Pitsos, Balay, Superser, and Crolls. Hotel operators are increasingly price-customizing their product and brand lines. Accor, the world's largest hotel company, offers a whole range of brands from higher-priced Meridien, Novotel, and Sofitel hotels through medium-priced Ibis to low-price Mercure and Motel 6 motels. The potential for cannibalization within such a broad line can become substantial if prices are not carefully attuned.

Beyond complementary and substitutive interrelations between individual products of a company, we note more general interdependencies (see arrows 3 and 4, Figure 8-1), which are relevant for pricing.

Arrow 3 in Figure 8-1 denotes the potential traffic-building effect of an attractive price for product A. A lower price of product A attracts more buyers to the outlet who then buy the other product B. (The negative sign on arrow 3 signifies that as the price of A goes down, traffic at the outlet goes up.) This is the typical purpose of a "loss leader." Profits are not made on the low-priced product but on the sales of other products with higher margins.

In many countries, super- and hypermarkets are successfully selling gasoline much cheaper than the classic gasoline stations of the multinational oil companies. The hypermarkets find their overall profitability enhanced by their extremely low gasoline prices because the customers who come to fill up their tanks buy a basket of other goods on which the firms make money. In Germany, two coffee chains, Eduscho and Tchibo, are successfully using their lead product, coffee, to create demand for the gamut of nonfood items they now carry.

The fourth product line effect shown in Figure 8-1 relates to the image of the product line, the brand, or the company, as indicated by arrow 4. An individual product price that is consistent with the image of the larger entity (product line, brand, or company) can have a positive, image-enhancing effect, while the reverse is true for an inconsistent price.

It is important to know whether the overall price image of a firm is primarily influenced by the prices of a few prominent products or by the prices of many products—or the whole assortment. This question is particularly critical for retailers, since the price image of a store determines its power to attract customers.[3]

The research on the issue of image formation is somewhat equivocal. The recent view is that consumers observe a rather large number of prices in the formation of price images. This suggests that the product line should be consistently priced instead of selling only a few selected articles at attractive prices or as special offers. The very successful Wal-

Mart in the United States, Aldi in Europe, and Ikea worldwide embody this principle.

The linkage mechanisms across a product line or a whole company can differ in type and intensity, and thus affect the cross-product price effects. The company name is an important linkage whose strength depends on the proximity of the products. For example, the impact of General Electric washing-machine pricing on General Electric aircraft-engine demand is small relative to the linkage between Compaq servers and Compaq personal computers. Another mechanism is a brand name with the company name suppressed. This is usually a strong link, like that between Pritt glue stick and Pritt liquid glue from Henkel.

The price positioning of one product linked to another can hurt the other product. Black & Decker, for example, saw a negative impact on its power tools business from its household products business. The Black & Decker brand name was one of the ten most powerful in the United States and proved valuable in establishing Black & Decker's small household appliances such as coffeemakers, popcorn poppers, waffle irons, and toasters. The positioning of these products was as mass-market items and they were appropriately priced for this positioning. However, the low price of Black & Decker brand household products had a negative impact on its brand image in the critical craftsman segment of its power-tools business. Black & Decker was forced to break the link between the products by adopting a new brand name in this professional segment of the power-tool market.[4]

Within a product line, one must also consider how a given product conveys a price image for the line. Its role here goes beyond what it actually does for the firm in terms of unit sales. For example, Hartmann Luggage wants to have its product line represented at the top by a truly superior product. This top premium variant can be used in the retail sales presentation with a potential customer to help define what a high-priced, top-quality briefcase looks like. This product defines a reference price and product. The customer then "trades down" from this standard. But Hartmann provides the same construction and durability in all its luggage; the covering—leather vs. cloth—is the main difference. The high price for the top item presents an image and facilitates an educational process which brings the right image to the whole line.

FIGURE 8-2
Saab Product Line and Prices—U.S. Market 1992

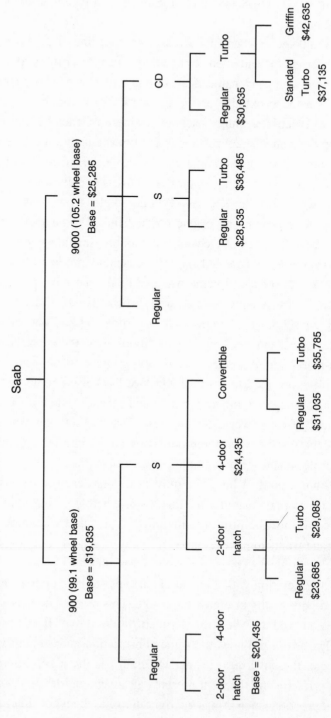

Source: Ward's Automotive Yearbook 1992, p. 270

The strategy of Saab's automobile pricing, shown in Figure 8-2, illustrates these tactics in further detail.[5]

Saab obviously tries to work on both ends of the price spectrum, offering 13 different models. The price range extends from $19,835 to $42,635. The basic Saab 900 is "less than $20,000." A special limited-edition Griffin model is $5,000 more expensive than any other car in the line. Saab made a very limited number of these exclusive cars. Clearly, the idea here is image and showroom appeal rather than any profit to be made directly from the Griffin.

Thus, there are a number of ways in which the individual products of a multiproduct company can be linked, indicating need for coordinated price setting. In some cases, the best strategy is to bundle products together and sell them as a package. Due to its importance in many different industries, we treat price bundling separately in chapter 9. In the current chapter we focus on determining optimal prices for individual products in a product line. We begin by considering complementary products.

PRICING COMPLEMENTARY PRODUCTS

Complementarity means that an increase in sales volume of product A leads to an increase in sales volume of product B (see arrow 1 in Figure 8-1). How does this affect the optimal price of product A?

We show this impact by first considering the optimal isolated price for product A in the upper part of Figure 8-3. The "isolated" price does not take into account the complementary effect. We know from chapter 2 that the optimal isolated price is exactly in the middle between the "maximum price" and the "variable unit cost."

Now suppose that each customer who buys product A effectively brings with him additional purchases of other complementary products. These products bring the firm additional margins and profit that can be casually attributed to the sales of product A, and thus are equivalent to a reduction of the variable unit cost of A. We can speak of "corrected variable unit cost," which we apply to setting the optimal product-line price. This is illustrated in the lower part of Figure 8-3. The optimal product-line price for the main item in the complementary-products case is lower

FIGURE 8-3

Isolated vs. Product-Line Pricing with Complementarity

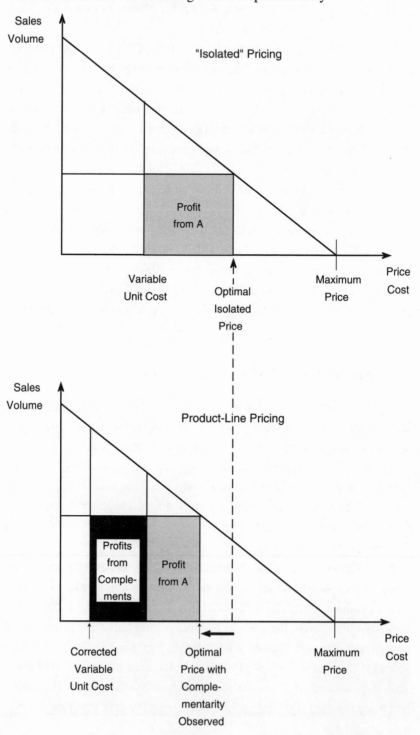

than the optimal isolated price. We sacrifice some profit from A in order to get an overall higher profit from the whole line.

To illustrate an actual complementary-products situation, consider a large men's clothing store. Based on a simple study of scanner data at the store, we documented the hypothesis that the sale of a suit generates additional sales of shirts and ties. Specifically, we found that on average a suit purchase led to the purchase of 0.8 shirts and 1.2 ties. The margins for shirts and ties averaged DM 15 and DM 10 respectively. The price response curve for suits was estimated by expert judgment (see chapter 3) and the optimal "isolated price"—the price that maximizes profit from suit sales alone—was about DM 350 per suit. At this price, the direct price elasticity was 2.33 and about 300 suits were sold per day. With an average unit cost to the store of DM 200 per suit, the unit contribution margin was DM 150 per suit; thus the total contribution from suits was DM 150 × 300 units or DM 45,000. In addition, suit buyers purchased 240 shirts at a margin of DM 15 per shirt, for a total contribution from shirts of DM 15 × 240 = DM 3,600, and 360 ties at a margin of DM 10 per tie for a total contribution of DM 3,600. Thus total margin realized for suits sold with shirts or ties or both added up to DM 45,000 + DM 3,600 + DM 3,600 = DM 52,200. In this case, 86% of the contribution came from the lead item—suits—because the follow-on "tail" of purchases was low in margin compared to the suits.

The optimal "isolated" suit price did not take into account the additional contributions gained from the shirt and tie sales. Considering these effects, and seeking to optimize total profit from suits and related purchases, we found the optimal suit price to be DM 338, about 5% lower than the optimal "isolated" price. At this price, the company sells 324 suits per day, 24 more than at DM 350, but the profit from suits decreases slightly—by almost 1% to DM 44,712—due to the lower unit contribution. This profit sacrifice on suits is more than made up by the increased profits in shirts and ties, which add up to DM 7,775 instead of DM 7,200. Overall a slightly higher profit is achieved through observing the interdependencies between these complementary products. The improvement is only slight because the follow-on product flow is small in the overall system.

Stronger effects, and a greater cost of ignoring complementarity, were observed in the case of an auto dealer. This dealer's objective was to find the optimal current car prices, taking into account future loyalty and service contributions. The price for the most popular car model was DM 15,000, if complementary effects on service and future loyalty effects were not considered. A long-term profit of DM 1.12 million per year was achieved with this strategy. Accounting for the effects of higher current car sales on services and future car sales, the optimal car price decreased by 12% to DM 13,200; but the long-term profit per year increased by about 5% to DM 1.17 million.

Even larger bottom-line impact was found in a complex study for a pharmaceutical company and its five-item product line. Taking into account both complementary effects between pairs of products and dynamic effects (customer loyalty), the profit with product-line pricing was 10.1% higher than with isolated pricing.[6]

From these cases and general considerations, we infer the following recommendations: for complementary products, the optimal product-line price:

- is lower than the optimal isolated price
- decreases with the absolute magnitude of the cross-price elasticity, i.e., the strength of the complementary relationship
- decreases with increasing margins of the complementary products; the more profitable the complements are, the more rewarding it is to sacrifice profit on the main products to generate complementary product demand

An addition of a complementary product to a product line affects the optimal prices of incumbent products in the direction addressed above. Thus, the addition of a complementary product requires consideration of price adjustments to existing products.

Complementarity considerations can have great bottom-line impact. For products which induce strong complementary effects, such as Polaroid cameras, mobile phones, and service-intensive machines, the cross-price effects can be more important than the direct price effects. Such products can well be sold at negative margins or even given away free, because of the demand for the complementary products or services. Providers of cellular-phone services sell the phone sets at extremely low prices if the customer signs a one-year contract for phone service. Book clubs offer their first books at virtually zero if the customer agrees to buy additional books within a certain time period. In all these cases, it is reasonable to sacrifice the profit of one product or even accept a loss there in order to get an overall higher profit. If priced in the right way, the "loss leader" can actually become a "profit leader."

These considerations show that the proper approach is to give up the perspective of "product margin" in favor of "customer margin." The focus should be less on how much we earn on a specific product and more on how profitable a relationship with a customer can be.

This customer-oriented profit perspective redirects our attention from the product price and margin to the customer contribution. This approach requires a customer-oriented accounting system, which is already prevalent in industries like banking, insurance, information technology, and industrial goods and which holds promise for many other sectors.

From these discussions it is evident that the information requirements for product-line pricing are high. It may be difficult to quantify precisely the causal interrelationships between products. But this information is indispensable to arrive at the right prices. A key point is that quantifying them, even somewhat imprecisely, is better than ignoring them altogether—since that is equivalent to asserting that the causal relationship or cross-elasticity is zero. Implicitly or explicitly, a pricer is always attaching a certain cross effect. Power pricers assess this cross effect rigorously and price in light of it.

PRICING SUBSTITUTE PRODUCTS

Pricing substitutes confuses some firms because of imprecision in defining the nature of the substitution in the first place. The initial consideration must be to understand the true interrelationship among elements in a product line of similar items. Figure 8-4 shows five fundamentally different types of situations to contrast, each with different pricing implications. We briefly discuss the first three and focus on the remaining two.

In situation 1, "diverse specifications,"[7] a firm markets a group of similar items to fill the diverse needs of its customer base. For example, an industrial-pipe supplier has an extensive catalogue of a particular type of pipe in many different diameters: 1/2", 1", 2", 3", 5", 6", 8", 12", 18", 24", and so on up to many feet in diameter. The reason for the large num-

FIGURE 8-4

Five Types of Relationships Among Similar Products and Examples

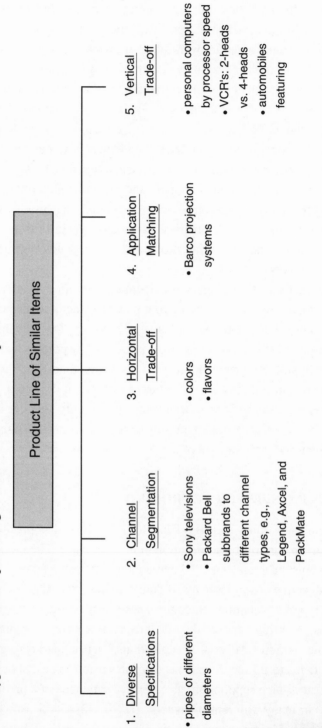

Product Line of Similar Items

1. Diverse
   Specifications

   • pipes of different
     diameters

2. Channel
   Segmentation

   • Sony televisions
   • Packard Bell
     subbrands to
     different channel
     types, e.g.,
     Legend, Axcel, and
     PackMate

3. Horizontal
   Trade-off

   • colors
   • flavors

4. Application
   Matching

   • Barco projection
     systems

5. Vertical
   Trade-off

   • personal computers
     by processor speed
   • VCR's: 2-heads
     vs. 4-heads
   • automobiles
     featuring

ber of pipe sizes is that the manufacturer serves a customer base with diverse specifications. And, in this case, those specifications are "tight," meaning if the plumber needs six feet of 4" pipe for a repair job, he needs six feet of 4" pipe—not three feet of 5" and three feet of 3"; nor would a deal of the nature "I'll give you a five-incher, but only charge you four inches" work. The customer does not trade off between different pipe sizes based on price. He expects some logic in the pricing of the items in the line, e.g., a higher price for 12" diameter pipe than for 8", because more material is required. However, although the products are "similar" in some sense, they are not substitutable for one another; relative prices do not shift a buyer from one specification to the other. Thus, the pricing indication for diverse specifications is merely that of relative consistency across items.

Situation 2 is "channel segmentation," in which a firm markets many "similar" items, offering the same basic product platform in slightly different "trade-dress" or subbrands in order to reduce competition among retailers. In many cases, retailers guarantee consumers the "lowest price" for each item they offer. The best way for a retailer to fulfill this promise is by making sure he is the only one selling that item. Sony offers a wide variety of television sets even of a given size to retailers, differentiated by the specific combination of features included. Production technology, which allows modular "drop-in" of a feature to a product platform, helps achieve this variety at low manufacturing cost. With only four incidental features that can be either added or not added, a manufacturer effectively can create $2 \times 2 \times 2 \times 2 = 16$ different products within the line.

Others, like Packard Bell Electronics, Inc., the personal-computer manufacturer, and various fitness equipment manufacturers, sell under different brands or subbrands to different channels. Many retailers wish to avoid being subject to price comparison with WalMart, for example. With this naming strategy, the manufacturer is able to satisfy those who need "something different from what you are selling WalMart." The idea is to restrict price competition within the channel. Since the product names are restricted to specific channel types or customers, at the manufacturer level these products really are not "substitutes." Again, however, there is a need to consider the degree of pricing harmony required.

Situation 3 is a "horizontal trade-off" by customers. By "horizontal," we mean that the inherent quality of the items is the same and which one a given customer prefers is a matter of taste; that is, choosing between a blue BMW 525i and an identically equipped green one or choosing between spearmint-flavored Dentyne chewing gum and regular flavor. These products do substitute for one another. The pricing focus for situations such as this is sensible harmonization given the brand linkage.

Basically, situations 1–3 are fairly straightforward to deal with. Due to the particular nature of product interrelationships, sensible harmonization of prices is key. Situations 4 and 5 present more complex pricing issues. In both situations, the firm produces products that differ in their inherent quality level. By "differing in inherent quality level," we simply mean that all target customers with any understanding of the products would prefer one item over the other if the prices were the same; for example, all other things equal, everyone would prefer a four-head VCR to a two-head; a faster PC to a slower one; a highly durable and reliable item to one less so, and so forth. Consumers may very well differ in how important the inherent quality difference is to them; for grandparents buying a VCR for their vacation home to be used only for children's videos brought along by grandchildren on a visit, the relative value of a four-head VCR over a two-head is small. But for a home-theater system use by an aficionado, the four-head is almost a requirement.

The distinction between situations 4 and 5 is a subtle but important one. Situation 4 we call "application matching," wherein products are designed to meet the needs of different segments of applications in the market. For example, Barco, the Belgian-based producer of industrial projection systems, had three different projection systems for the video, data, and graphics segments of the market.[8] In 1989, the products and their prices in Belgian francs (Bfr) were:

Segment	Product	Scan Rate	Price
Video	BV 600S	KHz: 16	Bfr: 360,000
Data	BD 600	KHz: 45	Bfr: 480,000
Graphics	BG 400	KHz: 72	Bfr: 1,000,000

The different segments required different levels of performance—in particular with respect to the scan rate. The video segment—e.g., for showing motion pictures in airplanes—was the least demanding, its needs being adequately serviced by the BV 600S with a scan rate of 16 KHz. At the top of the line, the BG 400 had to meet the demanding specifications of the graphics segment, scanning at 72 KHz. The BV 600S or BD 600 would not work in a graphics application; it simply could not scan fast enough. The graphics customer cannot trade down to 45 KHz or 16 KHz machines, no matter how attractive he finds their price relative to the BG 400 price. A data customer may "trade up" to the BG 400 machine, if he anticipates someday possibly needing a scan rate of 72 KHz, even though 45 is fine for his current requirements. But it cannot go the other way; an application implies *requirements* that must be met; customers can "trade up" but not down.

In situation 5, "vertical trade-off," things are more fluid. Customers trade off the price vs. functionality of all offerings. For example, customers *like* more speed rather than less, and they are willing to pay for it, but do not require it and hence they will trade off performance on this attribute against price. We now set forth a simple situation to illustrate the product-line and pricing impacts of these demand relationships.

ILLUSTRATING IMPACTS OF RELATIONSHIP AMONG PRODUCTS

Recall that chapter 3 discussed the use of conjoint analysis to indicate the optimal price and amount of a specific attribute to include in a product. The top graph of Figure 8-5 is similar to Figure 3-10, which was used to illustrate the concept of target pricing. In this case we use linear value functions to simplify the calculations and explanations—without affecting the general argument. Here, we focus on the single attribute of machine speed. As the speed increases the business user's value and the firm's costs go up. As we know from the discussion in chapter 3, the optimal speed is point S1 in Figure 8-5's top graph, that being the point at which the distance between the value curve and the cost curve is greatest. With this speed level designed into the machine and pricing at the business user's value, the firm's contribution would be this maximum distance.

The middle graph of Figure 8-5 now shows what happens if we add a casual user who has a different value curve. Considering the two customers independently, we achieve maximum contribution by selling the

FIGURE 8-5

Machine Speed, Cost, and Value to Three Different Users

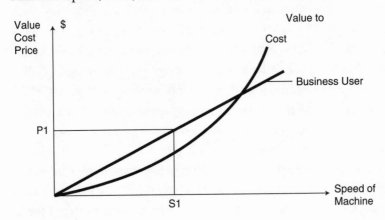

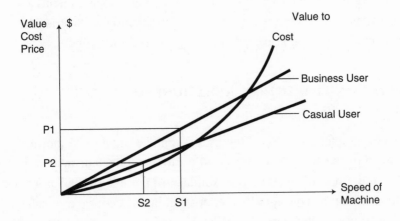

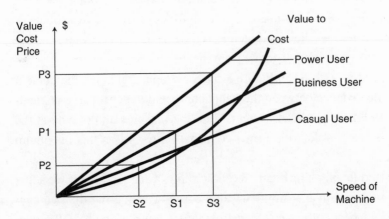

casual user a machine of slower speed at a lower price. Based on the valuation curves, the firm customizes both the product and the price to the individual customers. It sells a machine with speed S1 at price P1 to the business user and another machine with speed S2 at price P2 to the casual user. As long as the firm has built a fence between the business and casual users, this works fine. In the bottom graph of Figure 8-5 we introduce a third user group, power users, with a different value curve.

Consider an example. UNIPRO, a PC manufacturer, needs to figure out a product line and pricing strategy given three types of users: power, business, and casual users. Casual users value speed at $10 per MHz, that is, a casual user is willing to pay $1000 for a 100 MHz machine. Business users value speed at $20 per MHz and power users at $30 per MHz. This corresponds to the value curves shown in the lower part of Figure 8-5. Also shown is UNIPRO's cost curve, which represents the fact that the per-unit cost of a machine is the square of its speed, i.e., $\text{cost} = S^2$.

With these curves, it is easy to see that if the firm can "build a fence" between these users, to recall the terminology of chapter 5, it should offer three products:

- 150 MHz @ $4,500 for power users
- 100 MHz @ $2,000 for business users
- 50 MHz @ $500 for casual users

Each of these maximizes the distance between the value curve of its buyer type and the cost curve.

Our situation 4 of Figure 8-4, "Application Mapping," is really about fence building. Barco's graphics customers cannot trade down to machines for other segments. Effectively, the product has no value if it does not operate at a scan rate of 72 MHz for Barco's graphics customer. UNIPRO wants to do the same thing as Barco, i.e., keep the power user from even considering the model designed for business users, and keep the business user from even considering the casual-user machine. Conceptually, the idea is to build a fence that changes the value curves as shown in Figure 8-6 (a) and (b). If there are no fences the power user is better off buying the business user's machine—representing a lost profit opportunity for the firm. In the upper part the power user has a value for UNIPRO's machine of less than 150 MHz speed. In the lower part of

FIGURE 8-6

Building Fences in a Product Line

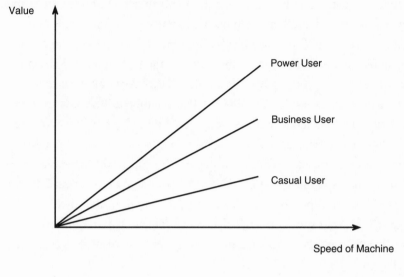

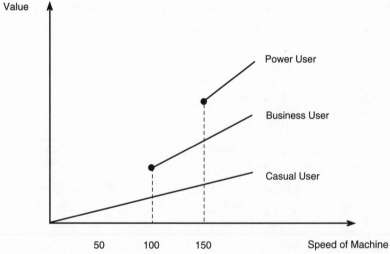

Figure 8-6, the power user's curve "kicks in" at 150 MHz, i.e., he perceives that this is the minimum MHz that enables him to "do the job."

Situation 4 in Figure 8-4 refers to building fences by applications. As we have seen previously, building fences can be the key to profits. Situation 5 in Figure 8-4 refers to a more fluid situation, where we are unable to build fences and customers will freely sort themselves out among the products available based on their functionality and price. Not being able to build fences—effectively leaving the valuation curves as shown in the upper part of Figure 8-6—has important product-line and price-rationalization implications. Without any fences, the power user would consider the business machine, the 100-MHz machine at $2,000. Since he values speed at $30 per MHz, he would in fact find this a better buy. The process for determining the optimal products and prices in this fluid situation is a little complicated[9] but if casual users are 20% of the potential market, power users 30%, and business users the rest, the optimal strategy is to:

1. Cut product-line length by deleting the MHz-50 machine altogether.
2. Downgrade the 100-MHz machine to 80 MHz and charge $1,600 for it.
3. Keep the 150-MHz machine at 150 MHz, but reduce the price to $3,700; so the power users would prefer this to the 80-MHz machine.

This reduces profit compared to the "fence" case, but it is a 10% profit improvement over the best single product strategy, which is a 100-MHz machine at $1,000. This simple example shows that fences are best. Recall that these fences can be to some extent mental ones, developed through the potential buyer's perception. Also, a product line can be used to segment the customer base and improve profit. It does require simultaneous prices and product design. We now consider some actual examples.

Illustrative Examples

In the chemical industry, a firm was introducing a new special-use chemical NEW. It was expected to substitute partially for the firm's incumbent product, OLD. Both products were used in the paper industry. OLD had a market share of 39% and was the market leader. The supply side was characterized by an oligopoly with a price stability that the company did not want to upset. Therefore the chemical firm imposed the constraint that the price of OLD should not be reduced, as such action could have triggered competitive reactions. NEW had clear environmental advantages over OLD and other incumbent products, but also had high manufacturing costs. The management requested that the price for NEW be set to maximize product-line profit.

A conjoint measurement study was carried out to estimate price and cross-price response between NEW and OLD and competing products. Based on the responses obtained, we developed the market share curves shown in Figure 8-7.

The curves show that if NEW were priced at DM 27.50 per kilogram, rather than DM 32.80 per kilogram, its market share would go up from 12% to 21%. But NEW's 9% market-share gain comes largely from OLD, which loses 6 market share points or 17.6% (6/34) of its original business. The cross-price elasticity estimated between the price of NEW and the market share of OLD is 1.09. We observe a strong cannibalization between the two products.

This interrelation has a clear impact on the optimal price of NEW. Pricing NEW in isolation, i.e., to maximize contribution from NEW, yields DM 27.50 per kilogram. If we consider the cannibalization effect and seek to maximize total profit from OLD and NEW together, we get an optimal price of DM 32.80. Table 8-1 summarizes the consequences of isolated and product-line pricing. Of course, product-line pricing sacrifices some profit with NEW. But the additional profit we get for OLD is higher than this sacrifice. In total, the profit with product-line pricing

FIGURE 8-7

Pricing for Substitutive Products—the Case of Two Special-use Chemicals

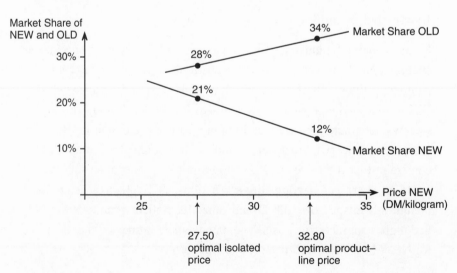

TABLE 8-1

Isolated and Product-Line Pricing for NEW and OLD

	Optimal Values	
	Product Line	**Isolated**
Price NEW	32.80 DM/kg	27.50 DM/kg
Market share NEW	12%	21%
Profit NEW	177.60	199.50
Market share OLD (Price OLD 18.50 DM/kg)	34%	28%
Profit OLD	289	238
Total profit	466.60	437.50

is 6.7% higher (DM 466.6 vs. DM 437.5). In addition to the higher price for NEW, the company tried via communicative measures to position the two products as far apart as possible in order to minimize cannibalization. In fact, a competitive price reaction was avoided and the equilibrium in the market was retained after the introduction of NEW.

From this case and a general derivation of optimality conditions[10] we can infer the following recommendations. For substitutive products,

- the optimal product-line price of a product at the upper end of the price scale is higher than the optimal isolated price.
- the optimal product-line price of this product increases with the cross-price elasticity, i.e., the strength of the substitutive relationship.
- the optimal product-line price of this product increases with the margins of the substitutes; the more profitable the substitutes are, the more costly cannibalization becomes and the more it should be avoided.
- the optimal product-line price of a product at the lower end of the price scale tends to be lower than the optimal isolated price. (This

statement does not hold in all cases but typically applies.) Thus, two products are priced farther apart if they are substitutes and belong to the same product line than if they do not belong to the same line.

• an addition of a substitutive product to a product line affects the optimal prices of incumbent products in the direction addressed above.

In many cases, more than two products have to be included in the product-line price decision. This can make pricing very complex. In an application for an automotive company we included a dozen of their models and about the same number of competitive models. A complex decision-support system was developed that revealed how certain price actions would affect the subject product line and competitive offerings. The high degree of projected cannibalization came as a big surprise to the management, and prevented several intended price cuts that would have mainly cannibalized other products in the subject line and led to overall negative profit consequences.

QUALITATIVE ASPECTS OF PRODUCT-LINE PRICING

Beyond the quantifiable relations there are numerous qualitative and strategic aspects that must be considered in product-line pricing. Some of these aspects have been addressed in chapter 5, where we discussed general price customization. In the context of this chapter we confine ourselves to specific and pressing product-line issues.

Less Expensive Alternatives/Second Brands/Fighting Brands

One of the most prevalent problems for premium brands is how to deal with aggressive "no-name" products or private labels. One possible answer is to cut prices permanently, switching to everyday low pricing, the route selected by Procter & Gamble for some of its products. A second alternative is to cut prices temporarily and to do this repeatedly in order to keep aggressors at bay. This is the classical promotional pattern adopted by many frequently purchased consumer-goods companies (see chapter 10).

A third alternative is to introduce a less expensive alternative (LEA) of the product in the form of a second brand, a generic/no-name label, or a private label of a retailer. The most critical consideration in deciding on the LEA and its price concerns the product-line effects. Is the LEA primarily cannibalizing the premium brand or does it mainly take market share from the price aggressors? How can the cannibalization effects be minimized through different product designs, separation of the distribution channels, exclusion of services, etc.? What is the optimal price differential between the brand and the LEA on the one hand, and the LEA and the aggressors on the other hand? Is there a risk that the image of the premium brand will suffer if it becomes known that the LEA comes from the same manufacturer? Or will the LEA profit from goodwill transfer and eventually replace the premium brand?

A leading manufacturer of lighting products chose the LEA route in 1994 because it was seen as the only possible defense against extremely cheap imports from China. Price cutting on the flagship product was not a viable alternative. Compared to the premium brand, the LEA product was slightly modified and mainly sold through a push strategy. Figure 8-8 shows the positioning structure. While the LEA's price was about 40% below the premium brand's, the company avoided attacking the Chinese products too aggressively (their price was 60–70% below the premium brand's price). At the same time, the company strove to keep the LEA's quality image clearly above that of the imports and paid a lot of attention to separating the distribution channels for its premium and LEA offerings. This is similar to Kodak's strategy with its Funtime film—a less expensive product available only in large packs, at certain times of year, and not supported by any advertising.

This LEA strategy was not confined to price but employed a whole battery of differentiation instruments. After two years the strategy seems a success, as the company has won back market share. About 40% of the LEA's sales came from the premium brand, and 60% came from the imports. Time will tell whether the strategy can be retained and whether the premium brand can defend a viable position. The price pressure is continuously increasing.

Some companies consciously employ "fighting brands" or private labels against price-aggressive competitors. According to *Business Week,* "fighting brands are spreading everywhere and scoring victories."[11] A case in point is Storck, a leading German candymaker. In addition to several well-known brands Storck has a number of little-known, cheaper brands whose main purpose is to keep competitors at bay in low-price channels.

FIGURE 8-8

Product-Line Pricing—A Case of a Less Expensive Alternative (LEA)

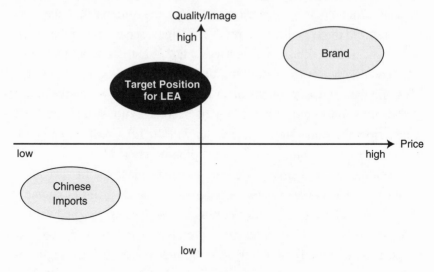

Fighting brands are judged less on their own contribution than on their effectiveness in keeping competitors off the backs of the main brands. Thus, their price is mainly determined by their competitive effectiveness.

In many cases LEAs have proven a failure. Many R&D-oriented pharmaceutical companies have either started or acquired generic divisions, but few of those have been successful. Many of these operations have been discontinued by the mid 1990s. Obviously, running a cost- and price-driven business requires competencies that are different from the capabilities which R&D- or brand-oriented companies master. An important aspect to consider in this context is whether or not the LEA can backfire on the brand. Jil Sander, a leading high-priced fashion designer, commented when asked whether she planned to introduce a second cheaper brand: "It's always the beginning of the end to launch a cheap line. You get a short-term sales boost, but you eventually lose your core customers with whom you really make money."[12] Indeed, if we look at brands which once had a premium price position and lost it, a common pattern is that they either became mass products (Lacoste shirts, Perrier water) or added LEAs (Opel cars, many hotel chains). Therefore, the "trade-down" decision to introduce an LEA has to be very carefully considered.

Entry-Level Products

A variant of LEAs is entry-level models, by which we mean the cheapest model in a product line. The main purpose of entry-level models is not to fend off price-aggressive competitors but to attract customers who then remain loyal in their future purchases. Entry-level models are aimed particularly at young customers and play an increasingly important role in the auto industry. The very successful strategy of BMW over the last three decades relied on this concept. For years BMW's slogan in Germany was *"Das Auto für Aufsteiger"* ("the car for people on the rise") and BMW's excellent market position has been built in this way. In a similar vein, Mercedes-Benz's introduction of the C-class ("Baby Benz") in the 1990s was motivated by the desire to lower the entry price level. As mentioned in the introduction to this chapter, this path will be continued in the late 1990s by adding an even less expensive model, the A-class, to the product line. In the mid 1990s Porsche, the sports-car maker, announced a similar strategy: "In 1997, Porsche is to introduce a coupe priced under $39,950, further lowering the hurdle for entry-level Porsche buyers."[13] Sony too follows this strategy, with its deep product lines and the introduction of the "My First Sony" line for children.

The entry-level concept of product-line pricing holds relevance for many industries both in the product sector (computers, household products, consumer electronics) and in services (information, communication, tourism). It takes into account that the purchasing power of people develops over time.

Premium Extensions

The opposite of adding a less expensive model to a product line is a premium extension. Sometimes this is called trading up. This upward move on the price scale is usually difficult to achieve, because the historic image of the product line is in a lower price category. Therefore a decision has to be made whether the existing brand should be used for the premium product or a new brand should be introduced. In the German market, Audi has been trying for 15 years to reposition its products towards higher price and prestige categories. Only in the mid 1990s does it seem to succeed. The Japanese manufacturers employed a different approach and achieved success more quickly when they introduced their new luxury models Acura (Honda), Lexus (Toyota), and Infiniti (Nissan) in the 1980s. The American auto companies went a third way by acquiring high-prestige European brands like Jaguar (Ford) or Lotus and Saab (General Motors). The risks of trading up are limited for the existing products since the more expensive new products are unlikely to cannibalize the cheaper old product line—but if they do, this is welcome, since a higher margin is earned from the higher-priced models.

Pricing Variants and Add-On Features

Should variants of a product be sold at the same or at different prices? Should certain add-on features of a product be included in the base price or priced separately? And if they are priced separately should the margins be higher or lower than those of the main product?

Different firms evidently adopt different perspectives on these questions. For example, Figure 8-9 shows the price premium charged for station wagons over sedans of the same model in Germany.

The Ford Mondero, Volvo 850, and Renault Laguna lines feature both a station wagon and a sedan at the same price (in spite of different

FIGURE 8-9

Price Differences Between Station Wagon and Sedan for Different Models (Year 1995)

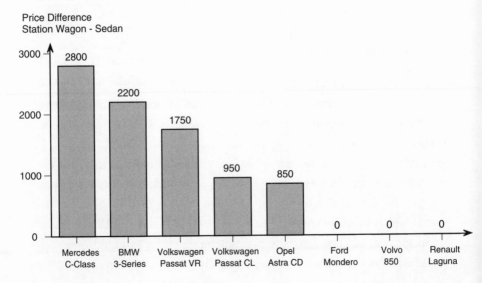

manufacturing costs). Other manufacturers apply a different pricing strategy, charging a premium for their station wagons over sedans in the same line. It is difficult to reconcile these differences. Our finding has been that consumers who want to buy station wagons at all usually value them higher than sedans. We think that this comparison points to substantial improvement potentials in this kind of product-line pricing.

Add-on features pose a further interesting pricing challenge. We will address some aspects of this problem in the following chapter, on price bundling. A general recommendation is not possible but our experiences suggest some proven rules. Often the price elasticity seems to be smaller for add-on features than for the base product. This suggests applying a higher margin on them. It can also be effective to include add-on features in the base price, instead of cutting the base price. In the same vein customers often accept extras in lieu of price concessions. The power pricer develops a deep understanding of consumer behavior as a guide to resolving these complex issues.

LIFE-CYCLE-RELATED PRODUCT-LINE PRICING

In the purchasing process of industrial products like trucks or machines, the initial purchasing price declines in importance relative to the total life-cycle costs, which are influenced by the prices of spare parts and services, the resale value, and operating costs. Many of these factors are affected by price decisions for the various components of a manufacturer's product line. Therefore the effects of each price decision on the life-cycle costs have to be well understood and taken into account.

In specific cases, it can be important to realign product and service prices. Some organizations, such as hospitals, often have limited investment budgets for new equipment but sufficient budgets for maintenance. In such a case, the seller of equipment should obviously keep the price of the machine low—within the budget limit—and charge higher prices for maintenance so that the overall profit goal is achieved.

A further aspect concerns pricing over the life cycle. The service cycle follows on after the product cycle. In the course of this development the relative pricing conditions for product and service change. For discussion purposes we consider an example of a machine that has a sales life cycle of five years and achieves the sales shown in Figure 8-10. The life of a

FIGURE 8-10
Product and Service Pricing over the Life Cycle

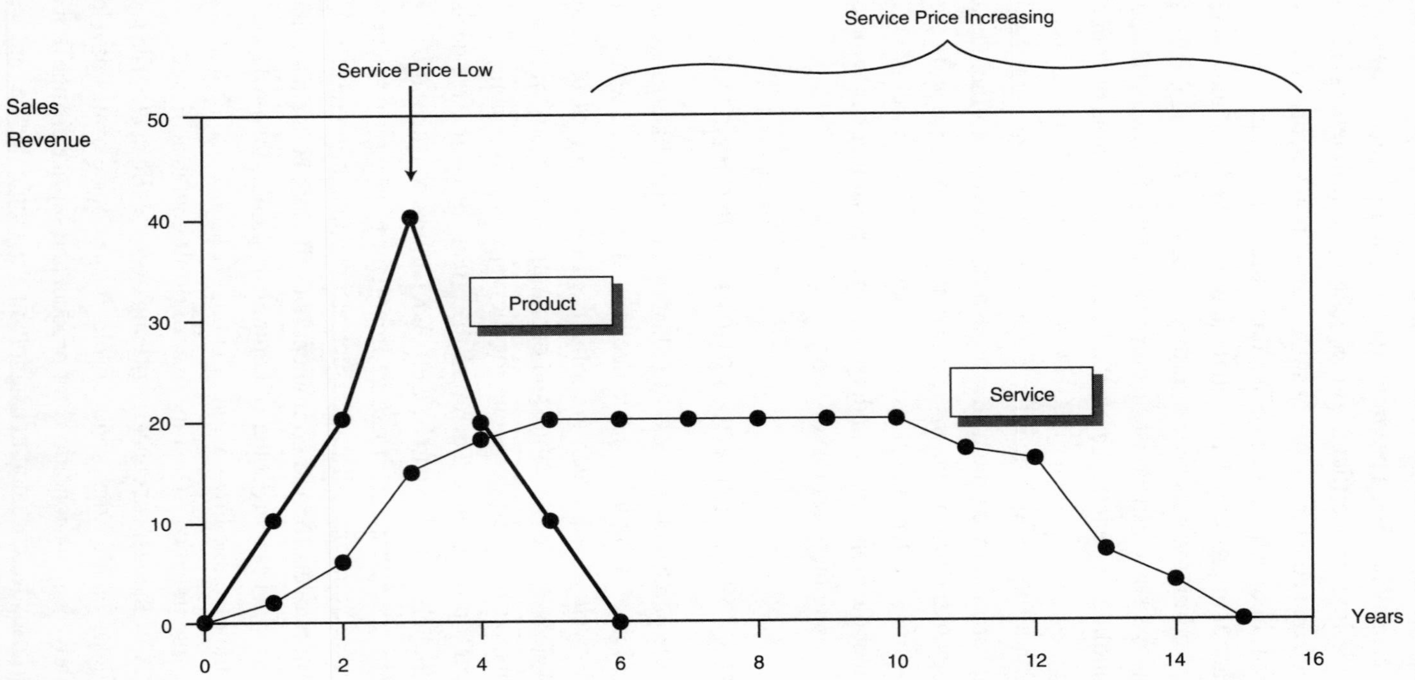

unit of the machine is assumed to be 10 years, during which service is required; per year the service revenue is 20% of the product's price.

As Figure 8-10 shows, the service cycle in this example is three times longer than the product cycle. In some cases, such as elevators, the service cycle can be ten times longer.

The pricing for the product obviously has a direct effect on the service revenue. But the pricing of the service has also an impact on the product's sales. If the initial service price is too high, customers (particularly those who apply life-cycle costing) will not buy the product. This suggests a relatively low service price at the beginning; this price should not be raised too early. The primary goal in the first phase is to sell as many products as possible and to build a service base. Later on, when the product's sales decline, a price increase for the service may be considered. Negative effects on product sales are no longer relevant and the customer may have little choice with regard to the service. In the declining stage of the service cycle, the service price may be further increased; an additional motive could be to encourage the customer to switch to a follow-up product. In one instance in the computer industry in the 1980s, the annual service price was higher than the purchase price of a new product with equal performance. Of course, one should be careful not to annoy a customer by exploiting the captive service position. Product and service price impacts on customer behavior have to be understood and considered simultaneously.

IMPLEMENTATIONAL ASPECTS OF PRODUCT-LINE PRICING

Obviously, product-line pricing implies that several products have to be included in making a pricing decision and that profit has to be sacrificed for at least one product to achieve an overall higher profit. This requirement can run counter to organizational separation into profit centers and is a potential cause of conflicts.

This was the case in a large medical-products company where product sales and service belonged to different profit centers. Of course, neither profit center chief had an interest in sacrificing any of his profits for the larger whole, particularly since no mechanism was available to transfer profits internally. In order to achieve optimal product-line pricing, the profit centers had to be redefined in a way that generated products with strong interdependencies. Too much decentralization will definitely impair product-line pricing. The only recourse then is to shift the price problem to the next higher level in the hierarchy, to an upper-level manager who can limit the pricing latitude of the profit centers and take charge of the price coordination. The problem is similar to the one encountered in international pricing when individual countries pursue their own goals. It is, however, usually less serious and easier to solve than the international problem.

A further implementational aspect concerns the gathering of information. As already mentioned, power product-line pricing requires a high information level on difficult-to-measure issues. Today, most product-line pricing is done on subjective feelings rather than on well-founded objective data. But this situation is gradually improving. On the retail level, scanner data allow firms to assess easily the copurchase pattern of products. Some supermarkets already use this powerful tool professionally. As far as substitutes are concerned, better competitive models, often based on conjoint measurement, allow one to predict cannibalization and to optimize prices considering cross-price elasticities. Again, the higher profits attainable through better customized prices come only through better information.

SUMMARY

Most companies in the real world offer multiple products. The power pricer takes interdependencies between products into consideration. The price of a product should be customized depending on how strong the demand interdependencies within this line are. In the same vein, additions to and deletions from a product line may affect the prices of all products. In product-line pricing, the following points should be observed:

- Product-line pricing implies that some profit is sacrificed for an individual product in order to attain a higher overall profit for the product line.
- Solid, ideally quantitative information is required on the interrelations between the products within a product line.
- Only strong and clear interrelations of either a complementary or a

substitutive nature should be explicitly taken into account in product-line pricing.

- Substitutive relations lead to product-line prices that are higher than the optimal isolated prices at the upper end of the price scale. At the lower end of the price scale the product-line price may be lower in order to position products farther apart and reduce cannibalization.
- Complementary relations lead to product-line prices that are lower than the optimal isolated prices. Complementary relations are often asymmetric (as with suits and ties). In these cases it is sufficient to consider the interrelation in setting the price for the main product.
- Not all aspects of product-line pricing and positioning can realistically be quantified. It is therefore important to also consider these problems in a strategic competitive context. This is particularly important when it comes to adding less expensive alternatives (LEAs), second or fighting brands, entry-level models, or premium extensions to a product line.
- The pricing of variants and add-on features should not only reflect the costs but should pay utmost attention to the valuation and the price elasticities. Very often, the price elasticities of the basic product and of these features differ strongly.
- Product-line pricing should include dynamic effects such as the influence of product sales on future service revenues. The varying roles of product and service over the life cycle should be considered in setting and changing prices for these components.
- Product-line pricing requires a coordination of several products. Thus it can be impaired if the responsibilities for these products are organizationally separated. If strong interdependencies exist, an organizational mechanism has to be found which takes care of this coordination task.

Power product-line pricing is probably one of the trickiest challenges in the area of price customization because the information requirements are high and the interdependencies can be very complex. Therefore, a perfect optimization may not be attainable. However, it helps already if the directions of the right price adjustments are understood. The power pricer will gradually learn how to deal with these intricacies and fine tune product line prices over the course of time.

9

Price Bundling

INTRODUCTION

In the preceding chapter, we analyzed the pricing of products in a multi-product company. But a multiproduct company has pricing options that go beyond setting prices for its individual products. Profit opportunity lies in determining not only what price to charge, but also *what* to price in the first place, i.e., individual products or bundles of them. For example, should a computer company sell computer and monitor together or separately? Should software be "preloaded" and sold as part of the system? And, should after-sale service be priced and tied in with the computer purchase?

Bundling is the core of some business strategies. A renowned case is Vobis, the largest computer retailer in Europe. Since its inception in the mid 1980s, this company has consistently offered bundles of computer, monitor, and printer at very attractive prices and heavily advertised these offers. In August 1995, one such bundle consisted of a Sky Tower 500 ZE-75, a 17-inch monitor, and a CD-ROM drive at a price of DM 3,998. By buying the bundle the consumer saved DM 466 or 10.4% of the sum of the individual component prices, which was DM 4,465.

Price bundling is also very popular in the software industry, where it is known as suite selling. Microsoft's "Office" bundle contains three programs, Word 6.0 for Windows, Excel 5.0, and Powerpoint, which purchased individually cost DM 829 each. The suite of three costs DM 1,269, a discount of 49% relative to the sum of the individual prices. "Office Pro," which additionally includes Access 2.0, sells at DM 1,599, a 52% discount relative to the sum of the individual software prices. In-tuit, the U.S. market leader in personal-finance software with its Quicken product, bundles in free customer support forever with its soft-ware. Black & Decker recently complemented the one-year warranty typical in the power-tool industry with bundling in free service, e.g., cleaning, oiling, and generally maintaining for one year as well on its new DeWalt professional power tool line.

In 1995, Ford offered a "Transit Plus" bundle for its vans comprising ABS, power windows, one-touch locking, airbags, and other features for DM 1,500. The individual prices of these features add up to DM 4,220, so that the bundle discount amounts to 64.5%. Similarly, U.S. car manufac-turers offer "value packages" of popular options at substantial discounts from individual rates. By offering only packages the manu- facturer standardizes the demands on the factory, as compared to the case where each user picks and chooses from multiple individual options. This can lead to production efficiencies.[1]

In 1996 BMW started to include antitheft and hijacking insurance in the price of new models in South Africa. According to the *Financial Times*,

> The decision has been taken to challenge the soaring price premiums charged by insurance companies because of the perception that BMWs are the favorite target for the country's thieves and armed hijackers. The policy costs BMW about 5 to 10% of a car's retail value but it creates a higher per-ceived value in the eyes of the customer.[2]

Mercedes-Benz and Swatch have formed a joint venture, called Micro Compact Car, which will produce a radically new city car, called the "Smart." Micro Compact Car is thinking of selling this car together with new apartments. Price bundling, thus, can even combine products from different companies.

In both the United States and Germany, McDonald's has been hugely successful with bundle offers combining food items and a beverage at discount of about 15%. Fine restaurants follow a strategy similar to

McDonald's: complete dinners consisting of appetizer, entree, and dessert are usually cheaper than the individual courses added up. A Chicago restaurant includes a ticket for admission to a movie theater in the price of meals, bundling the dinner and after-dinner entertainment.

In the pharmaceutical industry, price bundling has become popular with the changes in the purchasing processes, particularly in the U.S. market. The *Wall Street Journal* stated, "Companies that bundle their branded products with generics have greater pricing flexibility and are received favorably by managed care buyers."[3] Similar practices abound in the crop-protection sector, where companies try to sell bundles of products to farmers. Typically, such bundles include "lead products" that are superior to the competition and some products in weaker competitive positions.

Price bundling is also popular in the service sector. Holiday packages like the famous bundles of Club Med include air travel plus hotel plus meals. Mannheimer Versicherung, a German insurer, offers policy packages for various professions, such as lawyers, artists, etc., which cover all the risks specific to these groups at favorable prices.

Publishing companies sell so-called "title combinations" to their advertising customers. A company advertising in several magazines of the same publisher earns substantial rebates. The same is true for television companies that operate several channels, or channels in several viewing areas.

A special form of price bundling called block booking has been popular in the film industry for decades. The film distributor does not provide single films to the movie-house operators—these would most likely "cherry pick" the attractive titles—but supplies them with a "block" or bundle of more and less attractive films.

In some forms of bundling, the buyer of a product has to agree to buy other products from the same supplier (so called tie-in sales). Mobile phone companies offer phone sets at low prices provided the buyer signs a contract to buy phone services for a certain period (as discussed later in this chapter).

Most of these cases concern complementary products, i.e., products that are somehow used or consumed together. While complementarity certainly fosters price bundling, it is not a necessary precondition for the application of this strategy. Typically the bundle price is lower than the sum of the separate prices. However, a discount is not a necessary condition for price bundling. If the individual products alone offer little benefit to the user and really require someone to build them into a system, some customers are willing to pay a premium over the individual component prices for the assurance that system elements will complement each other optimally and are assembled properly. Also if some components are hard to obtain there can be a premium for compiling the full system. For collectors' items, the complete set can be much more expensive than the sum of the individual components of the set.

WHAT THIS CHAPTER WILL DO

This chapter addresses the following questions:

1. What are the relevant forms of price bundling?
2. Under which conditions and why is price bundling optimal?
3. Which information is required to determine the optimal bundle prices?
4. Which considerations are there in the implementation of price bundling?

Knowing the answers to these questions will help you to:

1. better understand when and how to apply bundling as a price customization technique
2. select the right form of price bundling
3. collect necessary and adequate data
4. know when to unbundle
5. implement price bundling successfully and avoid pitfalls

FORMS OF PRICE BUNDLING

The examples above show that price bundling has many forms, the most important of which in practice are:

• *Pure price bundling:* Only the bundle is offered. The products cannot be bought individually. Block booking is a form of this.
• *Mixed price bundling:* Here, both the bundle and the individual products are offered for sale. Normally prices are set for each of the individual

products in the bundle and for the bundle (so-called "mixed-joint bundling"). Microsoft uses this form for its "Office" bundles. Alternatively a discount is given for the second product if the full price is paid for the first (the "leader product"). This is the so-called "mixed-leader bundling."[4] A company in Germany is applying "mixed-leader bundling" to veterinary products. The "leader product" is innovative and priced high, whereas the second product is mature and priced low for those who have bought the "leader" product.

• *Tie-in sales:* The buyer of the main product (tying good) agrees to buy one or several complementary goods (tied goods), which are necessary to use the tying good, exclusively from the same supplier. Often the tying good is a durable—a machine, a copier, a computer—while the tied goods are nondurables like toner, paper, X-ray film, etc. The typical offers of mobile phone companies fall into this category—a package of a low-priced phone and a small activation fee when the customer agrees to obtain service from the company for at least a minimal time period, usually one year. Some goods are automatically tied to another—for example, a Polaroid instant camera works only with film purchased from Polaroid as well.

• *Sales rebates:* Frequently, companies offer customers a year-end rebate on total annual sales across all the company's products. These bonuses are mainly aimed at increasing customer loyalty. Overall, sales bonuses fall between price bundling and nonlinear pricing, since it does not matter whether the total sales value comes from one or from several products.

• *"Cross couponing":* U.S. consumer-goods manufacturers frequently use coupons to promote other products from their assortment. For example, Coca-Cola reached diet soft-drink users by distributing coupons for Diet Minute Maid on its 2-liter Diet Coke bottle. Cross-couponing is often used to introduce new products and/or increase the sales of weak products by linking them with established products in the firm's product line.[5] This is structurally similar to price bundling, in that a buyer of both Diet Coke and Diet Minute Maid willing to redeem the coupon would pay less than two individuals each buying one of the two flavors.

For more detailed discussion of the underlying economics of bundling, see Adams and Yellen, and Schmalensee.[6]

The prevalence of bundling in practice suggests that it is an effective strategy. Why is this so? When should one bundle and when should one unbundle? Which information is required? How do power prices utilize bundling? These are the questions we now address and illustrate through cases from various industries.

An Example of Pure Bundling

We illustrate the rationale for price bundling with a case from the cellular-phone industry. In addition to the basic mobile-phone service provided at a fixed monthly fee, the company offered a number of value-added services including voice mail and a hot line for customer support. What prices should be charged for the add-on services? While the fixed cost of providing each of the two services was substantial, variable cost per customer was low and was set to zero for pricing purposes, i.e., sales revenue for the two services was to be maximized.

To facilitate exposition, we simplify the case somewhat while retaining its essential elements. A market study revealed that a large number of customers valued the two services together at less than DM 5 per month. These customers were considered not worth pursuing and were excluded from further analysis. The remaining four customer groups differed in relative valuations of the two services. The maximum prices for voice mail and hot line that these four groups are willing to pay are given in Table 9-1. Customer group 1 was attracted to voice mail but valued the hot line little, whereas for group 4 it was just the other way around. Groups 2 and 3 were intermediate cases. The four groups were of about equal size. The willingness to pay for both services was calculated by summing up the two maximum prices.

The optimal prices for the individual services are easy to calculate. For voice mail, this is DM 8 per month. Customer groups 1 and 2 buy at this price and sales revenue (= profit) is DM 16. Analogously, the optimal price for the hot line is DM 8.50 per month. At this price, Groups 3 and 4 buy the hot line service and the revenue (= profit) is DM 17. Thus, if the two services are priced separately, the optimal prices shown in the top of Figure 9-1 yield DM 33 per month.

If we apply pure price bundling, selling only the two services together, the optimal bundle price is DM 10.50 per month. As can be seen

TABLE 9-1

Maximum Prices for Voice Mail and Hot Line Services

Customer Group	Maximum Prices (DM per month)		
	Voice Mail	Hot Line	Voice Mail + Hot Line
1	9.0	1.5	10.5
2	8.0	5.0	13.0
3	4.5	8.5	13.0
4	2.5	9.0	11.5

from the last column in Table 9-1, all four groups would buy at this bundle price and a revenue (= profit) of DM 42 would be obtained, a 27.2% improvement over the optimal individual prices.

Figure 9-1 illustrates the situation. In the upper graph we see the effect of separate pricing, where Groups 1 and 2 buy only the voice-mail service and groups 3 and 4 only the hot line. The lower part shows the situation with pure price bundling. All groups buy the bundle.

Why does price bundling lead to such a profit increase? The variability in the customer groups' evaluation of the individual services causes two problems for individual pricing. Consider the group 1 customers. They are willing to pay DM 9 for the voice mail, but have to pay only DM 8 because it is optimal for the firm to price in such a way as to induce group 2 to buy as well. The firm leaves DM 1 "on the table" for Group 1 in optimal individual pricing. Second, group 1 is willing to pay DM 1.50 for the hot line and our variable cost is zero. But group 1 does not buy it, because it is optimal to price the hot line at DM 8.50 to obtain good revenues from groups 3 and 4. However, if we combine the two services in a bundle, the valuation across the groups has little variability—the column 3 values in Table 9-1 jump around less than those of columns 1 or 2. Bundling effectively allows us to transfer the "money left on the table" or consumer surplus from one service to the other. By pricing the bundle of voice mail plus hot line at DM 10.50, we get group 1 to buy both services because their maximum prices add up to DM 10.50. This holds for the other groups as well.

FIGURE 9-1

Separate Pricing and Pure Price Bundling for Voice Mail and Hot Line

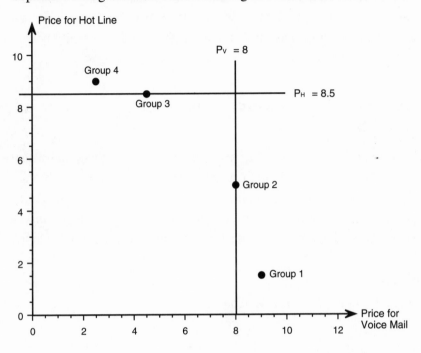

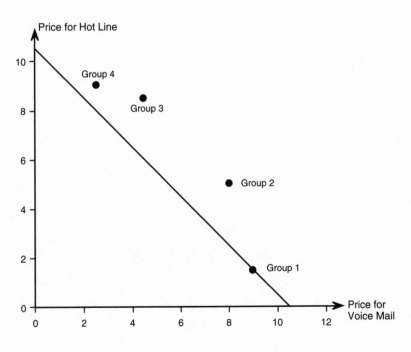

In addition to transferring willingness to pay from one product to the other, the optimal bundle price is usually lower than the sum of the separate prices (in our case DM 10.50 vs. DM 16.50). Due to the combined effect of lower price and surplus transfer, the bundle is usually bought by many customers.

DOES IT PAY TO SELL SERVICES INDIVIDUALLY AS WELL AS BY THE BUNDLE?

While the firm does a lot better with pure bundling than with individual pricing, the picture is still not perfect. Customers in groups 2 and 3 are getting "too good" a deal, i.e., they obtain services they value at DM 13 for only DM 10.50. The firm can capture more revenue by "mixed bundling," selling both the bundle and individual services. For example,

FIGURE 9-2

Mixed Bundling for Voice Mail and Hot Line

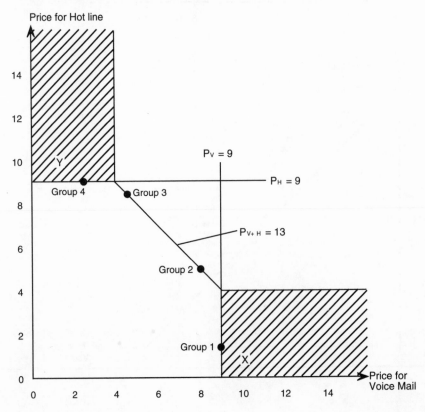

consider the price schedule: DM 9 for voice mail alone, DM 9 for the hot line alone, and DM 13 for the bundle. Customer groups 2 and 3 would buy the bundle, group 1 buys only voice mail, and group 4 buys only the hot-line service. The profit is now DM 44—about a 5% improvement over pure price bundling. Figure 9-2 illustrates the situation for mixed-price bundling.

In general terms, customers with maximum prices in rectangles X and Y of Figure 9-2 will become buyers of only one of the products. Mixed bundling allows a more fine-tuned segmentation of the market, into four segments: nonbuyers, buyers of the hot line only, buyers of "voice mail" only, and buyers of both.

Table 9-2 provides an overview of the three options: separate pricing, pure price bundling, and mixed price bundling for the two mobile phone services. In this case, mixed price bundling led to the highest profit. However, it is not possible to make a general recommendation on the optimality of either method; the optimality depends on the distribution of the maximum prices. The following rules provide rough guidelines.

- If customers display similarity in their valuations—all viewing one product as relatively high value and the other low—separate item pricing tends to be the best form.
- If the market is characterized by two customer groups with dissimilar relative valuation of products, pure price bundling is recommendable.
- If the market is characterized by a combination of customers—both

TABLE 9-2
Optimal Prices, Sales Volumes and Revenues for Different Forms of Pricing

Forms of Price Bundling	Optimal Prices			Sales Volume			Sales Revenue (= Profit)
	Voice Mail	Hot Line	Bundle	Voice Mail	Hot Line	Bundle	(Index)
No Bundling	8.0	8.5	—	2	2	—	33 (100)
Pure Bundling	—	—	10.5	—	—	4	42 (127)
Mixed Bundling	9.0	9.0	13.0	1	1	2	44 (133)

those with "extreme" preferences and those with "balanced" preferences (seeing the products as equally valuable)—mixed bundling is
likely to be the best concept.

RATIONALE FOR TIE-IN SALES

In tie-in sales, the buyer of the main product (tying good) agrees to buy
one or several complementary goods (tied goods), which are necessary
to use the tying good, exclusively from the same supplier. Typically, the
tying good is a durable (e.g., a copier) while the tied goods are nondurables like toner, paper, or service. A combination of "yes:no" and
"variable quantity" demand cases was discussed in chapter 2.

A famous historical example of tie-in sales that illustrates the economic impact and rationale for tying is the former IBM pricing system
for punch cards. In the 1930s, IBM had a quasi-monopoly for tabulating
machines and obliged its tabulating-machine customers to buy all their
punch cards from IBM as well. Punch cards were available from a number of alternative sources. In the 1930s, punch cards accounted for more
than 30% of IBM's total revenue.[7] Through tying, IBM customized its
prices to customers. Consumption of punch cards measures machine utilization and thus provides a good measure of the machines' value to the
customer: the more cards a customer uses, the more valuable is the machine. Tying thus customizes price across customers, according to the
intensity of their machine utilization. If the customers were allowed to
buy the cards from other suppliers, the value differentials would have to
be "skimmed" solely through the machine price. Price customization via
machine pricing alone would have been difficult to implement. While
the customers decide on their consumption of punch cards, they actually
determine the "total" price (or bundle price) they pay for the tabulation
process. In this way, they reveal the value they get from tabulation. In
1936 the Supreme Court banned this practice, rejecting IBM's claim that
it had to be the supplier of the cards or the machines would not work
properly, would be damaged, and IBM's reputation would be tarnished.

IBM bundled its computers and services until the late 1960s. Thomas
J. Watson, Jr., IBM's chief executive, sheds light on the centrality of this
practice to IBM and the reasons for its shift to "à la carte" prices:

It had always been our custom, whenever we rented or sold a machine, to lump everything together in a single price—hardware, software, engineering help, maintenance, and even training sessions for the customer's staff. This practice dated all the way back to the days of Herman Hollerith, the inventor of the punch-card machine, and it had been a powerful method for making customers feel secure enough to try computers when the technology was still new and hard to understand. Burke Marshall [an IBM lawyer], however, was shocked to find IBM doing business in this way. He saw bundling as a glaring violation of antitrust law known as a "tie-in sale," such as when a local electricity company tries to dictate the appliances you buy for your house. By requiring customers to buy our products by the bundle, we were making it almost impossible for independent companies specializing, say, in software to break into the business. At first people at IBM had trouble grasping this. No one could understand what Marshall objected to—bundling was like the Apostles' Creed at IBM, and since we looked at what we were doing as selling a service, it seemed perfectly natural that there should be one all-inclusive price. . . . I decided that we ought to follow Burke's advice rather than risk a showdown in court. In June 1969, after months of hectic preparation under the apt code name "New World," we announced à la carte prices for our system engineering services, customer training, and some of our software. Some executives thought we were giving up our birthright, that unbundling meant the death of the systems-selling technique on which my father had built IBM. But to me the bundle was simply another tradition that had to go, just as we had agreed in 1956 to sell our machines as well as rent them, and to license our patents to other companies.[8]

This quote illustrates the power of bundling in strengthening a firm's market position.

The basic issue of whether controlling the tied good is critical to overall quality is a key legal argument.[9] Because of the possibility of limiting competition in the market for the tied good, tying arrangements have not been generally looked upon favorably by the U.S. federal courts. However, the courts have allowed tying when there was some substance to the quality-control argument. If, however, the firm exerts market power in the tying good and there is substantial volume of sales foreclosed to competition in the tied market, the arrangement is subject to close scrutiny in the legal process. Note, however, that many arrangements which for all practical purposes function like tying arrangements arise naturally. At a remote resort hotel, the use of the room naturally carries along with it food, beverage, and sport-facility fees. Company-supplied technical support is often just naturally preferred to obtaining it from an independent party that did not produce the good.[10]

COST SAVINGS

Bundling can also create cost savings—for the consumer saves time and effort by buying bundles. For example, in February 1996 Alamo Rent-A-Car began a new advertising campaign promoting their bundled pricing over the "add-on" policy that had confused and irritated customers, with separate fees for damage insurance, personal liability insurance, child seats, gasoline, drop-off fees, etc. The producer may decrease cost through increased sales (economies of scale) and through economies of scope, if the combined products are interrelated. (For details on the economies of this, see Paroush and Peles, and Friege.)[11] Another cost advantage may result from the reduction of complexity costs. In the automotive industry, the complexity of assembly and logistics can be radically reduced if more customers buy bundles instead of individual features. Bundling can also be an effective method to create barriers to entry, as outlined in the Watson quote above (also see, e.g., Porter, Guiltinan, and Lawless).[12]

APPLICATIONS OF PRICE BUNDLING

Having explained the theory and rationale for bundling, we now show its potential value in various industries with a discussion of illustrative cases.

Case Example 1: Product and Service Bundling—Machine Tools

A machine-tool manufacturer had to set monthly rates for the use and also the maintenance of his high precision milling equipment. Users of milling machines from competitors were also potential sources of maintenance business. So, the pricing decision included the issue of quoting individual prices for (a) use and (b) maintenance and/or (c) a bundle price.

A study employing the direct-questioning method described in chapter 2 assessed the maximum prices that current and potential customers were willing to pay for individual items and the bundle; no assumption was made that the willingness to pay for the bundle was the sum of the willingness to pay for use and maintenance. Based on the survey, customers were clustered into four segments of different size as shown in Table 9-3. Each user shown in Table 9-3 had the potential for a unit of each item. Their willingness to pay for machine use ranged from DM 1,080 to DM 1,450 per month and maintenance from DM 540 to DM 1,030 per month. Those with high machine use values tended to have lower maintenance values. As shown in the table, the marginal costs to the firm were DM 550 and DM 470 for machine use and maintenance, respectively.

Table 9-4 gives the optimal monthly prices for machine use and mainentance under the three strategies of separate pricing for each, pure bundling in which use and maintenance are only sold together, and mixed bundling where both individual items and a bundle are offered. For separate pricing, the optimum price for the machine is DM 1,390 since at this price groups 2 and 4 would use the machine. Lowering the price to DM 1,250 to induce the 12% of consumers in segment 1 to buy

TABLE 9-3

Price Bundling for Milling Machine Use and Maintenance

Market Segment Group	Segment Size (As % Of Market)	Maximum Prices in DM (per Month)			Remarks
		Machine Use	Maintenance	Bundle (both)	
1	12	1,250	990	2,310	
2	23	1,450	540	1,750	Companies with own service technicians
3	22	1,080	1,030	2,090	Very high usage
4	43	1,390	870	2,350	
Marginal Costs		550	470	1,020	

TABLE 9-4

Different Forms of Pricing for Sale (in DM) of the Same Machine Tool, with Resulting Sales Volumes and Profits

Pricing Strategy	Optimal Selling Prices in (DM)			Sales Volume (%)			Profit Index	Relative to Separate Pricing (%)
	Machine	Maintenance	Bundle	Machine	Maintenance	Bundle		
Separate Pricing	1,390	870	—	66	77	—	86,240	100
Pure Bundling			2,090	—	—	77	82,390	96
Mixed Bundling	1,450	1,030	2,310	23	22	55	103,970	121
Marginal Costs	550	470	1,020					

would lower total contributions. The marginal cost per machine is DM 550. Thus the contribution margin per machine is DM 1,390 – DM 550 = DM 840, 66% of the potential market buy; assuming that one percentage point represents one machine to get a profit index, and 66 machines have been sold, the profit index is DM 840 × 66 = DM 55,440. Under separate pricing, the optimal maintenance-after-sale price is DM 870 per month, inducing sales of maintenance contracts to groups 1, 3, and 4 of Table 9-3. These groups represent 77% of the market. Marginal cost of maintenance after sale is DM 470 per unit, as shown in Table 9-4. Therefore under the same assumption of one percentage point representing one unit of sale, the profit index for maintenance following these sales is DM 870 – DM 470 = DM 400 × 77 = DM 30,800.

Group 4 thus purchases both machine and maintenance contracts; group 2 purchases only the machine contract and segments 1 and 3 only the maintenance contract. The total profit index for all these transactions is DM 55,440 + DM 30,800 = DM 86,240.

With pure price bundling, as shown in row 2 of Table 9-4, the optimal price per bundle is DM 2,090. This is found by simply comparing the true values in the bundle column of Table 9-3 in concert with the marginal costs. This price results in sales of machine-plus-maintenance bundles to groups 1, 3, and 4 of Table 9-3. The marginal cost of each sale is DM 1,020. Therefore the profit index for all these bundle sales is DM 2,090 - DM 1,020 = DM 1,070 × 77 = DM 82,390. In this case we see that pure price bundling delivers only 96% of the profit from separate pricing. The last column of Table 9-4 shows this index value.

Mixed price bundling, however, provides a significant profit opportunity. With the mixed bundling strategy, the optimal bundle price is DM 2,310—meanwhile offering the machine alone at DM 1,450 and the maintenance-after-sale contract alone at DM 1,030. Groups 1 and 4 of Table 9-3 buy the bundle; group 2 buys machine use alone; and group 3 buys the maintenance contract alone. Bundle sales to groups 1 and 4 together yield a profit index of DM 2,310 – DM 1,020 = DM 1,290 × 55 = DM 70,950; machine-alone sales to group 2 yield DM 1,450 – DM 550 = DM 900 × 23 = DM 20,700; maintenance-alone sales to group 3 yield DM 1,030 – DM 470 = DM 560 × 22 = DM 12,320. Total profit index from these three transaction groups comes to DM 103,970, which is a 21% gain over the profit from separate pricing.

While these prices maximized the profit index, the firm wanted to encourage customers to buy a bundle for strategic reasons, so it actually set a somewhat lower bundle price and somewhat higher component prices. The actual monthly prices offered were DM 2,250 for the bundle, DM 1,490 for machine use, and DM 1,050 for the maintenance contract.

Case Example 2: System Component Bundling—Computers

A personal computer system usually consists of three major components, the central processing unit (CPU), the monitor, and the printer. In an application for a large computer dealer, the direct-questioning approach was again used to determine the customers' maximum willingness to pay for the individual components and the bundle.

The maximum willingness to pay for the bundle was mostly lower than the sum of the individual maximum prices. This may be explained by the heavy advertising for the bundle. Under the condition that the bundle price has to be smaller than the sum of the individual component prices, we obtained the optimal values given in Table 9-5.

As in the previous example, pure bundling is again inferior to separate pricing. Mixed-price bundling yields the highest profit, a 7.7% surplus over separate pricing. The CPU and printer are offered separately under the optimal strategy but the monitor is not to be sold to anyone separately in the mixed case. Thus, as shown in Table 9-5, the price for the monitor can be set arbitrarily above DM 900. A price at about DM 1,100 would demonstrate the advantage of the bundle price more strongly. High separate prices, as in the case of Microsoft's "Office," can be a strong motivation for customers to buy the bundle. One should, however, take care that high separate prices in components do not lead to an unfavorable price image with customers.

Case Example 3: Option Packages—Automobiles

A third case is from the automotive industry. The company was considering several bundle of "options" or "special features" geared to specific needs, instead of selling special features individually. Three bundles called "Comfort," "Sports," and "Safety" were conceived. They included various features related to these notations.

TABLE 9-5

Different Forms of Pricing and Resulting Profits—A Case from the Computer Industry

| | Separate Pricing | | | | Mixed Bundling | | | |
	CPU	Color Monitor	Printer	Pure Bundling	CPU	Color Monitor	Printer	Bundle
Price	1,500	700	600	2,700	1,500	>900	600	3,000
Marginal Costs	1,100	500	450	2,050	1,100	500	450	2,050
Unit Sales Volume	20	11	20	15	12	0	12	8
Profit	8,000	2,200	3,000	9,750	4,800	0	1,800	7,600
Total Profit	13,200			9,750	14,200			

A conjoint-measurement study revealed that adoption rates were quite sensitive to the amount of discount the bundles represented, as compared to buying the special features individually, and bundles offered strong potential for sales-revenue increase. In addition to the demand effect, considerable cost reductions could be realized due to lower purchasing prices for the components and reduced complexity in logistics and assembly. Management wanted to price each of the three bundles at the same discount from its prices for individual special features. Figure 9-3 shows the profit effect of price bundling for various discount rates on all bundles. For varying discount levels for bundles, the graph shows the profit index obtained from optional features not included in one of the discount bundles plus the profit indices for each bundle. Thus, as the bundles become a "better deal" the firm makes less on nondiscounted options. As shown, a 21% discount on bundles yielded maximum total profit. This drove down the profit from individual special features from 100 to 80 (index) but boosted profit overall to 124 (index). Thus, at this level, one-third of the profit from special features (a very substantial portion of overall profit in the auto industry) comes from the bundles. In this case, the "Comfort" bundle was the most popular package.

FIGURE 9-3

Optimal Bundle Discount and Profit—A Case from the Automotive Industry

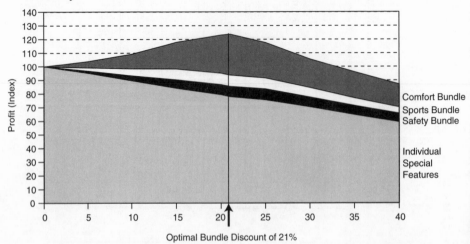

Case Example 4: Customer Sensitivity to Pricing Elements—Cellular Phones

Knowing which elements customers key on can be critical in constructing the right bundle prices. A cellular phone company's bundle consisted of four elements: (a) a Nokia phone at DM 188, (b) a one-time installation fee of DM 49, (c) a one-year contract with a fixed monthly fee of DM 44, and (d) a price per minute of DM 1.94. How important were each of these price elements to consumers? The perceived importance weights of these four price attributes were calibrated through 1,000 conjoint-measurement interviews. For each price attribute, an interval of ±25% was considered. In Figure 9-4, the importance weights in consumers' minds for the four price elements are compared to their objective cost share for a customer with an annual gross phone bill of DM 2,500—a typical magnitude.

We see from Figure 9-4 that the importance weight of the phone price is more than twice as high as its actual cost share (18.9% versus 7.5%) at current prices. In a sense, the customer is giving this price component more attention than he should. Price per minute, on the other hand, actually accounts for 69.4% of the total annual costs; but its importance weight is only 50.6%. It is extremely important to know these facts to get the prices in such a tie-in context right. In this case, given its salience to the customer, the phone price has to be reduced to the lowest possible level. Of course, this is precisely the current practice in the United States and Germany. In the United States, cellular phones are now given away free or priced at 1 cent to secure adoptions. Quelle, one of the largest cell-phone retailers in Germany, offers a phone set together with an annual contract at DM 29. Without the contract, i.e., unbundled, the phone costs 27 times as much, DM 799.

ESTIMATION AND IMPLEMENTATION ISSUES

Well-founded price bundling requires the knowledge of customer-specific maximum prices for both the individual products and the bundle. As our four case examples point out, several different methods can be applied to measure these variables, e.g., direct questioning (our machine-

FIGURE 9-4

Perceived Importance Weights and Actual Share in Total Cost of Four
Price Attributes—A Cellular Phone Case

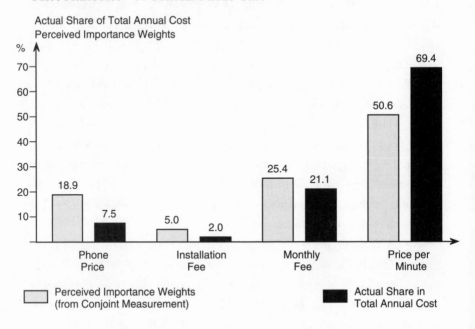

tool and computer examples) and conjoint measurement (the automobile
and cellular phone examples).

To use conjoint measurement, bundles are included in the preference
comparisons. Perceived values and maximum prices are indirectly
calculated, as described in chapter 3. The questionnaire design becomes rather complicated in this situation and the ability of the respondent to cope with this complexity has to be taken into consideration. In
any case, the number of bundles to be investigated should be kept
small.

A third possible method is expert judgment. However, in contrast to
estimating the aggregate price response curve, here at least segment-
specific maximum prices have to be estimated. Price bundling requires a
higher level of information than uniform pricing, and therefore can be
quite demanding on experts' judgments.

For small problems an optimization "by hand" is feasible. This applies also if the individual maximum prices have been aggregated into a

small number of segments. Optimizing separate and bundle prices for a large number of respondents and components is a complex problem. Hanson and Martin[13] developed an optimization program which includes both the price and the composition of the bundle. This program compares separate pricing, pure and mixed price bundling and selects the overall optimum. Consumers' maximum prices for all possible bundles, the size of the customer segments, and the costs of supplying customers in a specific segment with a certain bundle have to be known.

LEGAL PROBLEMS AND RESTRICTIONS

As reflected in the discussion of tying arrangements above, price bundling faces legal problems and restrictions. Certain practices are prohibited. In the United States, block booking for films had to be abandoned after the decision in the *U.S. v. Loew's, Inc.,* case of 1962.[14] As mentioned above, IBM had to abandon tying tabulating machines and punch cards in 1936. In 1969, IBM also stopped price bundling for computers in the face of a threatened antitrust suit. The basic question is whether the firm holds "economic power" in some good that it is trying to extend to others via bundling. If so, then the practice will likely be attacked. If not—as in the cases of the automobile option bundles and the computer retailer above—the practice is less likely to be questioned.

In Europe, the antitrust authorities show similarly negative attitudes toward price bundling. In Germany, Effem GmbH, a subsidiary of Mars and the leading manufacturer of pet food, had to rescind its annual sales-bonus system. However, it was allowed to grant sales bonuses on a quarterly basis, thought by the courts to be less binding on customers, and thus less effective in creating barriers to entry for competitors.[15] The European Supreme Court ordered Hoffmann-La Roche, the Swiss chemical giant, to discontinue its loyalty bonus system for vitamins. Loyalty bonuses are also considered illegal in the German jurisdiction. German antitrust agencies investigated title combinations for newspapers that offered attractive discounts if advertising space in various magazines put out by the same publisher was bought. And while "season tickets" are a fixture on the U.S. professional sports scene, the soccer team of Cologne, 1.FC Köln, was not allowed to sell block tickets that combined more attractive and less attractive soccer games. These legal restrictions apply mostly to companies with a dominant market position. In general, a legal opinion should be sought prior to implementing a specific program.

UNBUNDLING

There is no general rule stating whether price bundling or separate pricing is optimal. Changes in the given market can make it profitable to switch from one method to the other. In some cases we observe a trend to "unbundling." For example, Table 9-6 shows how a formerly bundled product, the SPSS software package, was unbundled in the mid 1980s.

In Version 2, a new basic product was created, essentially stripping out the advanced statistics and tables features included in the Version 1 product. To get equivalent functionality in Version 2, the buyer would have to obtain two modules at DM 530 each—resulting effectively in a 38% price increase. Version 3 offers an enhanced and broadened perfor-

TABLE 9-6

A Case of Unbundling: The SPSS Software

	Product	Prices
Version 1 **1984**	SPSS/PC+	DM 1,800
Version 2 **1985**	SPSS/PC+ • SPSS/PC+ • SPSS/PC+Advanced Statistics • SPSS/PC+Tables	 • DM 1,430 • DM 530 • DM 530 DM 2,290
Version 3 **1986**	SPSS/PC+ • SPSS/PC+ • SPSS/PC+Advanced Statistics • SPSS/PC+Tables • SPSS/PC+Graphics • SPSS/PC+Data Entry	 • DM 3,000 • DM 1,000 • DM 1,000 • DM 1,250 • DM 1,000 DM 7,250

mance. Frequently, unbundling is combined with a product modification, the introduction of a new product, or similar actions. Such a combination of product and price variations is essentially another form of price customization and is certainly recommendable—particularly when the unbundling involves a price increase, as in the SPSS case.

What are the reasons for the unbundling trend in certain industries? One of the main aspects is intensifying and more specialized competition.[16] One should consider unbundling under the following conditions:

• *Higher margins through unbundling:* These higher margins can result from a lower price elasticity for the individual products. This situation can emerge if the bundle price becomes very high. In the SPSS case, this motive may apply.

• *Market expansion through unbundling:* In certain cases new markets can be established if the products are sold individually. In the mid 1980s, Cummins, a leading diesel manufacturer, changed the positioning of its component division from internal supplier only to offering products on the open market as well. This created strong growth.

• *Increasing standardization and compatibility:* The more components are standardized and compatible, the riskier pure bundling becomes. Customers can compose their own system from separately bought components. A strong consumer preference for a particular component can turn a buyer away from a supplier totally if that supplier sells only on a systems or pure-bundle basis. For example, a computer supplier bundling monitor and CPU risks losing the CPU sale due to the preference a customer has for another monitor. In this situation one faces a dilemma between the closure of competition and the opening of a system in order to expand a market. Market dynamics can favor unbundling over the product life cycle.

• *Emergence of independent products/shift in contribution to value-added:* In many industries, the contribution to value-added is shifting from hardware to software and services. Information, technical advice, application knowhow, engineering, customer education, etc., are gaining in importance relative to hardware. Traditionally, these services were not billed separately but were integrated into the total system price. This traditional practice is becoming increasingly problematic if some competitors offer little ancillary services and the customer only looks at the hardware price when making his purchasing decision. Unbundling can lead to a better competitive position and to higher price transparency. A further argument for unbundling is that some customers try to get a "free ride" for services without paying later through hardware purchases. In one case, an equipment manufacturer asked a chemical company for a costly engineering concept for a new application center. The chemical supplier expected that the equipment manufacturer would remain a loyal customer of their chemicals for a long time. But this expectation proved false. Shortly after the new system was installed, the manufacturer changed to a cheaper supplier of generic chemicals. Customers sometimes perceive that they are being asked to pay for something they do not want because it is included in the bundle. Oracle shifted to "pay-as-you-use" pricing by stripping out functionality from the base platform and offering as add-on modules procedural databases, distributed databases, and parallel servers. This dissolved customer dissatisfaction of the type, "I have to pay for procedural databases and I don't even use them" which would otherwise cause the customer to seek other sources.[17]

The importance of these factors varies from industry to industry. Therefore, managers should carefully check whether and how the advantages or the disadvantages of price bundling are changing over time.

SUMMARY

Price bundling is a potentially powerful method to exploit profit potential better and to maximize profits in a multiproduct company. It does require careful analysis to see if the concept fits your situation; the information requirements are high, but it can be a big profit boost. In applying this pricing technique, the following points should be noted:

- Price bundling works when the customers are heterogeneous in their willingnesses to pay, i.e., in their maximum prices. Bundling can be optimal because unexploited consumer surplus, or "money left on the table," is transferred to a second product.
- Price bundling requires a relatively high level of information on individual customers or customer segments. Price response estimation for bundles is complex. Sometimes the only applicable method is direct

questioning of customers. We described the power of conjoint measurement in chapter 3, but its use in bundling application is sometimes too complicated.

- Price bundling can appear in the forms of pure and mixed bundling.
  The optimality of one or the other form depends on the distribution of
  maximum prices.
- Tie-in sales are a form of price bundling that must be carefully examined from a legal perspective as it sometimes makes for the extension
  of monopoly power from one product to another. For a sophisticated
  pricer, it may be a way to customize price according to usage.
- Based on our experience, power pricers often attain profit improvements through price bundling in the range of 20 to 30%.
- Under specific circumstances, unbundling can become advantageous.
  In dynamic markets the issue of whether to bundle or unbundle has to
  be checked regularly.
- The legal situation may restrict or prohibit price bundling for certain
  firms (particularly those in market-dominant positions).

In each individual case it has to be carefully investigated whether and
which form of price bundling is superior and how it compares to separate pricing for the individual products. There are no general or simple
rules but price bundling offers to the power pricer the opportunity to
turn superior know-how into higher profits.

10

Time Customization of Prices

The Short Term

INTRODUCTION

Every price has a life. Some of these lives are long. For example, the price of a basic Swatch watch has remained $40 since its introduction to the U.S. market in 1982. Others are short; many restaurants lower their prices for a few hours each day, offering "early-bird specials." This chapter and the next address the issue of time customization of prices. This chapter considers the short term; the next chapter focuses on the long term. Temporary price changes, i.e., short-term time customizations of prices, are common. For example:

1. Manufacturers distribute over 300 billion coupons to consumers in the United States each year, offering limited-time discounts ranging from 25¢ off a six-pack of soda to thousands of dollars off an automobile. On average, about 4% of these coupons are redeemed.
2. Manufacturers offer trade deals to retailers. These "deals" offer reduced prices to the trade for a specified period of time. The manufacturer may offer the deals one by one over time or provide the retailer a full calendar of deals for the year. For example, Colgate-Palmolive provided a $5.60 per case off-invoice allowance for Ajax laundry detergent, effectively cutting the price by 28% for a six-week period.[1]

3. At times, prompted by these trade deals or even without this incentive, stores offer items "on sale" for customers. Lechmere Sales, a consumer electronics retailer, has a substantial circular in the Boston newspaper virtually every Sunday, featuring hundreds of sale items for the upcoming week—for example, "Sauder Work Center—regularly $249.99, save $50—$198.98."; "Mr. Coffee 12-Cup Coffee Maker—regularly $49.99, save $10—$39.98."

4. Firms facing varying degrees of demand over time adjust prices accordingly. For example, electrical utilities use "peak load pricing" to vary rates with time of day to encourage demand shifting by consumers.

5. Sophisticated yield-management systems help airlines, hotels, and others manage inventory and time customize price to match demand optimally. American Airlines estimates the annual revenue contribution of its yield management procedures to be over $500 million.[2]

6. "Special introductory pricing" is used to build initial demand for a new product and "clearance sales" are used to move products whose demand never quite matched supply. For example, in the United States January typically finds men's fancy dress shirts not sold during the prime selling season at discounts of 40% or more. In Germany, consumers eagerly anticipate two annual sales events in which a broad group of retailers participate. The "Winter End Sale" and "Summer End Sale" find queues of customers awaiting the opening of stores and discounts of up to 80% to clear seasonal inventories. Some manufacturers attempt to clear out old inventory to make way for new models. For example, in late 1995, Saab attempted to clear out its inventory of cars in the United States by offering coupons of $1000–$3000 depending upon the model.

"Sales" are everywhere. In 1988, Sears sold 55% of its goods "on sale."[3] Seventy-five percent of major appliances are bought "on deal"[4] and some consumer packaged goods run to 90% on deal. This prompts two questions. First, can this be the right thing to do? What are the underlying motivations and conditions which make short-term price customization advisable? In spite of its prevalence, there are possible negative effects to this time customization. For example, some customers are now so accustomed to sale prices that they refuse even to consider buying at "full price." In light of this, how does one assess whether short-term time customization is well suited for the situation at hand? The second question is: if time customization is indicated, how does one set up the program? Poorly managed, sales activity can create peaks and valleys in demand—creating havoc in manufacturing, distribution, and inventory systems. However, a well-designed and implemented program of time-customized prices can be a key profit enhancer. The power pricer uses sale activity in a proactive way—not as a reaction to being saddled with excess supply of product. The power pricer builds promotion pricing into the pricing program from the beginning, carefully setting out purposes, triggering mechanisms, implementation means, and specific objectives of time-customizing price.

WHAT THIS CHAPTER WILL DO

This chapter addresses the following questions.

1. What are the underlying motivations for time customizing prices in the short term? We offer a three-class taxonomy of time-customization motivations to clarify thinking about the purpose of a sale.
2. How does one know when time customization is advisable? What are the counterarguments to it? Recently, many firms, most notably Procter & Gamble, have embarked on "Everyday Low Pricing" strategies instead of frequent trade promotions. What are the pros and cons of these "noncustomized" strategies?
3. If time customization is advisable, how should one go about setting the price levels, choosing the implementation method, and timing the offer?

Knowing the answers to these questions will help you to:

1. understand the information required to time customize effectively
2. know why and when to time customize prices
3. determine the beginning and duration of a customization period
4. assess the proper level of adjustment in prices
5. specify the implementation program necessary to reap the benefits

We begin by a detailed consideration of the variety of purposes for time customization, since clear specification of the objective is a critical prerequisite to profitable practice. Throughout the chapter, we will provide best practice examples to demonstrate the potential benefits. We conclude with general lessons on effective management of time customization.

MOTIVATIONS FOR TIME-CUSTOMIZED PRICES

As suggested by the variety of examples in this introduction, there is a set of fundamentally different motivations for time-customizing prices. We begin by developing a taxonomy of motivations to help clarify the proper objectives of time customization. As shown in Figure 10-1, we identify seven motivations in all. The first distinction underlying these approaches is based on the degree of knowledge about customer demand, the first branch in the tree in Figure 10-1. Working from the bottom of the figure up, if information on demand is initially limited, time-customizing prices can be used either as a way to learn about demand (A. Demand Probing, #6) or to respond to demand as it begins to reveal itself (B. Yield Management, #7). The upper "Known" demand section of the tree subdivides more extensively. The first subdivision is based on whether time itself is a good proxy for change in buying behavior or not. An example of a time-driven situation is the demand for accommodations at a Vermont ski area, which drops in April as mud replaces snow as the slippery surface on the hillsides. If time is a driver, prices may follow the "Peak Load" being adjusted upward to take advantage of the peaking in demand (A. Peak Load, #4) or adjusted in recognition of the peak, but with the added intention of shifting some of the peak demand to an off-peak time period (B. Peak Load with Demand Shift, #5).

If demand is "Not Time Driven" (the top branch of the tree), customized prices, particularly in the form of temporarily low prices, can be useful in three ways: A. Trial (#1), to overcome a customer's resistance to trial of a product with which he is unfamiliar—this can be either for a new product or for an existing product in an effort to attract new customers; B. Purchase Acceleration (#2), to induce a customer to buy more now rather than wait, e.g., to buy 60 days of consumable supplies into inventory rather than the usual 30 days; and C. Potential Build-Up (#3), to drop price temporarily to induce those who have not bought a durable at "regular price" to buy.

FIGURE 10-1

Three Classes/Seven Basic Motivations for Time Customization of Prices

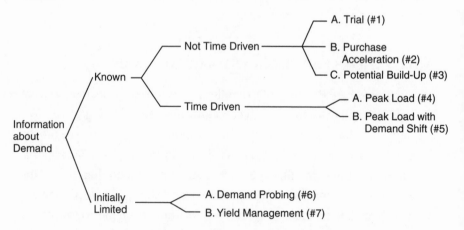

Thus, as shown in Figure 10-1, the specific nature of the demand situation implies seven different major motivations for short-term time customization of price. We now discuss these seven motivations to elaborate these rationales and show how the power pricer optimizes profit in each situation by incorporating short-term price customization.

Demand: Known and Not Time Driven

On Sunday, November 26, 1995, the Lechmere Sales circular in the *Boston Globe* offered 5 rolls of Fuji film (24 exposures) at $15.98, less a $10 manufacturer's mail-in rebate, valid until December 30, 1995. The circular highlighted Fuji's $5.98 "Final Cost After Rebate" or $1.20 per roll—approximately 60% less than the regular price. Lechmere features this offer to drive film sales and perhaps to build store traffic and demand for other products sold in the store as discussed in chapter 8, but what is the motivation for Fuji to offer such a temporary price reduction?

Fuji is likely pursuing motivation #1 of Figure 10-1, using the temporary price cut as a way to induce consumers to switch from long-time market leader Kodak and try Fuji film. Fuji has been a presence in the U.S. market since 1984, when it was the "official film" of the Summer Olympics in Los Angeles, but it still holds only about an 11% market share in the United States vs. Kodak's 70% share. The U.S. market is huge, at about 670,000,000 24-exposure-roll equivalents. The vast majority of consumers have been brand loyal to Kodak, the traditional market leader, despite Fuji being 10–15% cheaper on the basis of "regular prices" and studies in *Consumer Reports* citing virtually indistinguishable quality differences in their films. If Fuji can break the Kodak habit and induce Fuji trial, the consumer may thus develop the belief that Fuji is just as good as Kodak and, given its lower regular price, switch to it as his "regular brand," even when both Kodak and Fuji are at regular price.

Fuji also incorporates motivation #2: Purchase Acceleration. The $1.20 per-roll price, aided by the packaging in a five-pack of 24 exposures, accelerates purchasing. Few families ordinarily inventory four rolls of film. This pricing and packaging thus moves inventory that would otherwise be in the supply pipeline somewhere into the consumer's home. This "pantry loading" effect, as it is known particularly among consumer packaged goods marketers, may also have the beneficial impact of increasing the amount of film used—as no impulse-picture-taking occasions are missed due to a lack of film in the household. But equally important from Fuji's point of view is the benefit of the increased time the consumer has to recognize Fuji's acceptable quality until he is back "in the market" again making a brand choice decision. Effectively, the purchase acceleration limits Kodak's ability to regain its customer until the five Fuji units are used up.

Fuji implemented the time customization through a rebate, paid directly by the manufacturer, requiring the consumer to pay the $15.98 retail price to Lechmere and then mail in receipts to obtain money back from Fuji. Other mechanisms for enacting price customization of this type are:

1. *A coupon:* requires the consumer to see, clip, and bring the coupon to the store; this eliminates impulse purchasing, but allows the consumer to make a cash outlay of only the final discount price.
2. *An on-shelf price cut:* this requires no effort by the consumer, but makes the discount equally available to all customers, regardless of their patience with coupon or rebate-redemption procedures.

The rebate and coupon methods differ from the on-shelf price cut in two important respects. Research[5] has shown the importance of the notion of a "reference price" in consumer decision making. If a customer's perception was that he paid \$1.20 per roll for Fuji, this may become the reference price against which he compares future Fuji pricing. Thus, when Fuji returns to its regular price, instead of the customer seeing it as 10–15% less than Kodak, Fuji's price may be seen as "a lot more than I paid last time," thus having a negative impact on future sales. A coupon or rebate rather than an on-shelf price cut can mitigate against the formation of a detrimentally low reference price in the consumer's mind.

Second, a rebate or coupon can be applied more selectively than an on-shelf price cut. In the case of an on-shelf price cut, all buyers receive the savings on the spot. Rebates are similar in that they usually are available to all, as necessary materials are at the point-of-purchase or included in the packaging, but they require the effort of collecting proofs of purchase and forms and mailing them to the manufacturer. More price-conscious consumers will send in receipts and the required proofs of purchase, while less price-sensitive consumers may not. Coupons can be distributed selectively through various media. This helps to give the discount only to those who would not buy the product otherwise. If using coupons, Fuji would try to find a way to distribute them to Kodak users rather than current Fuji users. A key to the profitability of couponing is the extent to which it spurs incremental sales rather than representing a margin loss on sales that would have been made anyway. Several studies have been done on profiles of coupon redeemers.

Neslin and Clarke[6] studied a variety of coupons in a field experiment, finding that over 50% of coupon redemptions were by customers who "almost always" bought the brand anyway. Only 14% of coupons were true "trial" generators. However, this experiment did not attempt to distribute the coupons selectively to previous nonusers.

Bawa and Shoemaker's[7] study of panel data is summarized in Table 10-1. This documents the fact that regular users are more likely to redeem coupons than previous nonusers which again points out the benefits of selective distribution of coupons to previous nonusers if possible. In this study, the small percentage of the population being "frequent users" of the studied brands meant that, despite their higher redemption probability, "frequent users" made only 21% of the redemptions.

Ehrenberg, Hammond, and Goodhardt[8] have studied the ability of price promotions to draw new customers for established consumer products, such as detergents, toothpaste, and soups. Their finding is that 80% of buy-

TABLE 10-1

Profile of Coupon Redeemers

Prior	Probability of Redemption	% of Total Redemptions Accounted For
Nonuser	4.2%	28.5%
Infrequent user	17.8%	50.4%
Frequent user	31.3%	21.1%

ers during a promotion had purchased the promoted brand in the prior year. Their conclusion was that the boost in sales observed from a price promotion was driven by customers "merely choosing this already familiar brand instead of some other familiar brand which they would otherwise have bought on that particular occasion." Thus, price promotions directed to motivation #1, implemented through coupons, rebates, or on-shelf price price cuts, seem most well suited to low-share or new products. Motivation #2, in which "pantry loading" is sought, may be more appropriate for large-share, well-known brands. These brands typically have shown a larger promotional price elasticity than small brands in empirical studies.

Motivation #3, Potential Build-Up, the last of the "Not Time Driven" Class, is exemplified by the Mr. Coffee coffee maker example, i.e., on sale at $39.98 for one week and then returning to the $49.99 regular price the next. The objective of this time customization is to reach the maximum willingness-to-pay price of a growing proportion of the market that would not buy at regular price.[9] For certain durable goods situations, the optimal time cycle for customization of price is of the form shown in Figure 10-2.

The "potential build-up" phenomenon stems from all those who value the product above the "regular price" that is charged in periods 1 and 2 buying in periods 1 and 2—leaving a potential market in period 3 predominately characterized by those who would not buy at the regular price. For example, suppose potential customers for a coffee maker are of two types, one valuing the product at $60 and the other at $40. An

FIGURE 10-2

Price Cycle for Periodic Sale

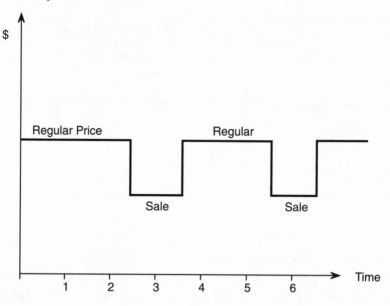

equal number, let's say 100, of each type become a potential customer each period due to the wearing out of the coffee maker currently owned. An individual customer follows a simple rule: he buys if the price for the period is less than his maximum willingness to pay. If the price is too high, he does not buy and makes do with his old coffee maker for a while longer. If the price is acceptable he buys and leaves the market. For this example, take the firm's cost to be $32 per unit.

Table 10-2 shows the evolution of prices. In period 1, 100 of each customer type become potential buyers due to their coffee pot wearing out. The firm can charge $60—in which case only the 100 high-value customers will buy; or it can charge $40, in which case both the high-value and low-value customers will buy. Charging $60 results in a unit contribution of $28 for each of 100 customers; charging $40 results in a unit contribution of $8 for all 200 potential buyers, for a total of $1600. Thus, in period 1, the optimal price is $60, as shown by the asterisk in Table 10-2. In period 2, an additional 100 buyers of each type become potential buyers due to wearing out, joining the 100 low-value types who did not buy in period 1. In period 2, the optimal strategy is still to charge $60, as a $28 unit contribution collected from each of the 100 high-value customers is more profitable than collecting $8 from all 300 potential customers. In period 3, 100 more of each type enter. This time, they join the 200 low-value types who did not buy in either period 1 or 2. Now that the low-valuation group has grown to be three times as big as the high-value group, it is optimal to lower the price to $40 to induce this group to buy, collecting $8 from all 400 customers for a total contribution of $3200—vs. the $2800 obtainable by holding the price at $60. Once these low-value customers have been cleared out of the market, 100 of each type enter in period 4, creating a situation identical to period 1. And thus the cycle would repeat.

In order to reveal the underlying dynamics most clearly, we have not considered issues such as customers anticipating and waiting for the sale, discounting of cash flows, or the peaking of unit demand in the demand pattern 100, 100, 400, 100, 100, 400, . . . and the resulting inventory implications. These factors would complicate the analysis somewhat but the basic motivation remains to cut price periodically in order to induce low-valuation consumers who have built up over time to buy. Some furniture manufacturers focusing on corporate accounts

TABLE 10-2

Price Evolution

Period	Number of Potential Customers: This Period Valuing At:		Contribution	
	$60	$40	P = $60	P = $40
1	100	100	$2800*	$1600
2	100	200	$2800*	$2400
3	100	300	$2800	$3200*
4	100	100	$2800*	$1600
5	◄———————— Same as Period 2 ————————►			
6	◄———————— Same as Period 3 ————————►			

* = profit contribution of the preferred price.

engage in sales activity of this type. A growing body of "at home" users with lower evaluations is tapped periodically through sale activity. For time customization of this type, one needs to understand the propensity of different groups to "buy now" or perhaps wait in anticipation of a sale. Some irregularity in the timing of sales can help guard against customers anticipating and planning ahead to wait for a sale.

This analysis of the first class of motivations—Demand: Known and Not Time Driven—shows that even if an individual's buying behavior is not evolving naturally with time, it can be a requirement of optimal profits to time customize prices. Low pricing can engender trials to educate customers and positively influence demand. This is probably the most intuitive use of time customization in the Not Time Driven case. Pricing can also pull demand forward in time. Even if this negatively impacts future demand it can be profitable, as it shifts inventory carrying costs from the firm to the customer. Finally, we show how periodic sales may be optimal even if *individual* buyers are not changing—but previous pricing changes the composition of the pool of potential buyers.

Demand Known and Time Driven

Motivations #4 and #5 in Figure 10-1 apply to a situation in which an individual customer's value for a product varies over time. For example, a business may value electrical power more during the business day than at night, and need auditing services more as it closes its fiscal year than at other times. A computer-industry executive values a hotel room in Las Vegas more during the COMDEX trade show than after. A family values a dinner at a local restaurant more at 7:00 P.M. than at 4:30 P.M. and a condominium rental at a ski resort more for the children's school vacation week than for the week before or after.

It makes sense to adjust pricing in recognition of varying demand. Indeed, electrical companies, accounting firms, restaurants, and ski resorts do customize their prices over time in recognition of the value fluctuations mentioned. As shown in Table 10-3, the time-driven value variation of interest can be by hour of day, day of week, week, month of year, or around some special event. For example, the value of a phone call to a business declines after work hours. Thus, NYNEX cuts its price for the first minute of a Boston-area call 39% from 29¢ to 17.8¢ for calls until

TABLE 10-3

Example Value Variation Over Different Time Periods

		Example
Time of day	• Value Change with Work/ Leisure Status	• NYNEX Rate for Initial Minute of Telephone Call Boston to Nantucket • .098 Night (11 P.M.–8 A.M.) • .178 Evening (5 P.M.–11 P.M.) • .29 Weekday (8 A.M.–5 P.M.)
Day of week	• Work Day vs. Not: ski lifts, golf course greens fee increase on weekends; car rental rates decrease on weekends	• Breakers Resort in West Palm Beach, Florida <u>"Centennial Package"</u> • $279/Night for Sunday–Thursday • $295/Night for Friday & Saturday
Week	• Holiday periods • Hotels • First/Last week of month as paycheck arrives	• EuroDisney Hotel Pricing • See Table 10-4
Month	• High season for resorts, demand for product influenced by weather conditions	• Hilton Head—3 Bedroom—Ocean Front • March–August: $2100 • September–October: $2000 • November–February: $1450
Special event	• Events causing convergence of people: Conventions, sporting events • Weather changes: heat wave impacts on value of electricity for air conditioning	• 4 Bedroom house in Atlanta listed on Internet for $1200/day during the 1996 Summer Olympics

11 P.M., and 66% for calls between 11 P.M. and and 8 A.M. Weekday vs. weekend drives the valuation of many things requiring an investment of one's time; for instance, recreational facilities geared to a local clientele typically have higher prices on weekends and some hotels have weekend rates—those in business areas dropping rates and some in resort areas increasing them. The Breakers Hotel in West Palm Beach, Florida, priced its basic package 5.7% higher for weekend nights for the 1996 winter social season.

EuroDisney used five different rate structures during the November 1995–March 1996 time period. The holiday period from December 22 to January 7 was priced above adjacent weeks by a factor that varied across the six hotels shown in Table 10-4.

TABLE 10-4

EuroDisney Pricing for Holiday Weeks of Christmas Season 1995–96 as Compared to Prices for Just Before/Just After (Adjacent) Periods

Hotel Rating	Hotel	Single-Occupancy Rate (in French Francs)		Premium for Holiday Weeks
		Adjacent	Holiday	
★★★★	Hotel New York	2395	2480	6%
★★★★	Disneyland Hotel	2035	2455	21%
★★★	Newport Bay Club	965	1330	38%
★★★	Sequoia	865	1230	42%
★★	Hotel Cheyenne	735	1120	52%
★★	Hotel Santa Fe	635	1020	61%

Table 10-4 shows that the percentage level of increase varies significantly and inversely with the quality rating of the hotel, suggesting that the overall boom of holiday demand lifts willingness to pay for these lower-priced options more dramatically. Absolute price differentials among the hotels, e.g., the 100-French-Franc difference between the Newport Bay Club and the Sequoia, are approximately the same in both types of price periods.

Similarly, rates vary by time of year as the weather pattern influences desirability of locations. An ocean-front home at Hilton Head costs 45% more in March than February. And special events such as the Olympics or unanticipated supply shortages of some materials can impact customers' willingness to pay. For the Formula 1 car-race event at the Nürnburgring, a very popular one-day affair, one hotel operator increases his rates by a factor of four, to DM 800 per night, and further, books only for a four-night minimum.

Most of these examples apply to services, because the importance of time customization of prices is greatest for those situations where the good cannot be economically inventoried for sale during the peak demand period. The principle behind time customization in these instances is clear. If demand is relatively high for a time, the price that maximizes the firm's profit is relatively high as well. If demand is relatively low, the short-term profit maximizing price is relatively low. For example, consider a "peak" period with 100 potential customers and demand as shown in Figure 10-3(a), i.e., customers' values are uniformly distributed between $50 and $150: one person values the good/service at $150, one at $149, one at $148, and so forth down to the last person valuing it at $50. This is the linear-demand-curve case discussed previously in chapter 2 (the POWER-STAR example) and then used in chapter 5's airline example. If the firm's cost per unit is $50, we know from chapter 2 that the maximum profit triangle under the peak sales revenue is swept out by charging $100, which is the mid-point between $50 cost and the maximum price of $150. Now consider an off-peak case as shown in panel (b) where each individual's value decreases by $50. Now, we know, the optimal price drops to $75.

As shown in Figure 10-3, in peak periods the best thing to do is price at $100 and sell 50 units. During off-peak, the best thing to do is offer a 25% off sale, cutting price to $75—but even then, sales volume during off-peak is only 25 units—half of that observed for peak.

This case covered the simple situation of a consumer potentially buying in both peak and off-peak periods. This corresponds to motivation #4 in Figure 10-1. Motivation #5 is Peak Load with Demand Shift. In

FIGURE 10-3

Peak and Off-Peak Pricing

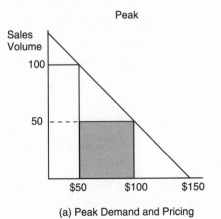

(a) Peak Demand and Pricing

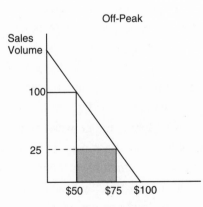

(b) Off-Peak Demand and Pricing

this case, a consumer buys only at the peak or off-peak, but not both. For example, the family takes only one vacation; the diner eats only one meal rather than both an "early-bird special" and a meal at the regular time. In this situation, relative prices at peak and off-peak have the effect of allocating demand between the peak and off-peak periods.

The rationale here can be explained via a situation similar to the Mr. Coffee one discussed for motivation #3, in that there are two groups of customers, one group of 100 people valuing the product during the peak time at a high-level $60 and the other group of 100 people valuing peak time availability at a lower level of $40.[10] The high consumers would generally find it quite inconvenient to switch to an off-peak period. Effectively, for them the value of the product off-peak falls to zero. The $40 type would rather have the product at peak than at off-peak, but do not find it quite as inconvenient to consume off peak. They value off-peak at $5 less, i.e., at $35. (This corresponds well to the behavior of business vs. pleasure travelers.) Each consumer knows both the price in the peak and off-peak before making his decision—what should the firm do? Does it make sense to have peak and off-peak pricing?

The valuations are as follows:

	Number	*Peak*	*Off-Peak*
High-value customers	100	$60	$0
Low-value customers	100	$40	$35

If costs are low relative to these values, the optimal pricing strategy is clear: charge $60 in the peak period and $35 in off-peak. The pricing shifts the low-customer-value-type demand to the off-peak period. Effectively, peak and off-peak time prices customize the pricing to low- and high-type customers. Note that for this situation, the sales rate off-peak may exceed the peak sales rate. If the number of low-value customers were slightly greater than 100, the pricing strategy would not change and off-peak demand would exceed peak.

The distinction between high- and low-value types of customers need not be so sharp for peak-load pricing to make sense. The key is that low-value types find it less inconvenient to consume off peak.

Deutsche Bahn, whose BahnCard was discussed in chapter 7 as a successful implementation of nonlinear pricing, has instituted an evening fare based on this principle. Called the "Guten Abend-Ticket" (GAT), this "Good Evening" ticket is valid after 7 P.M. It costs DM 69 for a 400-km ride, which before 7 P.M. is DM 96 for a second-class fare. The business traveler, headed home from work at 5 P.M., is time sensitive and is willing to pay very little for a train ride two hours after the time he really wants. A pleasure traveler with more discretion on time has relatively little value erosion and thus can shift. In a study, we observed that this 25% price cut induced 14% of those who conceivably could shift the time of their travel to do so. Thus, our "time-shift" elasticity was:

% change in peak demand/% change in price = .14/.25 = .56

Demand: Uncertain

A "sale" is a natural outcome of uncertainty about how much potential customers are willing to pay for the product. Pricing high initially and decreasing over time helps reveal the underlying demand, and prevents the costly mistake of selling at a price well below what the customers are willing to pay. If the high price does not generate sufficient sales, there is a learning benefit: the proper inference is that the product is not worth that much to the market and the price should be lowered. The process can continue sequentially. Filene's Basement in Boston is well known for institutionalizing and communicating a sales process like this. Its "Automatic Markdown" policy works as follows: the price of an article put on the selling floor falls by:

- 25% after 7 selling days
- 50% after 14 selling days
- 75% after 21 selling days
- and is given to charity after 28 selling days

A customer knows price will fall on a wanted item—but runs the risk of losing out to another customer if he plays the waiting game too long. If a $400 men's suit remains unsold for 7 days, that is useful information to Filene's about the value of the suit to patrons; specifically, it is unlikely anyone values it at over $400. After 7 days, Filene's has more information than it did when it set the original price and the markdown plan is the adjustment mechanism as the information about demand accumulates.

Pricing actions can be used to reveal the true underlying value for the product and the optimal "sales" discounts.

A simple example demonstrates these principles.[11] Consider selling a product to a single customer and three scenarios on information about a potential customer's valuation of a product, as shown in Figure 10-4.

1. You know he values the product at $5.00—panel (a) of Figure 10-4.
2. You know he values it somewhere between $4.00 and $6.00; but each valuation within that range is equally likely as far as you know. So, if the price is $4, he is sure to buy; if $5, there is a 50% chance he buys; at $6 or above, he does not buy. This is shown in panel (b).
3. You know he values it somewhere between $0 and $10.00; but again, within that range, each valuation is as likely as any other as far as you know. The map for probability of buy vs. price is shown in panel (c). This is the same as the linear demand case of chapter 2.

Note that in each scenario, the customer's expected valuation is $5.00, i.e., he is equally likely to have a valuation above or below this point. You have one unit of the good to sell him. He buys if the price you quote him is less than his value and there is no negotiation. But the good is not worth anything to you if you do not sell it to him. What price do you quote to maximize your expected revenues?

Scenario panel (a) is obviously trivial. Since you know he values it at $5.00, you quote $5.00, he buys the product, and you make $5.00. In the

FIGURE 10-4

Three Scenarios of Degree of Uncertainty About Product Value

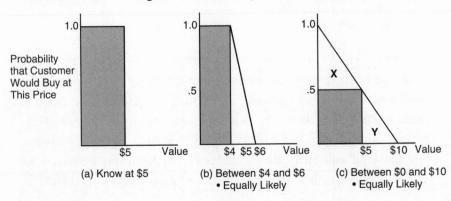

(a) Know at $5   (b) Between $4 and $6
• Equally Likely   (c) Between $0 and $10
• Equally Likely

scenarios of panels (b) and (c), as before, we look for the price that sweeps out the maximum area from under the sales response curve.

For scenario 2 in panel (b), the optimal price is $4 to sweep out the shaded rectangle shown. You make sure a transaction takes place by going to the low point of the range. For scenario 3 in panel (c), the best price is $5.00, the midpoint between maximum possible value $10 and the cost of $0. The odds of a transaction taking place are 50/50, so your expected revenue is $2.50.

While each scenario had the customer's mean value of the product at $5.00, the uncertainty associated with the value drove your expected profits down. Table 10-5 summarizes the optimal price, probability of a transaction, and expected revenue for different levels of uncertainty around the mean value of $5.00.

The "value spread" column represents the uncertainty. "$5 ± $1" is our scenario 2 of panel (b), where value is somewhere between $4 and $6 and any value in there is equally likely; "$5 ± $2" represents equally likely between $3 and $7, and so forth to our scenario 3/panel (c) above, here noted as the $5 ± $5 value spread.

With the high uncertainty of scenario 3/panel (c), we quote $5 but expect to make only $2.50. The interpretation given to the triangles left be-

TABLE 10-5
Pricing and Profits Given Different Levels of Demand Uncertainty

Mean Value	Value Spread	(1) Optimal Price	(2) Probability of Transaction	(1) * (2) Expected Revenue
$5	$5	$5	1	$5
	$5 ± $1	$4	1	$4
	$5 ± $2	$3.50	.875	$3.06
	$5 ± $3	$4.00	.667	$2.66
	$5 ± $4	$4.50	.563	$2.53
	$5 ± $5	$5.00	.500	$2.50

hind by any uniform price developed in chapter 5 can be used here to explain what happens due to the uncertainty. Triangle X in panel (c) is the "passed-up sale": we charge $5—but nothing happened because the price was too high. Triangle Y is the familiar "money left on the table." Now, in this scenario, let's suppose we get a second bite at the apple, i.e., we quoted $5.00 and got "no sale" yesterday but somewhat unexpectedly we bump into the same potential customer today. What do we do now?

This gives us the chance to sweep out a rectangle from Triangle X. We sweep out the maximum rectangle with a price of $2.50. Thus, if we got a second chance, we would offer a 50% discount off the first offer price of $5.00 which was rejected.

If we knew we would have two opportunities to quote prices in the beginning, the analysis is the same as we did in chapter 5 for expanding the airlines offering from economy class only to economy plus first class. Precisely as we did in chapter 5 for two classes, we would pick out the two prices that left over the smallest area in the triangles, as shown

FIGURE 10-5

Optimal Two-Day Sale Pricing

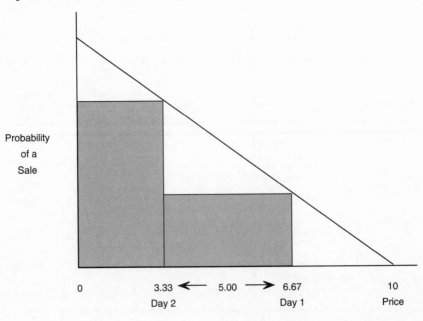

in Figure 10-5. The optimal strategy is to charge $6.67 on day 1; if no sale occurs, drop price 50% on day 2. The expected profit of this time customization strategy is: 1/3 (6.67) + 1/3 (3.33) = 3.33 or 33% more than the single price policy of $2.50.

Yield Management is motivation #7 in Figure 10-1, a more sophisticated version of the same demand-probing and revelation strategy discussed here. The best known users of yield management systems are airlines. American Airlines pioneered the concept in the late 1970s and in the early 1990s termed yield management "absolutely essential to profitable operations," as quantifiable benefits of its yield management were $1.4 billion for 1989–91 and American parent company AMR had net profit for the same time period of $892 million.[12] Whereas the demand probing motivation #6 in Figure 10-1 works with a single customer or homogeneous group of customers, yield-management systems developed because of different types of customers wanting to buy the same item. Leisure travelers and business travelers typically differ in important ways, such as these:

Leisure	*Business*
• Book well in advance	• Book on short notice
• Price oriented	• Less price sensitive
• Flexible on schedule	• Inflexible on schedule

Leisure travelers book well in advance, but are not willing to pay as much as business travelers. From the airlines' point of view, ideally, the plane would take off full—and at the same time no price-sensitive business travelers would be unable to get a seat at the last minute. A task for the yield-management system is to price and manage the availability of specific fare types over time as demand for a particular flight reveals itself. Norms exist for how full the flight should be X days before departure. If bookings are above the norm this is a signal to shut off availability of highly discounted fares; below the norm signals the need to lower prices or otherwise market that specific flight.

In car rentals, Hertz's yield-management system drives off a demand forecast at the level of a specific city/day/car type/length of rental.[13] This forecast is a combination of historical data for the day and recent booking data. The recent-booking data are similar to the demand-probing motivation. Based on prices in the market, reservations come in. The yield-management system processes this information into a demand forecast, and ultimately outputs prices that reflect the minimum net revenue which Hertz should be willing to accept for a particular city/day/car type/length of rental. These net revenue figures are dynamically updated over time based on the most recent bookings data. Thus, as demand reveals itself in bookings activity for future rentals, prices adjust upward or downward.

IMPORTANCE OF TIME CUSTOMIZATION

Figure 10-1 provides seven different scenarios in which short-term time customization of prices can prove profitable. Effective time customization is critical to the survival of some types of businesses (e.g., airlines, car rental agencies) and a strong profit enhancer for others.

Hertz reports an up to 5% increase in average revenue per rental with the time customization enacted through its yield-management system. This has tremendous bottom-line impact, as we know from chapter 1 that on average a 1% increase in price realization yields an 11% profit boost.

Power pricers implement effective time-customization plans by:

1. clearly understanding the underlying motivation for their program. Which rationale from Figure 10-1 is motivating the program is critical to its design, implementation, and evaluation.
2. specifying objectives for the program and measures by which it will be evaluated. Common metrics include the average revenue per unit sold and the percent of capacity utilized.
3. implementing the program in a cost-effective manner with a focus on incremental profit contribution.
4. developing the detailed customer data necessary to determine the timing and level of customization.
5. taking a broad view of the system-wide consequences of time customization.
6. assuring that the time customization program and/or its presentation does not create consumer attitudes and behavior which are detrimental to the firm in the long run.

PRACTICAL PROS AND CONS OF TIME CUSTOMIZATION

In some cases, the practical wisdom of time customization of price is clear. The customer impact is often great but the value requires careful analysis. For example, Blattberg and Wisniewski report deal elasticities much larger than price elasticities. For the product categories they analyzed, price elasticities were about 2.5, while promotional (i.e., temporary price change) elasticities were between 8 and 11.[14] This means that a 1% temporary price drop typically yielded an 8–11% unit sales increase. But does this take from competitors, or does it borrow against our own future sales? Despite the perceived power of time customization in impacting customer and trade behavior, some have raised concerns about such pricing moves. *Fortune,*[15] in the title of an October 1992 article, referred to widespread use of temporary price cuts to the trade in grocery products as "The Dumbest Marketing Ploy." The article documents the inefficiencies of extreme purchase acceleration generated by short-term price cuts by citing the average 84 days it takes a product to get from factory to store shelf.

In the United States, Procter and Gamble, among manufacturers, and Wal-Mart, among retailers, are the most notable proponents of reduced time customization of prices in favor of a strategy of "everyday low prices." A regional supermarket in Germany has not had a promotional deal in its 30-year history. Its market leadership comes from customer loyalty engendered by consistently offering good value for the money. Ortmeyer, Quelch, and Salmon[16] note four major classes of benefits from stabilizing rather than customizing prices:

1. *Reduced inventory requirements:* constant pricing stabilizes demand, reducing required safety stocks and stockouts. (This is true only if the competition is not following a heavily time-customized program. In that case, one's own time customization may be necessary to offset another's, if the objective is to have stable demand over time.)
2. *More efficient use of personnel:* less time is spent repricing items and managing the peak demand occasioned by a temporary price cut.
3. *Role/cost of advertising:* advertising can focus on product value and corporate image rather than price.
4. *Better customer relationship:* fewer stockouts mean less dissatisfaction; no "low" pricing means the consumer will not be upset that

prices were higher when she bought, whereas "high-low" pricing undermines customer confidence.

Whenever a firm contemplates time customization, the potentially negative consequences must be considered. Generally, the key considerations are:

1. Incremental or Substitute Sale

When customizing prices to a low-price period, the key is not to be simply cannibalizing sales that otherwise would have been made at a higher price. As noted, coupon redemption studies show that the most likely redeemer of a coupon is a regular user.

2. Cost of Customization

A time-customized price schedule is more difficult to communicate and implement than a uniform price schedule. The new Deutsche Telekom pricing system has four distance zones and six time brackets. Even senior industry executives do not know all the prices—let alone the consumers who are supposed to be time shifting in response to them. Also, when couponing one must consider not only the face value of the coupon but also distribution costs and processing fees. Given an average 4% redemption rate on coupons, the cost per redemption can be a significant consideration. Communicating the time customization through advertising or in personal selling can interfere with the other purposes of the communication, namely establishing the product value. The revenue enhancement potential is frequently sufficient to justify this cost, as we have discussed, but the customization must be significant to offset the costs. The Breakers, the resort hotel in Florida mentioned in Table 10-3, has a beautiful brochure effectively presenting the benefits a couple would receive on their package plan at $279 per night. But the flow of the presentation of benefits is disrupted by noting that $279 per night does not apply on Friday or Saturday—when the price increases to $295 per night. Is it worth the cost of disrupting the benefit message to try to customize prices by 5% for two nights—especially when consumers feel it is unfair to raise prices for a fixed capacity just because there is more demand? Such limited price customization seeks to raise the average revenue per room-night from \$279 to 5/7(\$279) + 2/7(\$295) = \$283.57—a 1.6% increase. Would The Breakers be better off at a \$285 price for all nights? The Hotel Elysée in Hamburg would seem to think so, having a fixed DM 270 rate per night.

Most price customization plans are more ambitious than that of The Breakers in their revenue enhancement goals and, consequently, can bear more communication and implementation costs. However, the cost side must always be recognized and taken into account in assessing the desirability of customization.

3. System Effect

A big boost in unit sales from a price promotion may not be a desirable outcome. The full impact on production, inventory, and other costs must be anticipated. A little bit of "pantry loading" or "forward buying" by the trade may be desirable; but, taken to an extreme, it can throw the whole supply system out of an efficient functioning mode. System-wide implications for those who hold inventory must be gauged. Buzzell, Quelch, and Salmon[17] estimated that "forward buying" stimulated by trade promotions causes the total cost of operating the manufacturing and distribution system for nonperishable food-store products in the United States to increase between 1.15% and 2.0% of retail sales.

With respect to consumer psychology, there are three important impacts to consider.

1. Reference Price Impact

Does a low price from time customization create a new reference price in consumers' minds which will make it difficult to attain higher prices in the future? For example, fare wars in the airline industry have caused many consumers to think \$99 is a fair price to fly from Boston to Orlando. Any price above that is forever unacceptable. The consumer's thinking is that "if they were willing to take me there once for \$99, they should be willing to do it again." The \$99 price of the past has a negative effect upon current demand if the current price is above \$99, because consumers see the price above \$99 as unfair. Research has documented this effect more generally. Coupons can be an effective way to lower price without the direct impact on reference price that a direct on-shelf price cut would have. Placing conditions on the sale for the low-price period—e.g., goods must be bought in a minimum lot size of 10 units—can also mitigate against the formation of undesirable reference prices.

2. "Wait for Sale" Mentality

One store uses the slogan "Where you never have to pay full price." Conditioned by the extent of sale and rebate activity, some consumers believe this "where" is "everywhere"—i.e., that one never has to pay full price. Trying to wean consumers off rebates has been a problem in the automobile industry ever since bloated inventories prompted a spate of rebate deals. In some cases, one wants particular customers to wait for the low prices, e.g., to engage in off-peak telephone and electricity consumption. In other situations, however, careful attention must be paid to educating the consumer about how best to buy. One mechanism to consider to counter the waiting-for-the-cut phenomenon is what is known as "most favored customer" clauses, in which the consumer is guaranteed the benefit of any future price cut. Lechmere Sales, the consumer-electronics retailer, like others, offers 30-day price protection. When Chrysler first offered $1,000 rebates on its minivans in late 1989, it guaranteed consumers that if it went to higher rebate levels any time between February and October 1990, the consumer would receive the additional rebate as well.[18]

3. Fairness

One has to be sure that the form and presentation of the time customization is such that it does not set up an adversarial relationship between consumers and the firm. When introducing his "Value Pricing" in 1992, Robert Crandall of American Airlines noted the importance of developing a fare structure that consumers felt was fair. As mentioned, the nature of the customization in the airline business was so complicated that companies were designing computer algorithms to search and find lowest rates even with bizarre routings; for a single trip some consumers were buying two different round-trip tickets and throwing away the back half of each. The fare wars were not simply Delta vs. American; but also the consumer vs. American.

Marketers must think through what consumers will regard as fair and what type of price customization is appropriate. A surcharge for busy times may not be regarded as fair, but a discount for off-peak times may be. Eliminating a discount may be seen as acceptable, while raising a price is not.[19] Generally, the better informed consumers are about the time schedule of prices before buying, the fairer the new process is seen to be. In the long term being perceived as "fair" is important, to prevent the detrimental buyer behavior and buyer-seller relationship found in the airline industry in 1992.

SUMMARY

Time customization of prices in the short term can be a powerful profit enhancer. However, effective and profitable implementation requires a well-researched and thought through plan.

- A number of different demand situations—as set out in Figure 10-1—provide the basis for effective time customization.
- The power pricer uses promotional pricing in a planned, proactive way rather than simply as a reaction to excessive inventory. The underlying motivation for the promotion is clearly understood and communicated throughout the organization.
- The information requirements for time customization are extensive. Also, it presents managers with new questions, such as what is the "time shift" elasticity? Subjective assessment may thus be inappropriate, indicating that more primary research-driven methods are needed.
- While there are potential benefits to time customization, implementation costs can be significant and must be weighed against the potential benefits.
- Time customization, especially when demand is fundamentally stable, can induce disruptions to the efficient operation of manufacturing and supply systems. This has led to some advocating "everyday low pricing" strategies. The power pricer has a full appreciation of the costs and benefits of alternative strategies.
- Full understanding of the customers' economic and emotional reaction must be developed prior to implementing the plan.

Short-term time customization is a widely exercised tool for attempting to improve profitability. In our experience, it is also an area in which practice needs to be thoroughly reexamined. With the exception of some yield-management systems, which have been the beneficiaries of major development investments, such practices are largely *ad hoc* and not well informed. Moreover, the payoff to improved management of time customization seems significant.

11

Time Customization of Prices

The Long Term

INTRODUCTION

Chapter 10 considered the short-term time customization of price. In this chapter, we examine how price decisions are linked together over time and we consider long-term evolution of prices in the marketplace. Figure 11-1 shows the proper systems context for considering longer-term price customization. All current effects are shown within the dotted box. The "current period price" works through the current sales response curve to produce a current quantity sold—which, through economies of scale, impacts our "current cost" and yields a current contribution. Figure 11-1 also shows four key dynamic effects whereby today's price decision impact the *future* context for pricing and marketing-mix decisions. These are the "ripple effects" of pricing, which extend the impact of today's decisions beyond today's profit. Ignoring these ripple effects can cost firms long-term profitability. As we will show, the power pricer maps out a long-term strategy that takes these effects into account. Properly accounting for the dynamic effects can result in a price path over time quite different from the one that would evolve if current profit alone were the driving consideration at all times.

Three of the four dynamic effects shown in Figure 11-1 impact the future position of the sales response curve:

- Current quantity sold can impact future demand; positively or negatively—positively if current users talk about their product in a favorable way; negatively if they discuss it in an unfavorable way.
- As mentioned in chapter 10's discussion of couponing vs. an on-shelf price cut, current price may impact customers' expectation of future prices and perceptions about what is "fair." Customers form a reference price that sets a benchmark against which future prices are judged.
- As discussed in chapter 4, current price may impact competitors' entry, capacity, pricing, or other marketing decisions.

The other potentially important dynamic impact is on cost position. Empirical data show that in many situations, costs decrease with the accumulated volume of the product sold through learning or experience curve effects. Hence, the lower the price now, the lower future costs will be in real terms.

This chapter discusses these dynamic factors and shows how to adjust pricing in light of them. Some dynamic effects are beneficial to long-term profit and should be fostered; others are not, but may be unavoidable. Ignoring these effects, though, is dangerous. In addition, we consider key long-term evolution in both competitors and customers that may be beyond the direct control of the firm, but should be anticipated and managed to the extent possible.

FIGURE 11-1

Systems Context for Strategic Pricing: The Four Key Dynamic Effects

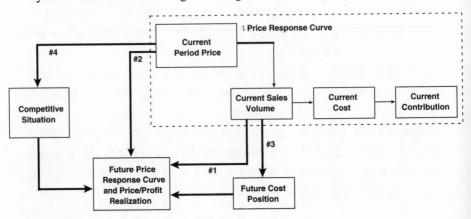

WHAT THIS CHAPTER WILL DO

This chapter addresses the following questions:

1. What are the long-term impacts of price setting and how do these effects operate?
2. What are the implications of these dynamic effects for developing an optimal time customized pricing strategy long term?
3. How can these effects be best managed?
4. How do competitive conditions typically evolve over time?

Knowing the answers to these questions will help you to:

1. assess the trade-off between reaping short-term profits and investing in future market position.
2. select a long-term strategy of time customizing price to influence the controllable factors in the system in the proper way
3. understand likely developments in the industry's price level and unit margins
4. control, to the extent possible, competitive developments
5. manage for long-term profit and forecast the unit margins attainable from the business over time

LINKING CURRENT SALES VOLUME TO FUTURE DEMAND

Dynamic linkage 1 in Figure 11-1 (see arrow #1) is from current sales volume to future position of the price response curve. An increase in current sales volume can impact future demand either positively or negatively. The major Type 1 links are shown in Table 11-1.

If a current sales volume has a positive impact on future price response, one should price lower than the level that optimizes short-term profit. Conversely, if a negative effect operates, price should be higher. Positive and negative effects could be operating simultaneously and the net impact would need to be assessed.

The first positive effect in Table 11-1 is an increase in sales volume, helping generate awareness. This is particularly true where the product's use is visible to others, as with automobiles or golf clubs. While awareness is only the first step to adoption of the product, it is a prerequisite. Second, increased sales volume may help to reduce customers'

TABLE 11-1

Current Sales Volume Demand Impacts on Future Demand

Positive Impact	Negative Impact
1. Awareness generation	1. Negative word of mouth
2. Uncertainty reduction/Positive word of mouth	2. Market saturation
3. Installed base or consumer franchise build-up	3. Exclusivity
4. Brand equity accumulation	
5. Network set-up	

uncertainty regarding the product's performance—leading to either new adoptions of the product or repeated use by adopters. Intuit in computer software and Lexus in automobiles have both followed a strategy of holding prices "low" upon entering the market, in order to gain adoptions and begin a favorable word-of-mouth process. Intuit introduced its personal financial software, Quicken, at a price of $35 to $45, supplemented by a program wherein the customer paid only shipping and handling costs and then paid for the product only if he liked it upon trial. The company did not even require that the product be returned if the customer found it unsatisfactory. Intuit's stated strategy is to have adopters of the product become "apostles," telling at least five friends about Quicken. Company research has shown that the "apostle" program works, being the major source of awareness and information about the product. Quicken became the market leader, so strongly positioned that Microsoft sold off its competing personal-finance software product and tried to buy Intuit for over $1.5 billion.[1]

In 1989 Toyota introduced the Lexus into the luxury segment of the U.S. market. While Lexus was a new brand name and not linked to Toyota in advertising, it was generally well known that the Lexus came from the company that had recently sold over one million mass-market cars in the United States in a year. The Toyota line-up was led by the Corolla and the Camry—cars with excellent reputations for reliability and good value but hardly the basis for a belief that Toyota could deliver a quality luxury car. The 1989 price for the Lexus LS400 was $35,000 and 16,000 units were sold. Figure 11-2 shows the evolution of prices for the LS400 model in the United States and its 48% price increase from 1989 to 1995. In 1990, sales jumped to 63,000. Early buyers of the LS400 provided extremely positive word of mouth for the product. In 1992 the *Consumer Reports* annual auto issue described the LS400 in glowing terms: "Combines advanced engineering with almost every conceivable comfort, safety, and convenience feature, making this the highest scoring car we've tested to date." The LS400 became the standard of excellence in the luxury segment, regularly topping customer satisfaction surveys. Any uncertainties customers had about Toyota's ability to deliver a superior luxury-car experience disappeared. So did prices in the $30,000 range. Toyota steadily boosted prices. The low price of 1989 helped Lexus penetrate the market quickly, get attention, and be seen as a great value. This is a classic example of a "penetration pricing" strategy. Lexus' 1989 price of $35,000 was too low if the objective was to maximize profits for 1989. Only when properly viewed as a tool for improving the demand situation for subsequent years can the $35,000 initial price be understood as the power pricing it was.

FIGURE 11-2

Lexus LS400 Price Evolution in U.S.A. 1989–1995 (Nominal Terms)

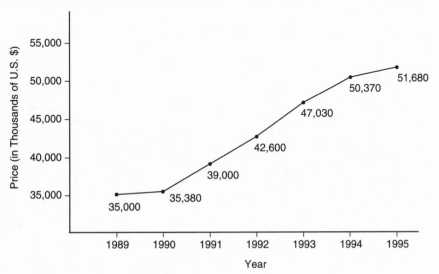

Another example of uncertainty reduction through low price and high sales volumes comes from the pharmaceutical market. As shown in Figure 11-3, Glaxo's U.S. pricing of its ulcer medication Zantac increased over time as the product's performance became more firmly established and uncertainties in the minds of prescribers and users faded away.[2]

We mentioned Glaxo's pricing in chapter 1 as a good example of adopting the customer-value perspective in pricing. Prior to Zantac's entry, Tagamet—the competing H2-antogonist medication from SmithKline—had become the best-selling pharmaceutical in the world, gradually decreasing price in the United States by 20% from 1977 to 1982 as Glaxo's U.S. entry neared. Some at Glaxo felt that as "second one in" to pioneer Tagamet, Zantac should be priced below Tagamet.[3] However, Sir Paul Girolami, the chief executive, recognized the inherent superiority of Zantac and decreed that it would be priced at a premium above Tagamet. Upon introduction in the United States, Zantac was priced at 56% above Tagamet. Glaxo and its U.S. marketing partner Roche, Inc. undertook the necessary marketing efforts to communicate Zantac's performance superiority. Over time, the safety profile of Zantac was convincingly established through sales rep visits to doctors and the growing number of clinical studies. Its efficacy was established in doctors' day-to-day interaction with patients who were now free of suffer-

FIGURE 11-3

Real Price of Tagamet and Zantac Daily Dosages (1982–1984 Dollars)

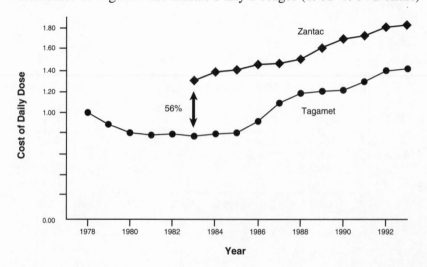

ing and the fear of stomach surgery. While pricing at 56% above the pioneer may have been a bold move by Glaxo, it was equally astute to move the pricing up with the increasing perceived value of the product to customers—a value that increased at an almost constant rate in real terms to a level 50% above the introductory price by its tenth year in the market. This was despite the entry of competing products marketed by Merck and Lilly after 1986.

The third positive factor in Table 11-1 is building the customer franchise or the installed base. Pricing "to get your foot in the door" at an account can be a useful approach. Intuit's low pricing is motivated by the "apostles" effect noted above, but also by the fact that an adopter of Quicken 2.0 is a good candidate for upgrading to version 3.0, 4.0, and so forth, as well as complementary products such as electronic bill paying. Thus, the pricing of the initial sale can be viewed as investment in the relationship. When Computer Associates entered the market to challenge Intuit, it gave away its product to the first million customers as an attempt to begin building the installed base. Similarly, the "launch carrier" of a new aircraft typically receives a favorable price. Universities are frequently offered attractive deals on computer hardware and software, serving as reference accounts and potential generators of future demand through students' familiarity with the products.

Related to this, the fourth impact is brand equity. In general, the power of the brand increases with its presence in the marketplace. Being among the volume leaders in the industry can improve the product's perceived value among customers.

Finally, the Network Effect applies in those situations where a product's utility increases with the number of other people who have it. An early example of this is telephones. More contemporary examples are found in computer software where, for example, Lotus 1-2-3 became the industry standard for spreadsheets. Its widespread adoption created value for individual customers, who had help nearby and the ability to transfer files within and between organizations. Similarly, the value of being able to send electronic mail increases with the number of people capable of receiving such messages. In order to spawn development of the network, prices are held below the level which would maximize short-term profits.

Many general recommendations have been offered about pricing over the product life cycle. However, these general concepts are not very useful. Empirical work has shown that it is very situation specific as to whether price elasticity increases or decreases over the product life cycle. Thus, each situation should be individually examined to assess the strength of each of these five dynamic effects. These strengths vary over time, typically being strongest during the early stages of the brand's life. At introduction, the dynamic effects can be such as to warrant a substantial reduction below the price that would maximize current profits—perhaps even below cost, as Computer Associates did in its "give-away" of the first million copies of CA-Simply Money. The appropriate reduction factor typically decreases over time, and the key is not to focus so long on pricing "to build the market" that the market is gone before profits are reaped. In markets with short life cycles, penetration pricing can be risky.

In addition to the five positive effects just discussed, Table 11-1 shows three possible negative impacts. The possibility of negative word of mouth must be carefully considered. A low penetration price that stimulates sales volume can create more demand than can be effectively managed. If there are uncertainties or potential "bugs" still in a product, a slower rollout—which could be effected by high prices—is recommended. A pharmaceutical company expected serious complications in one out of every million applications of a new drug. The company felt it could manage one or two of these incidents as it learned to specify the applications and potential side effects for the drug. Consequently, it wanted an initial price that would induce no more than one million applications in year one. As the manager put it, "If we price too low and generate ten million applications, we are sure to have ten serious problems on our hands. This would be the end of our product."

A simple example demonstrates the second possible negative effect, market saturation. Consider a set of potential adopters of a durable good who value it as follows:

% of Customers Valuing at:

- 25% at $100
- 25% at $90
- 25% at $70
- 25% at $40

The corresponding sales response curve is shown in Figure 11-4. Assume the firm's cost is $20 per unit. A price of $70 maximizes profit in the short term. Since the good is a durable, the only people left in the market are the 25% with $40 willingness-to-pay—so the strategy would then be to lower the price to this level. Given the assumed $20 unit cost, this results in an average unit contribution received of 3/4(50) + 1/4(20) = $42.50.

But maximizing short-term profit by charging $70 initially has taken too big a bite out of future demand. A better strategy is to charge $90 initially, selling to only 50% of the population. This results in 7% less profit initially but leaves 50% of the market still untapped for the future. Then selling to the 25% of the market who value the product at $70 at that price yields an average contribution of 1/2(70) + 1/4(50) = $47.50—so, even if one does not get to sell to the $40-valuation customers, contribution increases by 12% as a result of recognizing the finite market size and the market saturation effect. Clearly, if feasible, the best strategy is to step price down in accord with the sale response curve, practicing perfect time price customization, i.e., successively lowering the price from $100 to $90 to $70 to $40 and selling to an additional 25% of the market at each step. This yields an average contribution of $55, a 29% increase over the contribution yielded by maximizing short-term profit.

The third possible negative effect is exclusivity loss. Some products

FIGURE 11-4

Sales Response Curve for a Durable Good

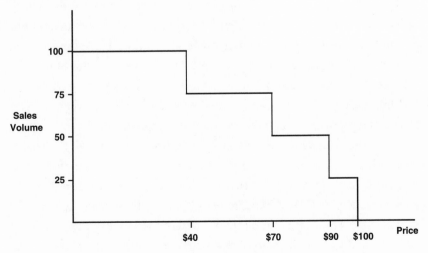

derive a portion of their value from their true target market from the fact that they are *not* priced within reach of many. For example, an elite luggage manufacturer's advertising plays off the familiar line "available at fine stores everywhere," and instead proclaims its exclusivity by proudly noting, "not available everywhere." A lower price now on a prestige item like a Hermes tie, a Mercedes automobile, or a stay at the Hotel Bristol in Paris may boost short-term profit—but at the cost of a decline in future value in the eyes of the long-term customer base.

As noted above, multiple dynamic factors may be operating simultaneously and the strength of any one force varies over time. Recognizing and managing these effects distinguish the efforts of power pricers.

DIRECT IMPACT OF CURRENT PRICE ON FUTURE DEMAND

The question often comes up: "If I am in an increase price mode, should I take lots of little price increases or bigger ones but fewer in number?" A chemical supplier facing this issue recently told us, "I have to get my prices up 8% this year—I would much rather try to do that selling in two 4% increases, rather then one 8% boost." This shows the practical concern with the concept of reference prices introduced in chapter 10. Current price often plays a role in customers developing an idea about what future prices should be. Deviations in the wrong direction from what the customer develops in his mind as a "should-be" price can have a strong negative sales impact. For example, consider an herbicide for crop protection priced at $12 for this selling season. In a static view of the world, we would say that the $12 price will determine a sales volume and limit our analysis to that. But would customers' reaction this selling season depend on the price last selling season? That is, would sales at the $12 price for this season depend on whether last season's price was: $12— and this year represented no price change; $8—and this year's was a 50% increase; or $16—and this year's was a 25% decrease?

There is a foundation for the answer that most people give: that the 50% price increase is quite different from the other scenarios, even though all net out at a $12 price for this season. Adaptation Theory,[4] which has been validated in a number of behavioral studies, holds that a response to a stimulus (future price) is determined by the strength of the stimulus and the relationship of that stimulus to preceding stimuli (current prices). Specifically in a pricing context, this effect was found in field experiments[5] which compared two scenarios:

Scenario A: product introduced at "normal" price and held at that level.

Scenario B: product introduced at lower than "normal" price for a brief period and then increased to the "normal" level of scenario A.

As would be expected from economic theory, during the introductory period scenario B's low prices generated sales higher than scenario A's. However, when both sets of stores sold at "normal" prices, the sales rate for scenario B was *less* than for scenario A for all five product categories studied, despite the equivalent prices. As Blattberg and Neslin[6] point out, there are a number of possible explanations of this result, but the data are consistent with Adaptation Theory, which basically holds that in scenario B the low introductory price became a reference price for some customers and when the "normal" price was instituted it was evaluated relative to the low introductory price. Hence, scenario B's sales at the "normal" price were depressed by the fact that "this is more than I paid before."

Figure 11-5 shows a common relationship between price increase or decrease and sales impact.[7] The customer develops a reference price, which becomes the foundation from which he judges the suitability of the actual price. A key point of Figure 11-5, as shown by the steep downward slope of the curve moving from the origin to the left of the reference price, is that the negative impact of a price "increase" relative to the reference price is greater than an equivalent price "decrease," i.e., the effect is asymmetric. If the actual price is above the reference price, the customer sees this is a "loss"—giving up more money than he expected to have to. The underlying theory, Prospect Theory, holds that losses "hurt" more than equivalent sized gains "please." How the customer develops this "reference price" depends on the situation and the actions of the firm. In a competitive market with lots of similar alternatives to choose from and price information easily available, the customer tends to use *competitive* prices as the key input for developing a reference point, e.g., "A Sony TV set should cost five percent more than an equivalent Hitachi or RCA." However, in markets where the customer is involved in a relationship with a seller and in-kind competitors are few or their price information hard to obtain, the *firm's own past prices* become key: "Since his labor cost went up three percent last year due to the new union contract, I'll accept a two to three percent price increase over last year, but anything more than that is just not acceptable."

Power pricers account for this future effect in setting and communicating prices. If the market situation is such that customers use the firm's past prices in forming reference prices, this is an argument for more price increases, each of a smaller amount than infrequent but larger increases. In addition, the power pricer manages reference price formation on the customer's part by messages directed to the market. For example, as suggested by the customer quote above, information about factor cost increases might be transmitted to the market. These implementation issues will be discussed more fully in chapter 12. In the heavy electrical industry, Sultan notes, "Utility customers wanted their equipment price increases to be 'cost-justified.' The rate of inflation in factor prices provided a handy benchmark for what appeared to be a just and reasonable rate of increase in prices. . . . [This] determined the basic upward trend

FIGURE 11-5

Asymmetric Impact of Prices Above and Below Reference

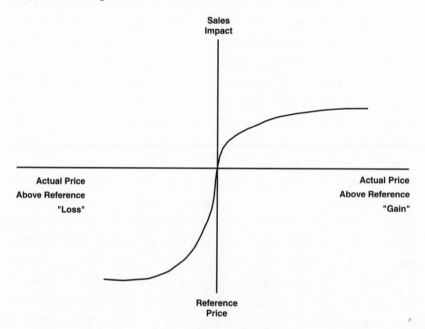

line for turbine generator prices under buoyant market conditions."[8]
While messages accompanying the prices can be very useful in shaping
reference price formation, the actual price paid most recently by the customer and his perception of recent product pricing (even if he has not
been in the market) are typically important, and ignoring this dynamic
effect is dangerous. As noted above, low penetration pricing, as with the
Lexus, can be a wise strategy but firms must be very careful about setting low prices that may come to represent a drag on future pricing. Noting prices as "special introductory prices" can help to mitigate this.

A related second impact of current prices is on the timing of purchases.
The well-known story of a potential customer for a personal computer
saying, "No matter what I buy or what I pay, I know I would be making a
big mistake—because I will be able to get it twenty-five percent cheaper
in six months" has some foundation to it. According to the data of the European Information Technology Observatory, the retail price of a Pen-
tium-based computer selling in Europe for $6,000 in mid-1993 fell 46%
by mid-1994 and then another 30% from mid-1994 to mid-1995. Some
describe the computer industry by a "2% per month" rule; that is, they anticipate that prices for a given model will decline 2% per month or
roughly 25% per year. What if the customer adopts this viewpoint? Unless
a customer really has to have a computer, how does he ever decide that
now is the time to buy? A steady succession of price decreases may erode
near-term demand as customers try to postpone purchase as long as possible. Even though they value the product above current prices, they see a
net benefit in riding the declining price curve a while longer.

There is no general answer to the price-increase question we started
this section with. It all depends on how reference prices are formed, and
that varies with the situation. The power pricer recognizes the importance of reference price formation, understands the formation process,
and manages that process and gauges prices in light of it.

CURRENT PRICE AND FUTURE COSTS

The third linkage in Figure 11-1 is the indirect impact of price on future
cost,

Price → Quantity Sold → Future Costs

A well-known form of this impact is the experience curve productivity model, popularized by the Boston Consulting Group in the early 1970s. As shown in Figure 11-6, this model posited a particular relationship between unit cost and the cumulative volume of production, i.e., unit cost declined in real times by a fixed percentage with each doubling of accumulated volume. Empirical support for this model has been reported in many industries, with cost declines generally between 15% and 25% with each doubling of cumulative volume.

The particular form of the relationship between cumulative volume and unit cost is situation specific. The important point is that if there is a link in which unit cost systematically declines with cumulative volume, then pricing in a way that maximizes short-term profit leads to prices higher than those which would lead to maximum profits over the long term.

Rather, one should "price to get down the learning curve." Dolan and Jeuland,[9] for example, show that if the demand situation is basically unchanging, pricing should anticipate the experience-based cost declines. Thus, the optimal strategy is at all times to have a price less than that which would maximize short-term profit. Prices should be set low to penetrate the market—with the low unit margins being offset by both higher volumes and lower costs in the future.

FIGURE 11-6

Experience Curve Model with Costs Declining by $(1 - C)$% for Each Doubling of Accumulated Volume (Typical Value of $C = .2$)

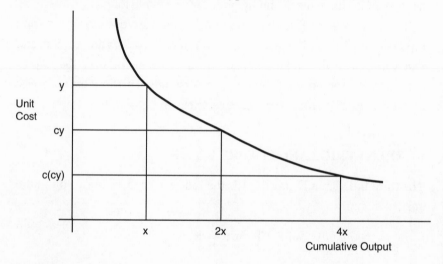

Experience-curve-based pricing can be a good guide to long-term profit. Boston Consulting Group's product portfolio matrix, with its cash cows found in businesses with high market share and low industry growth rates, was a very influential strategic framework growing out of experience-curve thinking. As Brock[10] noted in his analysis of the computer industry, "Market share can be thought of as a form of capital that is purchased through competitive actions and that can be sold through raising prices . . ." However, naive application of experience-curve pricing concepts has been disastrous for some firms as they pursued market share blindly; they attained share leadership but in a Pyrrhic victory as the share points failed to produce profit. The battle for share led to price wars and severely depressed prices as the product life cycle was exhausted during the battle. As discussed previously in chapter 4, a balanced look at market share and industry profitability is required.

CURRENT PRICE IMPACT ON COMPETITION

Chapter 4 discussed the interplay of competitive prices. In particular, we noted how the power pricer considers likely competitive reaction in price and other marketing mix variables with an eye to industry profitability. As shown in dynamic effect #4 of Figure 11-1, current price can have a broader impact on potential competitors' entry decisions and participants' capacity planning, which in turn impact future price realization.

The rate of capacity utilization in an industry has been shown to be a key to price realization in a number of situations; see for example Sultan's[11] detailed study of the electrical oligopoly, which linked price movements to the "competitive zeal" of the players—which, in turn, was impacted by "the state of the factory," i.e., the backlog and capacity utilization. The median retail price of a typical passenger tire in the United States dropped over 25% during the 1980s as capacity utilization slipped to 76%.[12]

Memory-chip prices had been falling over 25% per year through 1992. A 4MB DRAM chip declined from $38 in 1990 to less than $12 in 1992. From 1992 to 1995, however, prices stabilized and increased slightly to just above $12 as worldwide demand increased fourfold over the time period. This boom in demand exceeded the short-term ability of suppliers to increase capacity, and the demand/supply imbalance resulted in the four-year stabilization of prices. However in early 1996, with lots of new capacity on line, the supply of memory chips moved to a surplus, driving the spot market price from $12.50 in November 1995 to $8.50 in February 1996.[13]

Potential competitors' perceptions of "industry attractiveness" impact entry and capacity investment decisions. Scherer[14] notes Reynolds International Pen Corporation selling the ballpoint pens it pioneered at prices of $12 and more—15 times its production cost. This "precipitated the entry of some 100 competitors." He cites similar cases in industries ranging from instant mashed potatoes to aluminum extrusions. While it is generally difficult to deter entry into a market without either patent protection or a sustainable cost advantage, competitors' perceptions of the likely margins attainable certainly impact their decisions on capacity and entry or exit.

Here, again, pricing actions must be considered in light of the legal environment; in the United States, in particular, the Sherman Act makes attempts to monopolize a market unlawful. One specific prohibited activity is predatory pricing, which "includes cutting prices to unreasonably low or unprofitable levels in markets where competition is encountered in order to drive others from the market."[15] The appropriate way to judge when an action is or is not "predatory" is the subject of continuing debate and not always a simple matter. A commonly used guide though is the Areeda-Turner test, which defines predatory pricing as yielding a return less than either average variable cost or marginal cost.

The power pricer maps out and attempts to control, as far as is lawful, the number of competitors, capacity, and degree of product differentiation in his industry. The pattern of entry to an industry can be quite context specific, depending upon the particular dissemination of knowhow, patent expirations, and inventions in that industry. For example, Figure 11-7(a) shows the number of suppliers of H-2 antagonist-type ulcer medications in the United States, while Figure 11-7(b) shows the number of suppliers of a particular chemical product from introduction to product maturity. In the chemical example, one only new supplier entered the market in the first four years while 12 entered in the last two years as the product entered its maturity stage.[16]

FIGURE 11-7(A)

Number of Competitions in H2-Antagonists Ulcer Drug Medication in U.S.A. as Function of Years Since Tagamet's 1977 Entry

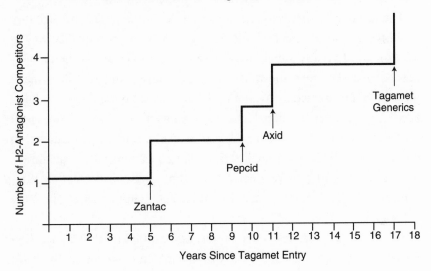

FIGURE 11-7(B)

Number of Chemical Product Suppliers Over Time

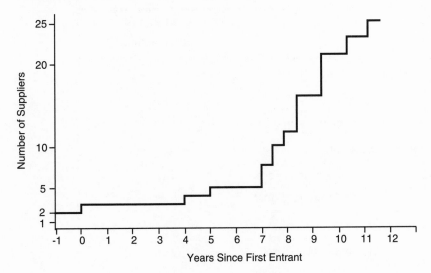

Three factors are now emerging to create a condition of limited *core product* differentiation opportunities. First, in many situations, industry standards are emerging. In order to "play the game" competitors must conform to these standards. Reinforcing this is the behavior of sophisticated buyers, who tightly define their own specifications.

The attitude is *"atarimae hinshitsu,"* a Japanese phrase for "quality taken for granted."[17] Second, the ability to produce in a quality way is widespread. In many situations, the key innovations are at the component level rather than the finished product level, and suppliers make these components widely available. Want to get into the computer business? Go see Intel for chips! The camera business? Go see Honeywell for autofocus mechanisms! Third, and relatedly, "clones" are quicker to imitate and deliver good quality. In many consumer goods categories, private-label firms now produce at a level of quality acceptable to consumers. This has created tremendous price and margin pressure in many situations.

For example, Northern Telecom lost $60 million on its Vantage Key System over three years as Pacific Rim manufacturers continually drove

TABLE 11-2

Approximate Rate of Annual Price Decline for Consumer Durables

	Average Annual Rate of Price Decline
Television	
B&W 1971–1984	3.5%
color 1971–1984	4.0%
Stereo Equipment	
turntable 1978–1989	4.5%
CD player 1983–1989	20.0%
Telephone	
corded 1978–1989	8.0%
cordless 1980–1989	14.0%
cellular 1986–1989	30.0%

prices down. Even in as hi-tech an industry as jet engines, *core product* differentiation is limited and "many engines have become commodities, albeit multimillion-dollar commodities."[18] This has led to intense competition between the Big Three suppliers—General Electric, Pratt & Whitney, and Rolls-Royce—particularly as the number of new orders declined by 80% from 1989 to 1994. Many in the industry claimed that Rolls-Royce captured Singapore Airlines' $1.8 billion order for engines on 61 Boeing 777 jets only at prices that would cost Rolls-Royce money. Bayus[19] provides data on the price trends of a number of consumer durables, as summarized in Table 11-2.

What to do about this? The first step is of course to understand the likely evolution of competitive intensity and resulting price pressure. One should understand whether the industry the firm participates in is one likely to be subject to price and margin erosion—or are there forces which will tend to support the price level?

This understanding needs to be developed at the level of the *market segment*—not the overall market—since segments' price evolution can differ. For example, Figure 11-8 shows the evolution of average selling prices of personal computers by market segment.[20]

As shown, while the price in the home hobby market declined by

FIGURE 11-8

Average Selling Price of Personal Computers by Market Segment (in thousands of dollars)

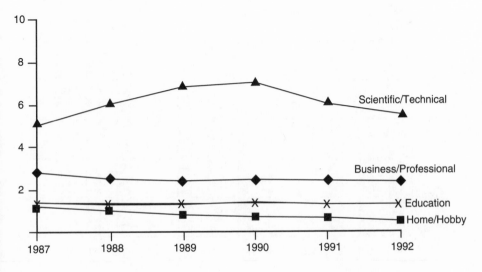

40% from 1987–92, it increased by 17% in the scientific/technical market. Different forces underlie the price evolution. The home hobby market was driven by cost declines and competition. But in the scientific/technical segment, added value in the computers, i.e., a different product mix, drove the price increases. One needs to understand whether the underlying force in the market is productivity/cost or value. Figure 11-9 shows the development of the average price paid for a new car in Germany from 1980 to 1991. The 1991 car is much improved in terms of performance and reliability and thus better customer benefit drives pricing up. In contrast, Figure 11-10 shows the price of wheat in real terms from 1913 to 1984, with productivity improvements driving the price down in a regular fashion. Figure 11-11 shows the variations in the real price for a haircut—a service not subject to great productivity gains or change in definition of the product and its value to customers. In real terms, this service price remained relatively constant from 1910 to 1984.

The second step is to follow the lead of Northern Telecom and take a "total-product" view to develop an effective differentiation beyond the core product itself. Based on a full understanding of buyer economics (to be discussed in chapter 13), Northern totally redefined the product from a telephone set or "Key System" to a "Key system delivered to installation site within 48 hours of order with installation times 25%

FIGURE 11-9

Average Price Paid for a New Car in Germany in 1980–91

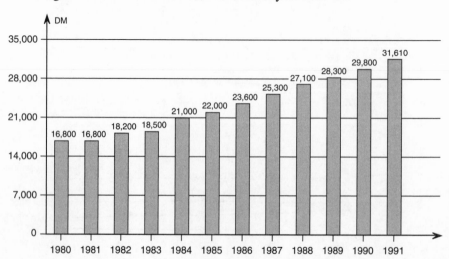

FIGURE 11-10

Real Price of Wheat, 1913–1984 (per 100 kg.)

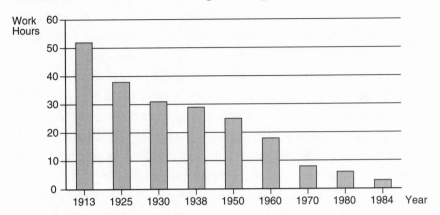

below historic levels." A serious problem for resellers had been the re-
supply times and the inventory they had to hold—when prices were regularly falling and new products being introduced. Northern responded to
this by providing for direct delivery to the reseller's customers, obviat-
ing the need for the reseller to make any investment in inventory. While
the core product Northern made had somewhat improved reliability, the
key was in providing real customer value by *augmenting* the core product with services people were willing to pay for. This differentiation re-

FIGURE 11-11

Real Price of a Haircut in Germany, 1910–1984

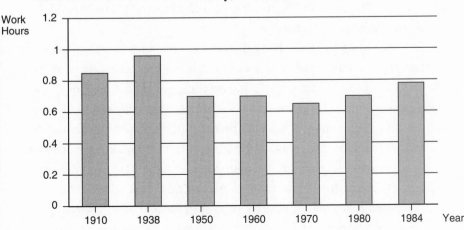

lieved Northern of the Pacific Rim manufacturers' price pressure as the latter could not supply the newly defined product-*plus*-service bundle. Thus, while industry prices continued a downward trend, Northern was able to free itself from the trend—stabilizing prices over time while costs continued to decline, generating margin improvement.

The critical part of differentiation through value-added services is to be sure that the services do in fact add customer value beyond what it costs to provide them. For example, a medical-instruments company provided (a) next-day delivery, (b) service availability from 9 to 5 on weekdays, but (c) no dedicated hot line. Customers complained and, when asked what they wanted, answered predictably: (a) deliver within 10 minutes, (b) 24-hours-a-day, 7-days-a week service availability, and (c) a dedicated hot line. The appropriate insight, however, came through application of conjoint measurement as described in chapter 3. In particular, the analysis showed the *value*—or customers' willingness to pay—for alternative levels of service differentiation to be as shown in Figure 11-12. On service response time, "within four hours" provided a significant customer value relative to cost, but the added value of going to a two-hour response time did not come close to justifying the cost. Analogously, for the service availability dimension, extending hours to 7 A.M.–10 P.M. was advisable; but going to the highest service level of 24 hours a day/7 days a week implied great cost and very small real benefit, or willingness to pay of customers. The dedicated hot line was worth the small added cost. This, then, is an example where to pursue differentiation by *maximizing* all service dimensions would have been to fall into a fatal trap: differentiation for its own sake and incurring cost beyond the value delivered to customers.

Understanding the underlying drivers of entry, such as patent expiration, component availability, and global initiatives, is necessary to assess the likely evolution of the firm's industry and possible means of favorably influencing it. Freedom from competitive price pressure, however, comes from innovation in the core product. Power pricing cannot compensate for lack of innovation in the long term. Lasting differentiation in the core product is generally becoming harder to achieve and one must also consider the true value to customers of adding services, which requires rigorous analysis of customers' cost in use and willingness to pay.

There is a variety of forces that drive the evolution of supply and

FIGURE 11-12

Price Value of Services—A Medical-Technology Case

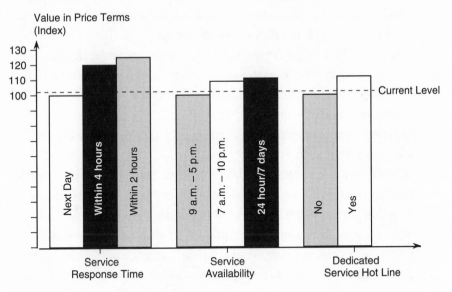

demand conditions over time. The power pricer is not myopic; he does not focus only on short-term profits. In addition to understanding the likely evolution of factors that he cannot control, like consumer disposable income or legal contexts, he considers the four dynamic factors set out in Figure 11-1 and discussed in this chapter. These dynamic factors link the present and the future. Reaping the harvest now and investing in the future are alternatives to be traded off in power pricing.

SUMMARY

A power pricer knows when to change price. In the last chapter, we considered short-term time customization, and here we have focused on the long term. In summary:

- Power pricers consider the dynamic effects as well as current effects of their pricing.
- The four major dynamic effects on current price identified in Figure 11-1 are:
  - future customer perception through reference price impacts, which provide a context for judging future prices.

- future demand working through the current sales volume. There are both positive and negative effects of high initial volume to consider.
- the future competitive situation, as entry and capacity decisions are made in response to industry attractiveness.
- future costs through the current sales volume variable. In many situations, costs have been shown to follow the experience curve. This promotes lower pricing initially to penetrate the market, build share, and gain cost position.
- Ignoring these dynamic effects can be very detrimental to the firm's long-term profitability.
- In today's market, relief from competitive pricing pressure comes from innovation. Power pricing does not substitute for substantive innovation, which increases the customer's perceived value of the firm offering. However, significant differentiation in the *core-product* offering is becoming increasingly difficult to maintain. Opportunity does exist to differentiate through value-added services. This requires rigorous analysis to ensure true value added rather than costly response to customer whims.

A power pricer helps the industry to realize a long-term price path that promotes industry profitability. His knowledge about and management of dynamic effects are key to this.

PART III

Implementation in the Organization

12

Organizing for Power Pricing

INTRODUCTION

How well are managers equipped with the informational and organizational means to develop and implement power pricing strategies? Usually not too well—as our findings show and the literature confirms!

In many cases, the information is just not available inside the company. For example, in a study at a company prominent on the list of the ten most admired American firms in the annual *Fortune* survey, we found that quantitative information on price response is available only in about 30% of its business units. Similarly, the manager of truck pricing at Navistar International, describing the introduction of their new pricing system, reported that "the first and most formidable problem in beginning a profit-based pricing strategy was the lack of basic profitability information."[1] Once a careful analysis was conducted, Navistar found that their fundamental assumption about the relationship between price level and profitability was incorrect. Less fully featured, low-priced trucks delivered higher margins than fully featured, higher-priced ones! The study elaborated, "Causes of the observed price-profit relationships were not understood, indicating several shortcomings in costing, accounting, and reporting systems." We have found this to be a common difficulty. In particular, many firms fail to understand the cost and value to the customer of "specials"—options or products not part of the standard line—and consequently underprice them.

Power pricing typically requires the involvement of various functions with different information backgrounds, but problems can arise if this involvement process is not carefully managed. The experience of a large electronics company is typical. Three functional areas—controlling, marketing, and sales—participated in pricing decisions. However, none of these functions had complete information. Controlling knew little about the effects of price in the market; marketing was not well informed on the cost-volume relationship; and sales was unfamiliar with the pricing methodology. No one understood the overall situation well enough or saw it as their responsibility to bring the pieces together in a fruitful way. In this environment, each party relied on mechanical formulas. The control people relied on cost; the sales people looked mainly at competitive prices; marketing proved unable to represent the customer side or to integrate all relevant information. The result was chaos, with conflicting pricing recommendations and no foundation or forum for a useful debate on the issue.

A chemical company suffered from the same lack of coordination: it had a pricing process in which marketing set the list price for the product. The sales organization then administered the discount schedule in the field, with some oversight from the finance/accounting function. Between 1990 and 1994, marketing pushed list prices up 22%. However, under competitive pressure, the sales organization responded to these list price increases by increasing the level of existing discounts and even inventing some new discounts to add to the stew! The net result? Actual prices rose by only 3.5%. The other 18% of list price increase was merely discounted away—and company headquarters was unaware of this while it was going on. Subsequently, management decided to prune back the "discount jungle" radically, reducing the pricing authority of the sales force. The focus at the company now is on actual price received rather than on "list prices." Price realization has improved.

A medical-products company had a similar price realization improvement through pushing decision-making authority back inside the organization from the field level. A new general manager set up a reporting system to flag high-discount situations. He commented,

When I started here about a year ago, I asked for a daily printout of all orders in which the products were sold at the lowest price possible given our discounts and approved concessions. In the first months, there were hundreds of items on that list every day. Now the printout contains approximately ten such items per day and these usually have been okayed by myself. Despite this stricter policy we have lost very few customers, but our profit has strongly improved.

In a British study on price decisions, 20% of the respondents could not specify where the pricing authority was located in their organization.[2] This finding is consistent with our own experience that it is hardly ever clear who is involved, what their role is, and what relative power they have in price decision making. In many cases, managers in one function area complain that they do not know how other functions influence prices and that such information is intentionally withheld in order to strengthen function positions. Goal conflicts are common in pricing. While finance/accounting tend to strive for high margins, sales people mostly pursue unit sales volume or sales-revenue objectives. Frequently sales incentive structures induce inconsistencies. In many firms the sales force is compensated on revenue, not margins, but nevertheless it has some pricing latitude, and thus an influence on the margin. For example,

FIGURE 12-1

Sales Commission Structure

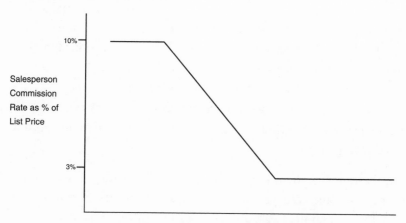

Discount % Granted Customer of List Price

Figure 12-1 shows the sales-force-compensation scheme of one company that left discounting authority to the field. The commission rate decreased with the size of the discount granted to customers, but leveled off at 3%. Consequently, the sales force had no incentive to limit discounting when it reached a high level—which it often does for big accounts. The Navistar study comments on the effects of goal conflicts: "The pricing process was inherently unstable, since there was no formal authority responsible for resolving conflicting objectives."[3] This statement holds for many companies we have encountered.

These cases prove that there is a large potential for improvement in the information, organization, and implementation of pricing strategies in most companies.

WHAT THIS CHAPTER WILL DO

This chapter addresses the following questions.

1. How should the pricing process be organized? How—and what—pricing information should be collected?
2. Who should have decision-making authority on price, and how should the various functions cooperate in making price decisions?
3. How should pricing actions be implemented—specifically with regard to preparation, communication, and negotiation?

Knowing the answers to these questions will help you to:

1. identify and design a process to collect adequate information
2. organize the pricing process effectively, getting the various functions to cooperate constructively
3. allocate the price decision authority properly
4. support price moves through concerted actions in other marketing instruments in order to achieve a successful implementation of profit-maximizing prices

On these issues, there is no adequate set of general rules to follow. Rather the specific context is key. Consequently, our focus in this chapter is on providing the key considerations to structure managers' thinking on these matters.

ORGANIZING PRICING INFORMATION AND PROCESS

The general information requirements for power pricing have been laid out in the preceding chapters. But it has also become clear that pricing situations show an amazing variety. Accordingly, the information to be procured and the process of analysis and decision making have to be geared to the specific situation. A product with a sales potential of a billion dollars warrants a much deeper analysis than one with only a million-dollar sales potential. Time is another essential aspect in preparing price decisions. Pricing of a major innovation may involve analyses over years, with repeated checks of cost and demand aspects. If, however, a quick reaction to a competitive move is necessary, a time-consuming analysis is hardly feasible as timeliness is critical. If a price is effectively fixed for a relatively long period of time (e.g., a year), the information requirements and opportunities for changing it are different from those in a situation where prices are easily adjustable on very short bases and have little carryover effect. Major price repositionings justify deeper research than minor price adjustments in the course of a product's life cycle.

The deployment of the full methodological and informational arsenal of power pricing as described in this book is particularly recommended under the following conditions:

- for products with large sales and profit potential
- for new products
- for major price changes/price repositioning
- if price adjustment opportunities are rare
- if a large pricing latitude is expected
- if uncertainty on price response or competitive reactions is high

Essentially, these aspects are related to two dimensions: profit potential and uncertainty. But even in cases where the application of the full arsenal is too costly or too time-consuming, rigorous thinking is still required. Simple methods—like expert judgment, characterized by systematic involvement of the various functions, explicitly considering both the cost and demand sides, and focusing on key aspects of the problem—will always improve your pricing. In general, given the highly leveraged effect of price on the bottom line, the costs of pricing analyses are more than offset by the higher profits resulting from setting the right price.

PROCESS FOR A NEW PRODUCT

Given the profit implications and uncertainty, the most comprehensive information collection and price analysis is usually done for major new products.

We illustrate the analysis process for a new product with a case from the private telecommunications sector. Initial considerations on target prices started with the R&D process about five years prior to the market launch. The actual pricing project of six phases and eight months' duration, as shown in Figure 12-2, began 18 months before the planned launch date.

A "kick-off workshop" was held to define the problem and formally set up the process by which it would be addressed. Two teams were set up: the project team and the Steering Committee. The Steering Committee consisted of two top managers and one outside consultant and was charged with keeping the process on track. Phases 2 and 3 began concurrently. A workshop for the project team got "buy-in" to the research methodology. Phase 2 was a two-month analysis of the firms in the market, particularly their pricing policies and market position, so that likely competitive reaction to entry and pricing could be assessed. Phase 3 was directed to research potential customers across five countries. Eight hundred potential customers were computer interviewed using the conjoint measurement methodology described in chapter 3. Field data were ana-

FIGURE 12-2

Process Chart for a Major Pricing Project

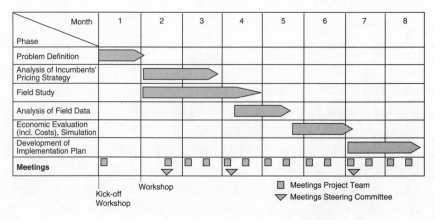

lyzed in phase 4; phase 5 was the development and use of a decision-support model to simulate alternative pricing and marketing scenarios for the firm and competitors. The team then spent two months (phase 6) developing the implementation plan, which was presented to top management about seven months before product launch. Discussions and decision processes at the top management level took one month. Thus, six months prior to launch there was a fully developed and supported plan. This allowed adequate time to develop the implementation details. This is a good example of what a process supporting a multibillion-dollar sales-potential product should look like. It featured broad involvement of company functions, formal definition of a process and timetable at the beginning, adequate description of research methodologies to management before their use, in-depth competitor analysis, a separate in-depth consideration of implementation issues, and a start date that was early enough to permit impact on decision making.

A second case concerning reaction to entry involved a more limited process at a leading manufacturer of special optical products. For years, its major competitor had been following its price lead; then a Korean company entered the market and began undercutting the market price—initially with little success. What should the incumbent market leader do? Since the customer base was highly concentrated, a representative survey was not considered an appropriate tool. Instead, an internal analysis was carried out, focusing on the most important customers. A project team developed several competitive scenarios, which were then discussed in two workshops with all functions involved. In addition, unstructured interviews were carried out with four especially trustworthy customers. Those proved to be very helpful in assessing customers' responses and collecting information on the new competitor. Based on this qualitative information, the project team recommended not cutting price across the board, relying instead on more account-specific responses. The management adopted this proposal and it was immediately implemented. The whole process from kick-off to implementation took only seven weeks.

These two cases illustrate that the methodology and complexity of pricing analyses should be attuned to the time constraints, potential benefits, and costs of a particular situation. An important point here is to tailor the approach to the potential of the situation—and not just accept the industry's conventional practice. One needs to benchmark against the best practice anywhere, not just best competitor practice.

We find huge variation between industries. In the car-rental industry, "[E]ven the most sophisticated companies lag far behind the airlines. Hertz can require as much as 24 hours to put a price increase into the main reservations systems used by travel agents—something the airlines can do instantly. . . . Budget had no idea what its competitors were doing; when a competitor changed its prices, Budget sometimes didn't notice for days—a factor in its huge losses."[4] Many industrial firms face serious problems regarding relevant pricing data. For example, Mohan and Holstein state, "Unlike consumer-product firms, industrial product companies are typically data-poor, or more precisely, marketing-data-poor."[5] The reasons are that (a) data needed for pricing are not collected (e.g., data on price response); (b) if useful data have been collected (as by the sales force in call reports), they are not captured in the computer; and (c) if data are available, they are poorly organized or not current.

The profit potential of price customization unleashed by having the right data has been established. Now, the opportunities for efficient data collection and analysis due to modern information technologies are everywhere. In the consumer-goods sector scanner data should be more widely used to improve price decisions. Many sectors with directly measurable customer response, such as direct marketing or telecommunications, do not exploit their measurement possibilities to understand price response deeply.

PRICING ANALYSIS: DO IT YOURSELF OR OUTSOURCE IT?

The application of the sophisticated pricing methods described in this book requires a high level of expertise and specialization. Should a company employ its own pricing specialists or hire consultants as needed?

In-house specialists or specialized departments are feasible for large companies with broad product lines and frequent major price decisions. The sought-after advantage is that these people can combine in-depth market and company knowledge with mastery of the full spectrum of research methods. The challenges for an internal pricing department are: (a) acceptance of the work by the line managers,[6] who are often suspicious of these methods and may be reluctant to accept the recommendations, and (b) keeping the internal know-how up to date. The development in new research methods is rapid and a continuous influx of new knowledge is crucial.

Many companies will be better off not employing pricing specialists permanently but hiring them if necessary. Strategic price decisions that warrant large-scale studies (as illustrated in Figure 12-2) are relatively rare in most firms. They are comparable to strategic projects typically done by outside consultants rather than to routine market research studies. Consistent with this observation, consultants are increasingly involved in pricing decisions. The driving factors behind this trend are the higher sophistication of the research methods and the recognition that pricing offers great potential for profit improvement.

ORGANIZATIONAL STRUCTURES FOR POWER PRICING

Pricing Authority

As noted above, in many organizations it is not fully clear who decides on prices or who is involved and to what degree. Mostly, finance/accounting/cost control and sales/marketing participate in the price decision. Often, general management has the final say. The findings in literature on these issues are scarce and somewhat equivocal. Table 12-1 gives the results of two across-industries studies on the allocation of the pricing authority.[7] The Atkin and Skinner study asked about the "ultimate decision authority"; the one in the German journal *asw* asked about "involvement." General management and sales/marketing management have a particularly strong influence, but the role of finance/accounting/cost control should not be underestimated. According to our experience, the latter function's weight is usually stronger than it appears in the table, particularly in its veto power.

Notably, the Atkin-Skinner study indicates that in about one-fifth of the companies it was not clear who has the final say in pricing decisions—a finding highly consistent with our own experiences.

Proper pricing requires input from both the marketing/sales side and the controlling/finance/accounting side. The recommended flow of information is illustrated in Figure 12-3.

TABLE 12-1

Allocation of Pricing Authority in Two Studies

Function	Atkin and Skinner Study Ultimate Decision Authority		*asw* Study Always Involved
	List Prices	**Negotiated Prices**	
General Management	38%	35%	65%
Sales Manager			76%
	31%	31%	
Marketing Manager			54%
Manager Finance/ Accounting/Cost Control	5%	5%	28%
Key Account Manager			40%
Manager Market Research			11%
Do not know	21%	24%	

Precisely where in the hierarchy the two sides flow together and the final decision is made depends on the specific situation. The authority should be placed higher

- the more important a specific product is for the company
- the better high-level managers are informed on products and markets
- the more homogeneous and less dynamic the markets are
- the more critical the consistency of pricing across segments is
- the less the culture and behavior of the lower organizational units are aligned to broad corporate strategies and goals
- the more important consistent signaling to competitors is.

The Marketing-Finance Interface

The necessity of cooperation between marketing/sales and finance/accounting/cost control in preparing pricing decisions is obvious. How these two functions interact can have a strong impact on the quality of pricing. The finance side naturally approaches the problem from a cost-plus and margin perspective. The marketing/sales people are more influenced by aspects like value to the customer, price acceptance/response,

FIGURE 12-3

Decision Authority and Participation in Pricing

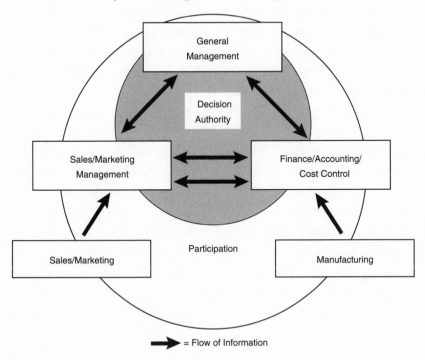

= Flow of Information

and competitive prices. As a result, the finance people usually prefer a higher price than the market experts. But even within the marketing/sales group a discrepancy is typical, with the sales people usually opting for a lower price than the marketing managers.[8]

Conflicts are unavoidable when several functions with possibly different goals are involved. In practice various approaches are used to deal with and resolve these conflicts:

• In the auto industry the "four-eyes principle" is prevalent in pricing: two people, one from the finance and the other from the sales side, have to find a consensus on the price, which they then recommend to the general manager. If the two sides adopt rational positions and refrain from power playing, this approach seems reasonable. We have experienced cases where it worked very well—but also situations where the two functions did not cooperate constructively.

• In the consumer-goods industry, multifunctional teams are frequently used to address the pricing problem. Unlike the first approach, where the two sides usually come up with their own proposals that they then discuss and "unify," the multifunctional team starts earlier and develops one price proposal. The team members are more broadly informed on one another's concerns, but the price information may also be more superficial than under the first approach. And the decision process can be more time consuming.

- A third approach is to employ a price manager who collects the information from both sides and develops his own price recommendation. He reports to the general manager. We observe this function increasingly in industries like airlines, telecommunications, services, pharmaceuticals, and industrial goods. Due to our as yet limited experience, we refrain from giving a definite recommendation on this model, but it seems an interesting and promising alternative. Ideally the price manager has worked on both sides during his career and is able to unite the financial and the marketing perspectives. It is crucial that the price manager be given sufficient power, since he may have to defend his position against two usually powerful players, the finance officer and the sales manager.

Delegating Pricing Authority to the Sales Force

In many markets, the buyer does not just accept the list prices set by the seller; instead, prices are negotiated between the two parties. In these cases, one has to decide whether and how much pricing authority should be delegated to the sales force.

In practice the following forms exist.

- The sales people have far-reaching (in extreme cases, full) pricing authority
- The sales people have limited pricing authority, negotiating prices or discounts down to a certain limit. Sometimes these limits of authority are differentiated according to hierarchical level (e.g., sales person 10%, group leader 20%, sales director 30%)
- the sales person has no pricing authority; each deviation from the list price must be approved by a central organizational unit.

The delegation of pricing authority to the sales force is structurally similar to the problem of delegating pricing competence to foreign subsidiaries, as discussed in chapter 6. And the problem is equally emotional. One author comments, "Letting the sales force set prices is about the same as hiring a fox to guard the henhouse."[9] This position is a little naive, since there can be good reasons for such a delegation in a particular situation.

Reasons for the delegation of pricing authority to the sales force are:

- the role of the salesperson is upgraded, thus improving his motivation
- the salesperson may be in the best position to assess the customer's willingness to pay, and thus to achieve the optimal customization of prices
- pricing is very flexible and delays are avoided when the salesperson can decide on the spot whether to accept a price or not
- the salesperson can react very quickly to changing market and competitive conditions
- negotiations often involve complex interactions between the precise product specification and price; the process can become very cumbersome if the salesperson has to consult frequently with management
- if the incentives are set right, i.e., if the salesperson is remunerated based on contribution and not on sales revenue, the objectives of the firm and the sales person are identical; hence, given his better customer knowledge, the salesperson should have a good measure of authority

But there are also aspects that speak against delegating pricing authority to sales people:

- the salesperson is sometimes too compliant in the negotiation situation (There is strong pressure to consummate the deal. As Nimer puts it, "there is the temptation to always play it safe to get the order."[10])
- the centralization of pricing authority relieves the salesperson psychologically (According to practitioners, most salespeople are afraid of the price negotiation. And the purchasing person may put less pressure on the salesperson if the latter does not have pricing authority. "An old purchasing axiom is: 'Find out if the salesperson can reduce the price. If he can, insist that he do so' "[11])

- centralizing pricing authority is more likely to prevent inconsistencies across customers, segments, or countries
- in some cases, the price decision requires complex analysis of costs, capacity effects, and so forth which cannot be effectively done decentrally or on the spot.

These pros and cons indicate that there is no simple solution to the problem. The empirical evidence relating to the wisdom of delegating pricing authority to the sales force is limited. Stephenson, Cron, and Frazier analyzed the relation between pricing authority and profitability for 108 hospital-supply companies.[12] They found a negative correlation between profit and the degree of delegation to the sales force. Wiltinger found that the specific customer knowledge of the sales representatives, the importance of the single customer, the customer's expectation of instant price quotation, and the sales force's orientation toward organizational goals have significant effects on the impact of delegation of pricing authority to the sales force.[13] These findings are largely consistent with the qualitative recommendations listed above.

In summary, the best course regarding delegation of pricing authority to the sales force is contingent upon the specific situation. Our own experience suggests using caution. It seems better to err on the restrictive side, i.e., less delegating rather than too much. In any case, the incentive system of the sales force must be made consistent with the company's objectives if pricing authority is delegated to a significant degree.

Implementing Pricing Actions

Once a price has been decided, it still has to be implemented in the market. This can be a very difficult step whose importance and difficulty are often underestimated. The seller does not impose a price on the customer. The customer has the money; he is the decision maker. The seller must motivate price acceptance by the customer. This is true for both fixed list prices and negotiated prices. To achieve this can require skill, smart tactics, effective communication, and the ability to negotiate. The implementation requirements strongly depend on the specific situation. They are different for new than for established products, and for price reductions than for increases. Under certain circumstances, prices should be kept on a need-to-know basis; under other conditions it may be better to loudly herald the new prices.

Implementing New-Product Prices

It is usually easier to achieve price acceptance for new products than it is to get acceptance of a price increase for an existing product. This is particularly true if the new product is not directly comparable to existing goods. If the new product is directly comparable to established ones, the existing price-value patterns need to be recognized and considered. Even novelties with strongly better price-value ratios may face acceptance problems, since low price may make consumers suspicious about the quality or decrease dealers' enthusiasm due to lower margins. For example, when Timex introduced its inexpensive watches in Germany in the mid 1960s, specialty dealers refused to include them in their assortment because the margins were too low and income from repairs would be lower than realized with conventional watches. Timex had to develop totally new distribution channels for its watches at gasoline stations and newsstands. In another case, the introduction of a new chemical with a much higher yield failed; it was boycotted by the retailers, who feared a reduction in sales revenue and refused to promote the product actively. In this case, it would have been better to introduce the product at a higher price (consistent with the established price-performance ratio) and to reduce the price later.

Setting the introductory price is a one-time opportunity since it marks the reference point for future prices, as discussed in chapters 10 and 11. This reference price needs to be managed. It can be better to introduce a new product at an official price of $100 and grant an introductory discount of 30% than to set the initial list price at $70 and increase it to $100 later on. The actual transaction price is identical, but the effect on price acceptance may be very different.

Another aspect of new-product pricing concerns the timing of the price announcement. It should be seen in the broader context of premarketing.[14] An early price announcement, although giving competitors information, can be useful to test the price acceptance of potential customers long before the actual product introduction, leaving time for price adjustment. For example, the maker of a new sports car announced a preliminary price two years before the introduction. This price was seen to be very low by the public and by the press, leading to a well-accepted actual introductory price that was 10% higher. In some cases, firms have rescinded announced price increases before they took effect due to competitor or customer reaction.

Implementing Price Reductions

While it is obvious that implementing price reductions is easier than implementing price increases, there are still some pitfalls that should be noted. Dealers do not always welcome price reductions. Lower prices may mean lower margins for them; if the volume does not increase accordingly, they may be worse off. A price reduction usually means that the inventories of the dealers are devalued, since they could buy the product now at the lower price. The dealers often require a compensation for this devaluation through "inventory protection" plan rebates.

In February 1996, Gruner & Jahr, a leading publisher, cut the price of *TV Today* in Germany from DM 2.30 to DM 1 and (after this was prohibited by a court as predatory pricing) then boosted the price to DM 1.80. But it also left the absolute dealer margin unchanged in the process. The price cut to the consumer was combined with a constant margin to the dealer to avoid the negative effect of a lower dealer margin.[15] This is, however, a costly way since Gruner & Jahr's margin declined out of proportion.

Price reductions may also annoy end users, as discussed in chapters 10 and 11. The customers who bought the product shortly before the price cut may feel cheated and complain. An early announcement of the intended price reduction can mitigate this problem. At the same time, such an announcement introduces another possibly undesirable effect—the postponement of purchases, which can mean a shift of sales from higher to lower margins and may cause temporary problems with capacity utilization.

A price decrease can be disguised. Instead of reducing the nominal price, reductions of the "specific" price can be implemented in the form of higher volume per pack. In this case the price figure remains unchanged but the specific price (per pound/kilogram, per gallon/liter) is reduced. For promotional purposes, this form is frequently used. For the company it has the advantage that it does not give away monetary value. The consumer gets more product at the same price and may be happy too.

Implementing Price Increases

The successful implementation of price increases, in the sense of achieving price acceptance, is one of the big challenges in pricing. Customers often strongly resist any attempt to increase price. This is particularly true for large retailers or industrial customers. For the sales force and even for top managers, price-increasing sales calls are often experiences fraught with anxiety. A top manager of a steel company told us that his "price-increase" visits to automotive-industry customers were his most dreaded experiences of the whole year.

In order to be successful in implementing price increases, the following tactics have proven useful:

- *long-term preparation and announcement*—It is crucial to prepare the market for the price increase. The necessity to increase price should be repeatedly communicated long before the intended date. The sales director of a brewery explained: "It is an illusion to increase prices out of the blue sky. You have to 'cook' your customers for a long time before you can dare demand a price increase. Only if they believe that the increase is unavoidable will they accept it."
- *choice of time*—It is advantageous to choose a point in time that facilitates explanation of the reasons for the increase. A price increase immediately after a wage increase is more likely to be accepted. As discussed in chapter 11, the same is true if prices for raw materials have increased or currency-exchange rates have changed. In addition to better acceptance by the customers, competitors are more likely to follow under such circumstances.
- *concurrent product modification*—If possible, the price increase should be combined with a product modification. Even a minor improvement of the product can distract from the price increase and mitigate its negative effect on sales.

- *number of steps*—If a large price increase is necessary, one should consider whether to implement the adjustment in one step or several smaller steps. The latter form may be less hazardous to sales but it takes longer to get to the desired price level.
- *reducing package size*—Instead of increasing the nominal price, the package size can be reduced. There are, of course, limits to the repetitive use of this tactic. If consumers are familiar with a specific size it may be dangerous. In the 1980s, Tchibo, a leading coffee company in Germany, wanted to avoid a price increase by introducing 400-gram packs instead of the familiar 500-gram packs. A public outcry occurred because consumers felt cheated, and Tchibo had to withdraw the smaller packs.
- *unbundling*—This technique, which we discussed in detail in chapter 9, can help to reduce the total amount to be paid for a certain transaction, while at the same time the sum of the unbundled prices is increased. In the 1970s computer companies used unbundling as a substitute for nominal price increases. The example of the unbundling of SPSS software given in Table 9-6 combines price increases with unbundling.

These tactics are more prevalent in consumer than in business-to-business markets. When using any of the above tactics, the emotional as well as the economic response of customers must be taken into account. Having customers feel cheated is a dangerous situation.

Communicating Price Changes

For customers' behavior to be impacted, they must be made aware of the price changes. Their perception is not confined to the price as such, but usually includes the value as well. To achieve the desired effects of a price change, it may be useful to support the implementation with communicative measures.

It is a different story for price reductions and price increases. The best message for a decrease is to highlight that the product is now less expensive, i.e., give out the reduced-price information. In the case of a price increase, the communication should emphasize the quality and the excellent image or service of the product, i.e., attempt to improve the value

FIGURE 12-4

The Effect of "Price Communication" and "Value Communication"

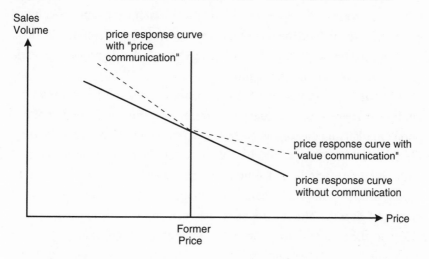

perception. Newspapers and magazines typically support their periodic price increases by emphasizing improved quality, professional journalism, etc.

The two opposite communication effects are illustrated in Figure 12-4. As price moves up above the "former price," a value communication can flatten the sales response curve; moving below, a price communication can make it steeper. We and other authors have found this pattern confirmed for several products.[16] It seems therefore advisable to support price changes by communicative measures, in the case of price reductions by "price communication," in the case of price increases by "value communication."

Implementing Customized Prices

Throughout part II of the book, we have shown that price customization is a highly effective way to increase profit. But price customization can cause implementation problems, both internally and with customers.

A customer is likely to be annoyed if he learns that he pays a higher price for the same product or service than another customer. In this regard, price customization is more dangerous; the more homogeneous the offering, the higher the price transparency, and the larger the price differentials are. These aspects have to be observed in the implementation. It can, therefore, be advantageous to keep prices confidential, i.e., revealed only in targeted communications to the individual customer. Confidentiality of prices can also reduce the risk of a competitive reaction. Another tactic is to reduce the homogeneity of the offering through design or package variants in order to diminish price transparency.

Another problem with price customization is that customers may get confused. There are more than 200 different rates in the German mobile-phone market and customers complain about the impossibility of finding the best deal. In 1996, Deutsche Telekom introduced a new price system with six time periods and four regional zones combining together to make 24 price points. The consumer confusion induced a wave of criticism and ill will. The discrepancy between the benefit of customizing prices to the firm and how hard it is to facilitate via communication the consumers' ability to understand complex price structures should be very carefully considered.

Overcustomization of price can be a major cause of internal price chaos. Too many different prices can create excessive demands on the sales organization. We made test queries to a transportation company and got different price quotes for the same service. The sales agents were unable to cope with the complexity of the company's pricing system. They did not understand it, and could not explain the system in all its intricacies or even its key aspects. The time needed to explain a price system to customers seems to increase exponentially with its complexity. Complex discount schemes lend themselves more easily to misuse by the sales force and require additional control.

Price Negotiations

Though conclusive empirical evidence is lacking, the majority of prices seem to be negotiated to some extent. In a German study of suppliers across different industries, 55% of the respondents said that their prices are negotiated and only 24% reported that they fix the prices and those prices are accepted by their customers.[17]

Price negotiations involve essentially three aspects: (a) the rational substance concerning the economic consequences, (b) the psychological interaction between seller and buyer, and (c) organizational factors. A special body of literature strongly influenced by game theory deals with the rational aspects and the economic consequences of negotiations. For details, see the work of Raiffa.[18] A totally different kind of literature, particularly popular with sales people, addresses the psychology of price negotiations.[19]

Here we confine ourselves to selected organizational aspects. Again the specific situation is of utmost importance, and general recommendations are of limited relevance. Ideally, negotiations should focus on the value rather than on the price. The value determines the customer's willingness to pay. A more effective communication of value is likely to lead to a higher transaction price or to a higher acceptance of a given price. Therefore the sales organization should be trained and prepared to focus on value in the negotiation. It is particularly important to get as much value information as possible to the customer before the price part of the negotiation starts. In many cases, the price negotiation is eventually unavoidable but it should start late in the process.

The current trend towards centralized purchasing affects the value perception and the price negotiation. We look at the case of a chemical company, called INTERCHEM here, which supplies plastic parts to a large car manufacturer, called GLOBALAUTO in this case. Traditionally the GLOBALAUTO plants had their own decentralized purchasing departments. INTERCHEM provided an excellent service, its delivery was superb, and its technical advice was appreciated. All this was perceived by the purchasing people in the GLOBALAUTO plants and recognized in the price negotiations. In 1994 GLOBALAUTO introduced global sourcing; now INTERCHEM's sales director had to negotiate prices with the central purchasing director, who was remote from and knew little about the value INTERCHEM contributed to the plants.

The director of INTERCHEM reflected,

> This is a totally new situation. Traditionally our value was known to and appreciated by my negotiation partners. Now I am dealing with a person who knows little about what we are delivering in the plants. The focus has shifted from value delivery to price and I am having a very hard time. The only value arguments that are accepted are hard economic savings, like through better just-in-time delivery. We have to reconsider our strategy. If we are not successful in translating our value delivery into cost advantages, we may have to give up the respective services in order to become more price competitive.

This case illustrates how strongly organizational developments can impact the negotiation position. There are no easy solutions to such problems.

These few cases illustrate the pivotal role of organizational aspects in price negotiations. It is impossible to give any useful general rules for these situations, but great attention should be paid to these problems. The final success in pricing often depends on the negotiation skills of an organization and its individual employees.

SUMMARY

Organizing for power pricing largely escapes general rules. We observe that many companies are not effectively organized with regard to pricing information, processes, structures, and implementation procedures. The following aspects should be observed.

- The scale of pricing analyses should be adjusted to the potential value. In-depth, large-scale studies should be confined to new products and price-repositioning projects with high profit improvement potential.
- The pricing process must involve both the marketing/sales and the finance/accounting/controlling functions. It is crucial that the two functions cooperate constructively.
- Since the final price decision has to balance both sides it is often seen as a general management task.
- Only large companies with frequent major price decisions should have internal capacities for sophisticated pricing analyses; smaller companies with less frequent price problems seem to be better off hiring specialized price consultants.
- The delegation of pricing authority to the sales force should be handled with caution; we recommend delegating rather too little than too much pricing authority to sales people.
- In the implementation of pricing actions a range of tactics should be applied as appropriate; such tactics can be particularly critical for the successful implementation of price increases.
- Price changes should be supported by communicative measures.

A smart analysis is only the first step toward power pricing. The ultimate success depends on a company's ability to implement the right prices. While there are hardly any general rules for successful pricing implementation, the organization of pricing processes and structures deserves the highest management attention.

13

Becoming a Power Pricer

Check Your Pricing IQ

INTRODUCTION

In chapter 1, we described some characteristics of the power pricer. Subsequent chapters elaborated upon these by providing examples of best practice. Some of the main points were that a power pricer: (a) builds on a solid fact foundation, rigorously analyzing demand conditions (chapters 2 and 3), (b) considers competitive reaction and how to influence it (chapter 4), (c) pursues price customization (chapter 5 for the motivation and chapters 6–10 on specific methods for accomplishing this) and (d) manages the long-term impacts of price (chapter 11). Our hope is that everyone reading the book finds at least a few ideas for substantial profit improvement. Given the breadth of the examples and the many possible routes to improved price realization discussed, we recognize that a reader may have some uncertainty about just how good or bad a pricing job his company is doing, and what ought to be the focus of his initial improvement efforts. Building on the prior chapters, this final chapter provides a structured process whereby a manager can check his organization's "Pricing IQ" and identify the most important activities to undertake to become a stronger power pricer. We do not present any new conceptual material here but we describe a Pricing IQ

Scorecard, which is a concrete way to self-assess the state of your pricing thinking and action.

WHAT THIS CHAPTER WILL DO

This chapter addresses the following questions.

1. How do you know how good a job you are doing on pricing?
2. How do you identify key improvement opportunities?

Knowing the answers to these questions will help you to:

1. Focus on your price realization improvement efforts.
2. Gain the maximum return from the improvement program.

ELEMENTS OF THE PRICING IQ

Figure 13-1 shows the three related domains of the Pricing IQ.

Domain A, The Pricing Mindset, refers to the way in which the organization approaches the price management process. Does it believe price is something that can be managed or does it regard price as something determined largely by external factors? Is pricing connected to the overall corporate and marketing strategies? Is top management involved or is pricing a concern left to lower management levels? What data and tools support pricing decisions? In short, does the company have a "commitment" to manage price? Domain B is the Scope of Understanding or true "Insight" the company has developed. Are external factors like customers and competitors understood, along with the internal issues of product design and costs? Domain C is Price Management Processes or "Action" aspects. These are the key processes for getting the pricing job done.

These domains are related. The Pricing Mindset is a prerequisite foundational element. If you don't really believe that price is manageable, that rigorous thinking will improve pricing performance, and that intelligence and hard work can have high profit payoffs through better pricing, the rest does not matter much. The Pricing Mindset is the commitment to analyze, think, and act. Domain B relates to having an appropriately broad

FIGURE 13-1

Three Domains of Pricing IQ

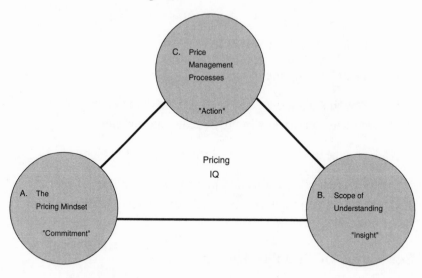

but also deep sense of the market, both the product-market fit and the product-company fit. Does the deep understanding extend to competitors, knowing how "dumb" or "smart" they are and how they can be influenced? Domain C is the existence of Price Management Processes to keep the pricing decision-making consistently focused on the right thing.

For each domain, we provide specific criteria by which to assess practice. Table 13-1, the Pricing IQ Scorecard, lists our 10 prescribed criteria across the three domains. The importance of a given criterion performance varies across situations, so the scorecard asks for a judgment of the relevance of the criterion to the particular situation. There may also be additional important considerations for a company's particular situation and these could be added to the scorecard criteria. However, in observing pricing practices and pinning down why some work and others don't, we have found this three domain/ten criteria scorecard an extremely reliable indicator of the overall quality of pricing practice.

Domain A: The Pricing Mindset

The Pricing Mindset reflects the way the organization approaches pricing issues. The power pricer meets two mindset tests. The first is the existence of a "real" pricing strategy, meaning a strategy that:

TABLE 13-1

The Pricing IQ Scorecard

	Importance: 1–5 Rating from Low to High	Current Performance Poor 1	2	3	4	Excellent 5
Domain A: Pricing Mindset						
Extent to which our process						
1. (a) is connected to corporate and marketing strategy						
(b) is understood by people in our organization						
(c) provides meaningful guidance						
2. rests on a fact foundation that is:						
(a) relevant						
(b) accurate						
(c) appropriately disaggregated						
(d) timely						
Domain B: Scope of Understanding						
Extent to which our understanding covers						
1. (a) value customers place on product						
(b) variation in value across customers						
2. likely competitive reactions and means for influencing						
3. product's role in company portfolio						
Domain C: Process						
Extent to which our pricing process formally analyzes						
1. customization strategies						
2. managing pocket price and account-specific costs						
3. today's pricing influence on future opportunities						
4. communicating/implementing pricing in the marketplace						
5. legal boundaries						

a. is connected to and reinforcing of the overall corporate and marketing strategy
b. is understood by everyone in the organization
c. provides meaningful guidance to their actions

A corporate strategy is "the way a company creates value through the configuration and coordination of its multimarket activities."[1] In this corporate level definition, "value" refers to that created for the various stakeholders of the company, including the stockholders. The marketing strategy is the mediating process for creating this corporate "value." A corporation has value for its stockholders only if it is able to take a set of inputs and use it to create value for its chosen customers. The *value creation* part of the firm's marketing strategy is the design, distribution of, and communication about its products and services to its chosen customers. Pricing strategy is the *value extraction* piece of the marketing strategy whereby a portion of the value created for customers is recouped by the company.

A power pricer has a clearly stated pricing policy that is "in synch" with the higher levels of company strategy. For example, he must know whether the company seeks to be a volume leader or a niche player, choose its product mix and associated costs accordingly, and translate this strategy into effective pricing. A good example of such a strategy is General Motors' Saturn division. GM's head of marketing described Saturn's strategy as a focus on "an overall shopping, buying, and ownership experience" standing for "dependability, intelligence, friendliness."[2] (This is meaningfully different from his description of his Pontiac division's positioning as "in-your-face styling.") Thus the Saturn pricing strategy needed to complement GM's marketing strategy and product positioning for this particular car.

The most important "reason for purchase" given by the American buyer of a small American car is "price."[3] In many dealerships, the importance of price to both the customer *and* the dealer reveals itself in the discussions between the two, which could hardly be characterized as relationship building. In creating "A Different Kind of Company, A Different Kind of Car" as proclaimed in its advertising, GM designed large sales districts for its dealers (so a dealer did not have to worry about customers cross-shopping Saturn outlets he did not control) and established a simple pricing policy: each model in the Saturn line had an economical price set with the price sensitivity of customers in mind. But an important second piece of the pricing strategy was that this price was not subject to negotiation at the point of sale. This "no-haggle" price policy perfectly fit Saturn's overall strategy of providing value through the shopping and buying experience as well as the ownership experience. *Advertising Age* described Saturn as "a textbook case of how to build a brand through a single-minded focus on how customers relate to the product and the company behind it . . . its pricing policy is genius. . . ."[4]

Other examples of the beneficial fit between pricing and higher-level strategy are Intuit software for "low" pricing and Perdue chickens for "high" pricing. As described earlier, Intuit priced its personal finance software product at $35–$45 even though some customers proclaimed its value to be many times this. This prompted one analyst to opine that it could double its price and see no impact on sales levels.[5] If this were true, prices would seem too low. However, when the pricing strategy is viewed in light of the overall marketing strategy of creating powerful word-of-mouth among adopters as the primary sales-generation vehicle, the pricing strategy's complementarity to the marketing strategy is clear. On the other hand, when Frank Perdue pioneered branded chickens and shot to market leadership, he did so at a 15% retail price premium over unbranded chickens. This premium pricing strategy was critical to his high overall strategy of quality differentiation, serving three purposes: (a) to reinforce the quality differentiation positioning of branded chickens over unbranded ones, (b) to fund the advertising campaign Perdue was running to educate customers as to the benefits of his brand, and (c) to allow the trade better margins, generating trade support and push.

Similarly, from its inception in 1973, Fielmann, now the second largest eyeglasses retailer in the world, has had a very clear pricing strategy. The industry traditionally focused on the optical-technical features of the eyeglasses. Fielmann in contrast emphasized beauty and good-looking glasses at affordable prices. DM 35 was the typical level of reimbursement to individuals from health-care plans. While others' DM 35 frames were hardly fashion statements, Fielmann has offered good-looking frames at this level.

Aldi, the leading discount retailer in Germany and just sweeping Europe, has a strategy that has no peer for the strength of its low cost–low price fit. A very limited assortment of about 600 articles combined with few prices allow for an incredible checkout speed. Because they have the prices in their heads, Aldi cashiers check out a basket with a value of DM 200 in 40 seconds, much faster than any scanner can go. Taking inventory in an Aldi store takes about 15 minutes; a truckload is a store's inventory. There are even no telephones in Aldi stores. These cost advantages are rigorously translated into everyday low prices. There are no price promotions; quality, while not high, is acceptable and absolutely consistent over time. There are neither quality nor price surprises at Aldi.

Bitburger, the premium beer brand in Germany, has gone the opposite route. Emerging from a small local brand franchise in the early seventies, "Bit" has consistently resisted the temptation to price-promote its product, even in the 1980s when beer was a favorite product for retailers' promotions. Bit fought against retailers' attempts to sell it at a low price and has, over time, established a very strong image of high quality, continuity, and consistency. The foundation for this strategy carried out over decades was the vision of Bit's management, which never succumbed to short-term price pressures. In the process, Bit has risen from nowhere to become the second largest premium beer brand in the huge German market.

Each of these companies had a pricing strategy logically linked to its corporate strategy and everybody in the organization worked in pursuit of it. In contrast, consider this pricing planning meeting for a company operating in a highly competitive environment. Four senior executives were present: the president, the controller, the vice president for marketing, and the vice president for sales. The initial issue in the meeting was simply to describe the firm's pricing strategy. When the question was first posed, silence resonated for a few moments. Finally, the V.P. for sales spoke up.

Well, it's kind of hard to describe because each of us has our own pricing strategy. I'm in sales. I want to book the business. That's what I am paid to do. So, I talk to the customer and then I come in and fight for the discount I need to book his business.

The controller chimed in:

Yes—and I have to approve any discounts above his authority level and I make sure we don't lose any money on the deal. I look at our costs for the products involved and factory load and I do push back some at the sales people—can't we get a little more?—but as long as we are making money on the deal, we are better off with it than without it—so we'll discount whatever's necessary to get it.

V.P. for marketing:

I don't care about the discounting so much. I want our list price to convey the kind of image that we want. People don't know all that much about who got what discount, so list-price level is the key part of the pricing strategy for me. It positions us in the customer's mind among the major players.

The president:

I just want to make money, so we can make the numbers we promised to the folks upstairs.

The vice president for sales was right in indicating that everybody had his own agenda but was wrong in saying, "Each of us has our own pricing strategy." If everyone has his own strategy, the firm really has none. This is an absolutely critical issue and a problem seen frequently. A perhaps well-intentioned but uncoordinated set of actions, not driven by a common vision of objectives, leads to poor pricing performance.

The power pricer's strategy is communicated and understood throughout the organization. Those responsible for implementing the strategy have no individual incentives to subvert it. The "real" pricing strategy is not a fantasy-land expression of hopes and dreams, but rather recognizes and realistically provides guidance on the trade-offs between price, sales volume, and profitability as discussed in the Pricing Goal Matrix diagram in Figures 2-9 and 2-10. Unrealistic pricing goals, such as "increase profitability, grow the market, and improve market share" provide no guidance for the real decisions to be made in the marketplace. These may be good long-term goals for new-product development activity, but pricing actions alone usually cannot accomplish all this.

Pricing Mindset check 2 is the underlying rigor of the approach and emphasis on the factual cornerstone. As we noted in chapter 1, the power pricer has data that are more relevant, timely, accurate, and disaggregated than the everyday pricer has. Often, the data that managers need to do pricing right are just not available—at least on a timely enough basis. We asked managers in a large company to rate the importance of eight possible inputs to setting and controlling price in the field. Ratings were on a 1–5 scale with 1 = not at all important and 5 = very important. Ratings ranged from a high of 4.5 for "Purchase by Account" to 3.7 for "Discounts by Account and Product." We then asked the managers to indicate if these data were available. Results for the eight data types are shown in Figure 13-2, with order of importance decreasing from left to right.

Figure 13-2 shows that data which are also useful for billing and financial reporting tended to be available—but some data which managers viewed as important to their pricing job, particularly account level profitability, are rarely available. Also, the picture changes dramatically if the question posed is "information available on a daily basis." These results are shown in Figure 13-3.

Hence, data available for real-time use in pricing are limited. The power pricer traps the right marketplace data and then summarizes it in a way to inform marketing decision making—not just to feed into monthly financial reports. In addition to market tracking data, the power pricer conducts market research using appropriate market research techniques—including power tools like conjoint analysis or other methods as described in chapter 3—to complete the needed database. For power pricers, there is a foundation of data relevant to the marketing decisions, available at the appropriate level of disaggregation (which often includes disaggregation by account), insightfully summarized and available in a timely enough way to inform decision making.

These two tests of the Pricing Mindset domain reflect the extent to which the firm believes it can control its pricing and is willing to invest in the necessary data and analysis to do so. We previously introduced the notion of pricing as a third front in profits, i.e.,

Profit = Price × Sales Volume – Cost.

For many firms, the focus is on sales volume and cost; price is subordinated to these. The power pricer moves pricing to the forefront, consid-

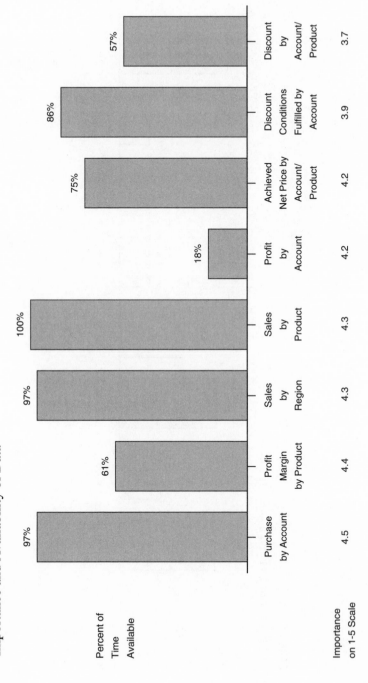

FIGURE 13-2
Importance and Availability of Data

FIGURE 13-3

Availability of Data on a Daily Basis

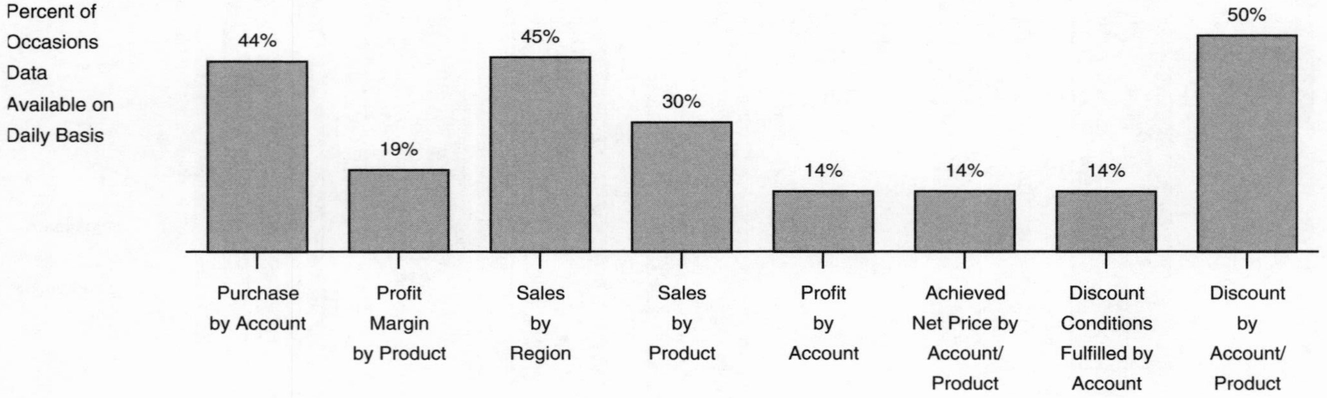

Percent of
Occasions
Data
Available on
Daily Basis

44%	19%	45%	30%	14%	14%	14%	50%

Purchase by Account — Profit Margin by Product — Sales by Region — Sales by Product — Profit by Account — Achieved Net Price by Account/Product — Discount Conditions Fulfilled by Account — Discount by Account/Product

ering it a controllable and key driver of profitability. Top management is as active in its pursuit of profits through price as through the other two means.

Domain B: Scope of Understanding

With the right Pricing Mindset in place, the power pricer follows through to the next level and develops the appropriate Scope of Understanding or "Insight." The three checks in this domain relate to understanding of customer value, competitors, and the company situation.

Domain B's first criterion relates to the centrality of customer value in the pricing process. The power pricer rigorously assesses the value of its products and services; sees how this value varies across customers; and understands the drivers of value variation. In business-to-business selling situations, this means developing an in-depth understanding of the potential customer's cost structure and how your products and services impact it. For example, this in-depth understanding was an important driver of the success that Northern Telecom (now NORTEL) had in turning around its key-systems (telephone systems for small businesses) product. Northern's direct customer was a reseller such as one of the Bell regional operating companies or GTE. Via in-depth field research, Northern was able to develop a precise understanding of the magnitude and relationship of six cost elements—the six elements as shown in Figure 13-4.[6]

Understanding this cost structure and the underlying drivers of each cost element was the basis for understanding not only the value that a product/service bundle would bring to the customer but also how to communicate that value to customers.

The second key element to customer value is understanding how and why it varies across customers. This gives insight into the potential trade-off between price and volume sold and the importance of price customization strategies, as discussed in chapter 5. Monsanto has followed a policy of aggressive price cutting over time with its Roundup herbicide even in markets with no competition, because it understood the potential to open up new markets around the world if the price could be lowered. Sales have doubled from 1990 to 1994, gross margins have been preserved at 40% due to cost cutting, and product contribution increased to

FIGURE 13-4

Cost Structure of a Northern Telecom Customer

6.   Overhead Costs
5.   Sales Generation Costs
4.   Training of End Users
3.   Inventory Holding/Materials Management Cost
2.   Installation and Repair
1.   Key System Product Cost

over $300 million.[7] The power pricer's scope of understanding includes these aspects of customer value and places them at the heart of the pricing process. Customer value is rigorously estimated via appropriate techniques such as cost-structure studies, surveys, and managerial judgment.

Domain B's second criterion relates to depth of understanding of competitors. As set out in chapter 4, the scope of understanding should extend to identifying competitors—present and potential, in-kind and not-in-kind—and understanding their business strategy and competencies. This understanding must extend inside the competitor companies to its key decision makers. In many cases, price reactions are fueled by individuals' emotional reactions more than by economic logic. This understanding is prerequisite, first, to predicting what competitive reaction will be, and second, to ultimately shaping competitive reactions in the most effective way, by market actions and associated signals. The power pricer knows enough to be able to think through the full sequence of marketing reactions with a broad array of reactions considered, such as price or other mix variable, in same market or other market.

Domain B's third criterion is an internal one. Just as a product's pricing has an impact on competitors that must be understood, so too is there typically an internal impact on some of the other product offerings of the firm. As discussed in chapter 8, there is a variety of possible product linkages, ranging from a product serving as a traffic generator for other company products to complementary-in-use products to substitutes. The power pricer has clearly specified the role of his product in the overall strategy.

Domain C: Price Management Processes

Domain C is the "action" domain, i.e., the processes formally in place as part of the pricing program. With the right mindset and appropriately broad scope of understanding in place, pricing performance rests on five key price management processes being part of the routine. They are:

1. developing price customization strategies—building "the right fences"
2. managing pocket prices and account-specific costs
3. linking today's pricing to future opportunity
4. communicating and implementing prices to the marketplace
5. sensing and respecting legal boundaries

Criterion 1 in this domain relates to a major theme of this book, the benefits of price customization. We have provided many examples of situations where "What price should I charge?" was the wrong question, and even if answered quite correctly might cost the firm dearly. We have set out in chapters 5–11 the many procedures for varying price across customers. Chapter 5 showed the limitations of a "one-price" system. Consequently, we have described the power pricer as one who understands the costs and benefits of price-customization opportunities. We have seen the possibility and value of creative "fence building" to separate customers and allow customized pricing through the discussions in chapters 6–11. The power pricer has a process in place to pursue regularly the opportunities for customization. He understands that customizing price and building the right fences are as critical as setting the right price levels.

Check 2 of the Process domain is on managing prices and contribution "net of any discounts," i.e., the power pricer looks at revenue actually derived from an account—and monitors contribution by account level while also assessing account-specific costs.

Marn and Rosiello[8] make an important distinction between "list" price and "transaction" or "pocket" price, meaning the money that is actually realized by the firm from the transaction. In one of their examples, the $6.00 dealer list price turned into a $5.78 invoice price after "order size" and "competitive discounts"—which, in turn, was transformed to a $4.47 "pocket" price after discounts for quick payment, annual volume bonus, off-invoice promotion, co-op advertising, and freight—a pocket price 22.7% below the list price. In general, substantial "revenue leaks" are possible from list to pocket. Marn and Rosiello term this process the "price waterfall."

Figure 13-5 presents a somewhat disguised example from our experience, where a manufacturer offered three brands which, though positioned differently, competed with one another to some extent. Product A was thought to be the "high-margin" item for the firm since its cost of goods sold, at 34% of list price, was substantially less than the 42% and 46% levels for B and C. However, product A, for a variety of reasons, was caught in a discount jungle, in that the 21% in dealer commissions shown in Figure 13-6 was supplemented by a percentage revenue loss of equal magnitude from five other assorted discount programs. Products B and C were less subject to discounting off list. Once the cost of these discount programs was fully understood the perceived profitability turned around, as product A offered only 25% "true" contribution compared to B's 40% and C's 43%.

In addition to understanding the difference in "pocket price" percentage across products, it is critically important to realize that one list price established for the market can consciously or unconsciously be translated into a wide range of pocket prices across customers because of their ability to access different discounts or simply negotiate better. Marn and Rosiello's research shows a difference between highest and lowest pocket prices of 220% for a chemical company and 500% for a fastener supplier!

The highest "pocket-price" customers may or may not be your most attractive customers. One price deduction that Marn and Rosiello make in getting to a "pocket" price is for cooperative advertising allowances. While this does represent a revenue loss in a sense, it also typically means that the customer puts up matching funds for advertising, and the ads may generate so much demand that his is a more attractive situation

FIGURE 13-5

List and Pocket Prices and True Margins for Products A, B, C

	Product Line		
	A	B	C
List	**100**	**100**	**100**
Dealer commission	21	15	7
Early pay discounts	5	1	1
Freight absorption	3	2	2
"Make goods"	8		
After the fact adjustments	2		
Rebates	2		
Total waterfall	41	18	10

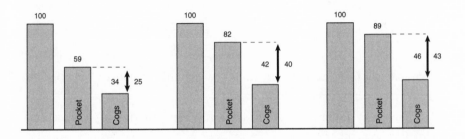

than those who did not take up the co-op ad offer. The lower "pocket price" customer may be more attractive because he performs other tasks in the marketing system. Second, true understanding of account desirability comes only from joining "pocket-price" information with cost data. Shapiro, Rangan, Moriarty, and Ross[9] proposed the "customer grid" as a way to look at this. As shown in Figure 13-6, this grid maps customers by the pocket price received and the cost-to-serve of the account, e.g., for technical support not charged, sales-force time, and special services "thrown in," such as custom paint or convenient shipping. The research of Shapiro et al. shows that it is by no means the rule for accounts to line up along the "equity axis" of Figure 13-6, which shows a high correlation between pocket price and cost-to-serve. They offer one example where accounts are almost uniformly dispersed across the grid. The lower-right-hand quadrant of low price/high cost-to-serve accounts can

FIGURE 13-6

Customer Grid and Equity Axis

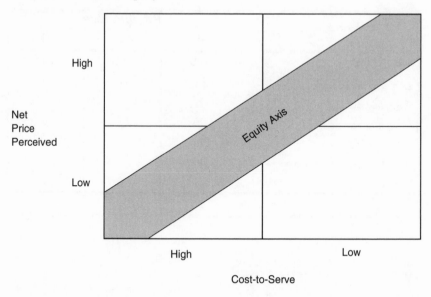

be populated by some large accounts—which the company would be better off losing completely!

The power pricer understands the full implications of its discount structure and other "revenue leaks" and has a process to monitor and manage price at the "net–net" or "pocket price" level; this "pocket price" is understood in terms of what tasks the buyer does for the marketing system, e.g., a reseller engaging in cooperative advertising, and the costs imposed on the seller. The customer grid can then be used to assess which accounts should be the target of price increases or export to the competition. It also identifies the accounts, i.e., the upper left box, most likely to become the subject of competitive interest.

Domain C's third criterion relates to the fact that the power pricer has a process in place to sense which way his market is moving; i.e., he knows where his prices and margins are going and what he can do to influence trends. Figure 13-7 shows four types of markets based on price and margin trends.

Cell 1 shows increasing prices—but not at a rate that can offset the increase in costs; thus margins are decreasing. A number of medical services and supplies fit this description. Cell 2 shows a case where price increases faster than cost, improving margins—like the Lexus in the United States, whose pricing we discussed in chapter 11. Mobile phones typify cell 3, with declining costs but margin compression due to price pressure, and prices declining more quickly. Finally, cell 4 shows a situation of declining prices but improving margins due to more rapid cost decline; some electronics firms display this pattern.

The power pricer first senses the direction of the market and then has a process in place that takes account of the factors described in chapter 11 whereby current price actions impact the future evolution of the market.

Domain C's fourth criterion relates to implementation of pricing in the marketplace: is there a process to consider how best to present the price or a price change to the marketplace? how will the customer come to pay the desired price? Consider this actual scenario at a high-end

FIGURE 13-7

Four Market Evolution Types

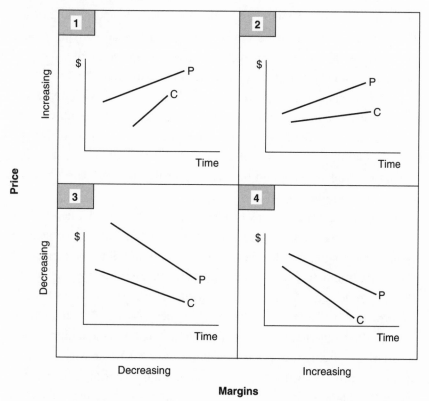

office-furniture showroom. A potential buyer looking for a quality desk chair for a home office sees an appealing one, but with a price tag of $3,000. The salesperson quickly explains, however, that $3,000 is the "catalogue" price and he can offer a 65% discount off the catalogue price, making the chair's actual price $1,050. How does the buyer react? Naively, one might suppose that he would be attracted by the big discount and would be more favorably disposed to buy than if the price tag just said $1,050 in the first place and the salesperson offered no discount. However, if the buyer is a novice in this territory, his response may be just the opposite. The "big discount" suggests that even bigger discounts are available to the savvy and as a novice he is sure to get less than the discount he should. Hence, he avoids this possibility of making a mistake in negotiation and leaves, even though he was willing to pay $1,050 for the chair. The way the price was quoted, rather than the price level, had a determining impact.

The power pricer systematically thinks through the myriad ways of expressing price and understands them from the customer's point of view. A critical point here is that different customers will react quite differently. A potentially large buyer with self-perceived "buying power" needs to be sold a price increase differently than the "mom and pop" buyer for whom other attributes of the transaction may be key. As described in chapter 12, the power pricer's thinking about price implementation leads to consideration of how the product line make-up can help attain price in the field. As in the Taurus G example presented earlier, a phantom product (i.e., one that the firm does not really expect to sell in any substantial quantity) on the low end of the line can help get to the desired price point.

There are, of course, many different contexts to consider here. Much, for example, has been written about how to behave in a price negotiation. Depending on the degree of product differentiation, price mode, industry traditions, type of buyer, and other factors, the specifics of the best implementation plan differ. The power pricer has as part of his pricing process systematic consideration of these issues. Rather than just leaving this to the field people to figure out, this implementation issue is a part of the pricing process. We recently observed a case where a failure to include this doomed a price move. A building materials manufacturer carefully analyzed his customers and found a 4% price increase advisable. However, the sales force was not prepared for it, it was not supported by a communication campaign, and no signals prepared either the customer or the competition. The attempted price increase failed, resulting in not only a missed opportunity to improve price realization but also damage to the firm's image.

The last criterion in this domain is that the power pricer takes a proactive stance on legal issues, because the pricing process requires an indepth review of the legality of the pricing practice under consideration. Products have "gone global" and pricing is impacted by different nations' situations; pricing practices have become more complex as terms and conditions have proliferated; and, as advocated in this book, price customization opportunities are being pursued worldwide. With this, the possibility of legal entanglements has increased for the unwary. Recent headlines attest to this:

"Printing-Press Importers Accused of Unfair Pricing"[10]
"Drug Makers Set to Pay $600 Million to Settle Lawsuits by Pharmacies"[11]

In addition, major airlines have recently made payments to consumers in settlement of suits for price fixing. Archer Daniels Midland is under highly publicized investigation for price fixing and many are currently involved in litigation regarding price discrimination. We have seen fines of hundreds of millions of dollars for price collusion in Europe. A good *beginning* for pricing managers is to be familiar with the relevant statutes by reading a reliable, comprehensive book on marketing law. However, in our view, this is a case where a little knowledge can be a dangerous thing, given the ambiguity and subtleties of some regulations—as discussed in part II of this book. Professional opinion should be consulted as a regular part of the process as new practices are proposed.

THE PRICING IQ SCORECARD

Evaluating your company's pricing practices with the scorecard of Table 13-1 will give a good sense of the quality of the pricing process within the company. It is important to recall the hierarchical nature of the domains, i.e., to bear in mind that a quality process builds on a foundation of Domain A's mindset and then Domain B's understanding.

"Good" performance on Domain C's process will not matter much if Domains A and B are not well founded. In addition to the elements listed in Table 13-1, one should add any other elements thought to be important to generate fruitful discussion.

In practice, we have found it useful to conduct this as a group exercise for four to eight managers involved in pricing for the business unit. It is important to note that while Domain A ratings are typically similar across products within the business units, Domain B and C ratings can vary across products and should be considered separately.

Figure 13-8 shows the self-ratings of one particular business unit that felt it was on track. The horizontal axis is the importance of the criterion and the vertical is the unit's rating of performance on the criterion. For this group, there was pretty good alignment between importance and performance and the mindset domain was highly rated. The key areas for improvement were seen to be generally better data to support decision making (DA-2), and specifically more focus on "pocket prices" (DC-2), representing better understanding of the impact of the discount structure on account profitability.

In contrast, Figure 13-9 shows the ratings for a business unit which had been experiencing severe frustration with pricing. The sources of the frustration and required areas for initial focus became readily appar-

FIGURE 13-8

Ratings of an "On-Track" Business Unit (D*i-j* means item *i* in domain *j*)

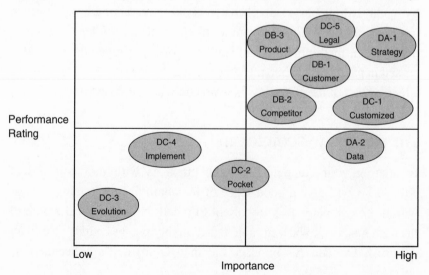

FIGURE 13-9

Ratings of a Frustrated Business Unit (Di-j means item i in domain j)

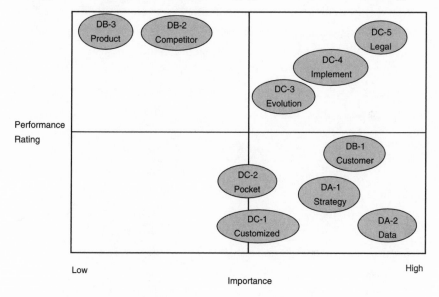

ent when the scorecard matrix was applied. The strategy (DA-1) and data (DA-2), both of the Domain A criteria being in the lower right box, created a situation where little else mattered. Middle managers felt that top management had no commitment beyond talk to better pricing.

SUMMARY

This chapter proposes a simple Pricing IQ Scorecard (Table 13-1) to self-assess your pricing performance. In using the scorecard, it is important to:

- involve a number of people from different perspectives involved in the pricing process
- recall the need to have adequate Domain A scores as a prerequisite to any reasonable performance
- focus on those criteria below the diagonal, i.e., where the performance is low relative to the ranking

This check can help get the serious marketer on the road to power pricing.

Notes

Chapter 1. Introduction

1. Figures for an individual company can be computed by taking 1% of net sales for the year and dividing by reported net income. McKinsey researchers have computed these statistics and reported them in a number of places, including R. Garda and M. Marn, "Price Wars," *The McKinsey Quarterly,* 3 (1993), pp. 87–100.
2. K. Clancy and R. Shulman, *Marketing Myths that Are Killing Businesses: The Cure for Death Wish Marketing* (New York: McGraw-Hill, 1994).
3. See for example the work of R. Cooper and R. Kaplan, "Measure Costs Right: Make the Right Decision," *Harvard Business Review,* September–October 1988, pp. 96–103, and "Profit Priorities from Activity-Based Costing," *Harvard Business Review,* May–June 1991, pp. 1–13.
4. W. Taylor, "Message and Muscle: An Interview with Swatch Titan Nicholas Hayek," *Harvard Business Review,* March–April 1993, pp. 98–110.
5. E. Berndt, L. Bui, D. Reiley, and G. Urban, "The Roles of Marketing, Product Quality and Price Competition in the Growth and Composition of the U.S. Anti-ulcer Drug Industry," working paper, Sloan School of Management, Massachusetts Institute of Technology, May 1994.
6. J. Mendes, "The Prince of Smart Pricing," *Fortune,* May 23, 1992, pp. 107–108.

Chapter 2. Price, Costs, and Profit: Economic Underpinnings of Pricing

1. M. Marn and R. Rosiello, "Managing Price, Gaining Profit," *Harvard Business Review,* September–October 1992, pp. 84–94.

2. Ibid., p. 84.
3. If the price response curve is linear and the marginal cost is constant the decision rule for the optimal price is simple. The optimal price is exactly in the middle between the "maximum price," here $150, and the marginal cost, here $60. This price of $105 maximizes the profit rectangle.
4. "Attack of the Fighting Brands," *Business Week,* May 2, 1994, p. 20.
5. See for example S. Wied-Nebbeling, *Das Preisverhalten in der Industrie* (Tübingen: Mohr-Siebeck, 1985), for empirical studies; W. Baumol, *Business Behavior, Value, and Growth* (New York: Harcourt & Brace, 1959), who argues sales maximization goals; and H. Simon, *Preismanagement: Analyse-Strategie-Umsetzung* (Wiesbaden: Gabler, 1992), p. 241, for Japanese market share discussion.
6. R. Hudson, "Escom Pays a Price to Boost European PC Market Share," *Wall Street Journal Europe,* November 8, 1995, p. 4.
7. *Wall Street Journal Europe,* January 12, 1996.
8. S. Weigel, "Wir bekommen aus Amerika nur das Drehbuch." Interview with Eurodisney president Philippe Bourguignon, *Frankfurter Allgemeine Zeitung,* December 18, 1995, p. 18.
9. D. Kirkpatrick, "Intel Goes for Broke," *Fortune,* May 16, 1994, p. 54.
10. H. Simon, "Pricing Opportunities—And How to Exploit Them," *Sloan Management Review,* Winter 1992, pp. 55–65.
11. First quote is from D. Nimer, "Nimer on Pricing," *Industrial Marketing,* March 1971, pp. 48–55, here p. 48; the second from S. Godin and C. Conley, *Business Rules of Thumb* (New York: Warner Books, 1987), p. 58.
12. Wied-Nebbeling, p. 137.

Chapter 3. Price Response Estimation

1. J. Cole, "Clipped Wings: Boeing Is Offering Cuts In Prices of New Jets, Rattling the Industry," *Wall Street Journal Europe,* April 26, 1995.
2. K. Pope, "British Mobile-Phone Firm Suffers Christmas Hangover," *Wall Street Journal Europe,* December 28, 1994, p. 4.
3. J. Little, "Models and Managers: The Concept of a Decision Calculus," *Management Science,* 16 (April 1970), pp. 466–485.
4. A. Gabor and C. Granger, "Price Sensitivity of the Consumer," *Journal of Advertising Research,* 4 (December 1964), pp. 40–44.
5. J. Abrams, "A New Method for Testing Pricing Decisions," *Journal of Marketing,* 28:3 (July 1964), pp. 6–9.
6. D. Adam, "Consumer Reactions to Price," in Bernard Taylor and Gordon Wells, eds., *Pricing Strategy* (London, Princeton: Brandon, 1969), pp. 75–88.
7. R. Dolan, *Managing the New Product Development Process* (Reading, MA: Addison-Wesley Pub. Co., 1993).

8. P. Green and V. Srinivasan, "Conjoint Analysis in Marketing: New Developments and Directions," *Journal of Marketing,* 54:4 (October 1990), pp. 3–19.

9. D. Wittink, M. Vriens, and W. Burhenne, "Commercial Use of Conjoint Analysis in Europe, Results and Critical Reflections," *International Journal of Research in Marketing,* 11 (1994), pp. 41–52.

10. R. Johnson, "Adaptive Conjoint Analysis," in *Sawtooth Software Conference on Perceptual Mapping, Conjoint Analysis, and Computer Interviewing,* Ketchum, ID, 1987, pp. 253–265.

11. H. Simon, *Preismanagement: Analyse-Strategie-Umsetzung* (Wiesbaden: Gabler, 1992).

12. P. Green and V. Srinivasan, "Conjoint Analysis in Marketing: New Developments With Implications for Research and Practice," *Journal of Marketing,* October 1990, pp. 3–19.

13. T. Elrod and S. Krishna Kumar, "New Conjoint Analysis Products on the Way," *Sawtooth News,* 5:4 (Fall 1989), pp. 1–3.

14. Dolan, *op. cit.,* and J. Wind, P. Green, D. Shifflet, and M. Scarbrough, "Courtyard by Marriott: Designing a Hotel with Consumer-based Marketing Models," *Interfaces,* 19:1 (January-February 1989), pp. 25–47.

15. R. King, Jr., "Packard Bell May Be Hurt By Wrong Bet," *Wall Street Journal Europe,* November 30, 1995, p. 4.

16. H. Simon, *Hidden Champions—Lessons from 500 of the World's Best Companies* (Boston: Harvard Business School Press, 1996), p. 145.

17. J. Carlton, "Low Prices Help Order Video-Game Players Outsell Next-Generation Machines in the U.S.," *Wall Street Journal Europe,* 27 (December 1995), p. 4.

18. A. Silk and G. Urban, "Pre-Test-Market Evaluation of New Packaged Goods: A Model and Measurement Metholology," *Journal of Marketing Research,* 15 (May 1978), pp. 171–191.

19. G. Tellis, "The Price Elasticity of Selective Demand: A Meta-Analysis of Econometric Models of Sales, *Journal of Marketing Research,* 25 (November 1988), pp. 331–341.

20. G. Assmus, J. U. Farley, and Don R. Lehmann, "Affects Sales: Meta Analysis of Econometric Results," *Journal of Marketing Research,* 21 (February 1984), pp. 65–74.

21. J.-J. Lambin, *Advertising, Competition and Market Conduct in Oligopoly over Time* (Amsterdam: North Holland-Elsevier, 1976).

22. R. Sethuraman and G. Tellis, "Analysis of the Tradeoff between Advertising and Price Discounting," *Journal of Marketing Research,* 28 (May 1991), p. 168.

23. H. Simon, *Preismanagement: Analyse-Strategie-Umsetzung* (Wiesbaden: Gabler, 1992), p. 139.

24. R. Dolan, "How Do You Know When the Price is Right?," *Harvard Business Review,* September–October 1995, p. 178.

25. P. Guadagni and John D. C. Little, "A Logit Model of Brand Choice Calibrated on Scanner Data," *Marketing Science,* 2 (Summer 1983), pp. 203–208.
26. E. Kucher, *Scannerdaten und Preissensitivität bei Konsumgütern* (Wiesbaden: Gabler, 1985).

Chapter 4. Pricing and Competitive Strategy

1. K. Alexander, "Continental Airlines soars to new heights," *USA Today,* January 23, 1996, p. 48.
2. P. Carty, "Who Will Lose Their Shirts in the Fleet Street Price War?" *Accountancy,* February 1994, pp. 30–34.
3. For details see R. Dolan, "Eastman Kodak Company: Funtime Film," Harvard Business School Case No. 9-594111.
4. E. Ross, "Making Money with Proactive Pricing," *Harvard Business Review,* November–December, 1984, pp. 145–155.
5. Philip Kotler, *Marketing Management: Analysis, Planning, Implementation and Control,* 8th ed. (Englewood Cliffs, NJ: Prentice-Hall, 1994), p. 37.
6. H. Takeuchi and I. Nonaka, "The New New Product Development Game," *Harvard Business Review,* January–February, 1986, pp. 137–146.
7. R. C. Blattberg and K. J. Wisniewski, "Price-Induced Patterns of Competition," *Marketing Science* 8 (Fall 1989), pp. 291–309.
8. K. Sivakumar and S. P. Raj, "Quality-Tier Competition: Impacts of the 'Whether' Decision and the Direction of a Price Change," Marketing Science Institute, Technical Work Paper No. 95-106, June 1995.
9. F. Scherer, *Industrial Market Structure and Economic Performance,* 2nd ed. (New York: Rand McNally, 1980), p. 177.
10. Polaroid sued Kodak for patent infringement and was eventually awarded over $900 million in damages by the U.S. District court.
11. R. McGough, "Fidelity Joins Mutual Funds on Fee-Cutting Bandwagon," *Wall Street Journal,* December 30, 1993, p. C1.
12. *Infoworld,* June 29, 1992, p. 98, and February 22, 1993, p. 33.
13. J. Lawrence, "Huggies price drops to match Pampers," *Advertising Age,* May 31, 1993, p. 12.
14. S. Sherman, "How To Prosper in the Value Decade," *Fortune,* November 30, 1992, pp. 90ff.
15. See S. Michael and A. Silk, "American Airlines' Value Pricing (A)," Harvard Business School Case No. 9-594001, for a detailed description of this new pricing policy.
16. L. Rublin, "Fare Wars Are Hell—At Least for Airlines' Bottom Lines," *Barron's,* July 6, 1992, p. 15.
17. B. O'Brian, "American Air Launches New Price Sortie," *Wall Street Journal,* April 21, 1992, p. B1.

18. W. Zellner, A. Rothman, and E. Schine, "The Airline Mess," *Business Week,* July 6, 1992, p. 50–55.

19. J. Lambin, *Advertising, Competition and Market Conduct in Oligopoly Over Time* (Amsterdam: North Holland-Elsevier, 1976).

20. W. Zellner, A. Rothman, and E. Schine, *op. cit.*

21. J. Hess and E. Gerstner examine the implications of these price matching guarantees in "Price-Matching Policies: An Empirical Case," *Managerial and Decision Economics,* 12:4 (August 1991), pp. 305–315.

22. R. Buzzell, B. Gale, and R. Sultan, "Market Share—A Key to Profitability," *Harvard Business Review,* January–February 1975, pp. 97–106.

23. McKinsey and Company, "Marketers' Metamorphosis," updated internal document.

24. N. Templin, "Compaq in Bid to Boost PC Market Share Declines to Cut Price by as Much as 20%," *Wall Street Journal,* March 3, 1996, p. A3 ff.

25. An article by O. Heil and A. Langvardt, "The Interface Between Competitive Market Signaling and Antitrust Law," *Journal of Marketing,* 58 (July 1994), pp. 81–96, provides a good summary of legal issues involved in signaling intentions.

26. J. Liesse, "Price War Bites At Pet Food Ad $," *Advertising Age,* 64:4 (April 5, 1993), p. 12.

27. I. Bejenke, "Bellicose TV Guides Compete in Germany," *Wall Street Journal Europe,* March 6, 1996.

28. O. Heil and A. Langvardt, *op. cit.*

29. A. Choi, "Digital to exit home PC computer sector, focus on PC for Business Customers," *Wall Street Journal,* January 30, 1996, p. A3.

Chapter 5. Price Customization

1. S. E. Prokesch, "Competing on Customer Service: An Interview with British Airways' Sir Colin Marshall," *Harvard Business Review,* November–December 1995, pp. 100–118.

2. E. Gerstner and D. Houlthausen analyze this specific point in "Profitable Pricing When Market Segments Overlap," *Marketing Science,* Winter 1986, pp. 55–69.

3. Reported in J. Birnbaum, "Pricing of Products is Still an Art, Often Having Little Like to Costs," *Wall Street Journal* article reprinted in B. Shapiro, R. Dolan, and J. Quelch, *Marketing Management Readings: From Theory to Practice,* Volume III (Homewood, IL: Irwin, 1985).

4. O. Suris, "Ford to Offer Dressed-Down Taurus Model," *Wall Street Journal,* February 6, 1996, pp. A2ff.

5. K. Bradsher, "Ford to Offer Cheaper Cars as Sales Sag," *New York Times,* February 6, 1995, pp. D1ff.

6. K. Bradsher, "Ford Tests the Price Barrier," *New York Times,* January 24, 1996, pp. D1ff.

7. L. Bird, "Victoria's Secret May Be that Men Get a Better Deal," *Wall Street Journal,* January 3, 1996, p. B5.

8. R. Blattberg and S. Neslin, *Sales Promotions: Concepts, Methods and Strategies* (Englewood Cliffs, NJ: Prentice Hall, 1990), p. 278.

9. Reported in J. Kamen, "Price Filtering: Restricting Price Deals to Those Least Likely to Buy Without Them," *Journal of Consumer Marketing,* 6:3 (Summer 1988), pp. 37–43.

10. N. Shirouzu, "Luxury Prices for U.S. Goods No Longer Pass Muster in Japan," *Wall Street Journal,* February 6, 1996, p. B1.

11. E. Tanouge, "Norplant's Maker Draws Sharp Criticism on Pricing of Long-Acting Contraceptives," *Wall Street Journal,* August 30, 1993, pp. B1–2.

12. D. Lavin, "Phone Firms Offer Shoppers Discount Deals," *Wall Street Journal Europe,* January 31, 1996, p. 9.

13. L. Cohen and E. Tanouge, "Drug Makers Set to Pay $600 Million to Settle Lawsuits by Pharmacies," *Wall Street Journal,* January 18, 1996, p. A1ff.; see also M. Freudenheim, "13 Drug Makers and Pharmacies Close to Accord," *New York Times,* January 19, 1996.

14. L. Stern and T. Eovaldi, *Legal Aspects of Marketing Strategy* (Englewood Cliffs, NJ: Prentice-Hall, 1984), p. 264.

15. L. Stern and T. Eovaldi, op. cit.; see also J. Welch, *Marketing Law* (Tulsa, OK: PPC Books, 1980).

Chapter 6. International Pricing

1. See "Millionen-Deal Grauimporte: Weit unter Preis" ("Million-Deal Gray Imports: Far Below List Price"), *Trierischer Volksfreund,* January 20, 1996, p. 41.

2. For more details see H. Simon, *Hidden Champions—Lessons from 500 of the World's Best Unknown Companies* (Boston: Harvard Business School Press, 1996).

3. "Cars in America: As American as Apfelkuchen," *Economist,* January 6, 1996, pp. 59–60.

4. For further details see "Don't Call Us," *Economist,* January 6, 1996, p. 61.

5. S. Wied-Nebbeling, *Industrielle Preissetzung (Industrial Pricing),* (Tübingen: Mohr-Siebeck 1975), p. 295.

6. For a further discussion see G. Albaum, *International Marketing and Export Management* (Reading, MA: Addison-Wesley, 1990), and P. Cateora, *International Marketing,* 7th ed. (Homewood, IL: Irwin, 1990).

7. S. T. Cavusgil, "Unraveling the Mystique of Export Pricing," *Business Horizons,* May–June 1988, pp. 54–63.

8. For a more detailed description of the price corridor concept, see H. Simon and E. Kucher, "Pricing in the New Europe—A Time Bomb," *Pricing Strategy & Practice* 3:1 (1995), pp. 4–13.

9. G. Assmus and C. Wiese, "How to Address the Gray Market Threat Using Price Coordination," *Sloan Management Review,* Spring 1995, pp. 31–41.

Chapter 7. Nonlinear Pricing

1. R. J. Dolan, "Quantity Discounts: Managerial Issues And Research Opportunities," *Marketing Science,* 6 (Winter 1987), p. 12.

2. R. J. Dolan, *op. cit.,* p. 13.

3. B. Gloede, *"Los Angeles Times* to Fight Order," *Editor and Publisher,* October 3, 1981, p. 11.

4. J. P. Newport, "Frequent-Flier Clones, *Fortune,* April 29, 1985, p. 113.

5. A. P. Jeuland, and S. M. Shugan, "Managing Channel Profits," *Marketing Science,* 2 (Summer 1983), pp. 239–272.

6. S. S. Oren, S. A. Smith, and R. B.Wilson, "Competitive Non-linear Tariffs," *Journal of Economic Theory,* 29 (February 1993), pp. 49–71.

7. R. J. Dolan, *op. cit.*, p. 12.

8. Tacke, Georg, *Nichtlineare Preisbildung* (Wiesbaden: Gabler, 1984).

9. L. W. Stern and T. L. Eovaldi, "Legal Aspects of Marketing Strategy" (Englewood Cliffs, NJ: Prentice-Hall, 1984).

Chapter 8. Product-Line Pricing

1. B. Pine II, *Mass Customization: The New Frontier in Business Competition* (Boston: Harvard Business School Press, 1993).

2. S. Wheelwright and K. Clark, *Revolutionizing Product Development: Quantum Leaps in Speed, Efficiency and Quality* (New York: Free Press, 1992).

3. For a profound discussion of this aspect see H. Nystroem, *Retail Pricing—An Integrated Economics and Psychological Approach* (Stockholm School of Economics: Economic Research Institute, 1979).

4. For details see R. Dolan, "Black & Decker Corporation A: Power Tool Division," Harvard Business School Case # 9-595-057

5. The prices and data are from *Ward's Automotive Yearbook* (1992), p. 270.

6. Hermann Simon, *Goodwill und Marketingstrategie* (Wiesbaden: Gabler, 1985), p. 175. If other marketing instruments were included the profit difference was even larger.

7. Professor Ben Shapiro of Harvard Business School introduced us to this example and the "Diverse Specifications" terminology.

8. For details, see K. McQuade and R. Moriarty, "Barco Projection Systems (A)," Harvard Business School Case 9-591133.

9. For methods, see G. Lilien, P. Kotter, and S. Moorthy, *Marketing Models* (Englewood Cliffs, NJ: Prentice-Hall, 1992), upon which this example is based.

10. For a derivation of optimality conditions see H. Simon, *Preismanagement—Analyse, Strategie, Umsetzung* (Wiesbaden: Gabler, 1992), Chapter 11.

11. "Attack of the Fighting Brands," *Business Week,* May 2, 1994, p. 22.

12. C. Rohwedder, "Jil Sander Lays Out Pattern for Success amid Fashion Slump," *Wall Street Journal Europe,* January 15, 1996, pp. 1 and 12, here p. 1.

13. O. Suris, "Porsche Hopes Lower-Priced Cars Will Push '90s Sales to '80s Level," *Wall Street Journal Europe,* February 4–5, 1994, p. 5.

Chapter 9. Price Bundling

1. G. Eppen, W. Hanson, and R. Martin, in "Bundling—New Products, New Markets, Low Risk," *Sloan Management Review* (Summer 1991), pp. 7–14, report that Chrysler reduced costs $1,000 per vehicle via this strategy.

2. R. Matthews, "BMW to Tackle Car Criminals in South Africa," *Financial Times,* January 17, 1996, p. 4. Theft and hijacking of luxury cars are major problems in South Africa, so that insurance premiums there are excessively high.

3. E. Tanouye, "Hoechst Celanese Offer for Copley Stake Confirms New Clout of Generic Drug Makers," *Wall Street Journal Europe,* October 12, 1993, p. 3.

4. J. Guiltinan, "The Price Bundling of Services: A Normative Framework," *Journal of Marketing,* 51 (April 1987), pp. 74–78.

5. I. Foster, "Cross-Couponing as Bundling," dissertation (Ann Arbor, MI: University Microfilms International, 1991).

6. W. Adams and J. Yellen, "Commodity Bundling and the Burden of Monopoly," *Quarterly Journal of Economics,* 90 (August 1976), pp. 475–498; R. Schmalensee, "Gaussian Demand and Commodity Bundling," *Journal of Business,* 57 (January 1984), pp. 211–230.

7. H. Simon, *Preismanagement—Analyse, Strategie, Umsetzung,* 2nd ed. (Wiesbaden: Gabler, 1991).

8. T. Watson, Jr., *Father, Son & Co.,: My Life at IBM and Beyond* (New York: Bantam Books, 1990).

9. See L. Stern and T. Eovaldi, *Legal Aspects of Marketing Strategy* (Englewood Cliffs, NJ: Prentice-Hall, 1984), for a good overview of relevant U.S. laws.

10. Ibid.

11. J. Paroush and Y. Peles, "A Combined Monopoly and Optimal Packaging," *European Economic Review,* 15 (1981), pp. 373–383; C. Friege, "Angebot und Zusammenstellung von effizienten Leistungsverbunden auf der Basis von Economies of Scope," *Arbeitspapier* (working paper), December 1994, pp. 1–35.

12. M. Porter, *Competitive Advantage* (New York: The Free Press, 1985); J. Guilti-

nan, "The Price Bundling of Services: A Normative Framework," *Journal of Marketing,* 51 (April 1987), pp. 74–85; M. Lawless, "Commodity Bundling for Competitive Advantage: Strategic Implications," *Journal of Management Studies,* 28 (May 1991), pp. 267–280.

13. W. Hanson and R. Martin, "Optimal Bundle Pricing," *Management Science,* 36 (February 1990), pp. 155–174.

14. L. Phlips, *The Economics of Price Discrimination* (Cambridge: Cambridge University Press, 1989).

15. W. Möschel, "Umsatzbonussysteme und der Mißbrauch marktbeherrschender Stellungen," *Marketing—Zeitschrift für Forschung und Praxis,* 3 (1981), pp. 225–232.

16. L. Wilson, A. Weiss, and G. John, "Unbundling of Industrial System," *Journal of Marketing Research,* 27 (May 1990), pp. 123–138.

17. "Oracle Policy Prompts Pricing Worries," *Computerworld,* March 23, 1992.

Chapter 10. Time Customization of Prices: The Short Term

1. R. Blattberg and S. Neslin, *Sales Promotion Concepts, Methods and Strategies* (Englewood Cliffs, NJ: Prentice-Hall, 1990), p. 319.

2. The underlying economic theory for this rationale is described in E. Lazear, "Retail Pricing and Clearance Sales," *American Economic Review,* March 1986, pp. 14–32.

3. Reported in G. Ortmeyer, J. A. Quelch, and W. Salmon, "Restoring Credibility to Retail Pricing," *Sloan Management Review,* Fall 1991, pp. 55–66.

4. W. Wilkie and P. Dickson, "Shopping for Appliances: Consumers' Strategies and Patterns of Information Search," Marketing Science Institute paper, November 1985.

5. A. Doob, J. Carlsmith, J. Feedman, T. Landaauer, and T. Soleng, "Effect of Initial Selling Price on Subsequent Sales," *Journal of Personality and Social Psychology,* 11:4 (1969), pp. 345–50.

6. S. Neslin and D. Clarke, "Relating the Brand Use Profile of Coupon Redeemers to Brand and Coupon Characteristics," *Journal of Advertising Research,* 27:4, (February–March 1987), pp. 23–32. See also the general discussion in Chapter 10 of Blattberg and Neslin, *op. cit.*

7. K. Bawa and R. Shoemaker, "The Coupon-Prone Consumer: Some Findings Based on Purchase Behavior Across Product Classes," *Journal of Marketing,* 51:4 (October 1987), pp. 99–110.

8. A. Ehrenberg, K. Hammond, and G. Goodhardt, "The After-Effects of Price-Related Consumer Promotions," working paper, March 1994.

9. The underlying economic theory of this process is described in J. Conlisk, E. Gerstner, and J. Sobel, "Cyclic Pricing by a Durable Goods Monopolist," *The Quarterly Journal of Economics,* August 1984, pp. 489–505, and extended in J.

Sobel, "The Timing of Sales," *Review of Economic Studies,* 1984, LI, pp. 353–68.

10. The discussion draws on a model of E. Gerstner and D. Holthausen, "Profitable Pricing When Market Segments Overlap," *Marketing Science,* 5:1 (Winter 1986), pp. 55–69. Gerstner and Holthausen treat the issue of different markets, but their argument is easily reinterpreted as applying to time periods.

11. E. Lazear, *op. cit.*

12. American's system is described in B. Smith, J. Leimkuhler, and R. Darrow, "Yield Management at American Airlines," *Interfaces,* 22:1 (January–February 1992), pp. 9–30.

13. Hertz's system is described in W. Carroll and R. Grimes, "Evolutionary Change in Product Management: Experiences in the Car Rental Industry," *Interfaces,* 25:5 (September–October 1995), pp. 84–104.

14. R. Blattberg and K. Wisniewski, working paper, results reported in Blattberg and Neslin, *op. cit.,* pp. 351–57.

15. P. Sellers, "The Dumbest Marketing Ploy," *Fortune,* October 5, 1992, pp. 88 ff.

16. G. Ortmeyer, J. Quelch, and W. Salmon, "Restoring Credibility to Retail Pricing," *Sloan Management Review,* Fall 1991, pp. 55–66.

17. R. Buzzell, J. Quelch, and W. Salmon, "The Costly Bargain of Trade Promotion," *Harvard Business Review,* March–April 1990, pp. 141–49.

18. M. Guiles, "Chrysler's New Incentives on Minivans Take Their Cue from Appliance Stores," *Wall Street Journal,* December 18, 1989, p. B5. The underlying economic theory is discussed in I. Png, "Most Favored-Customer Protection versus Price Discrimination over Time," *Journal of Political Economy,* 99:5 (October 1991), pp. 1010–28.

19. Fairness of yield management systems in the hotel industry is the focus of S. Kimes, "Perceived Fairness of Yield Management," *The Cornell H.R.A. Quarterly,* February 1994, pp. 22–29.

Chapter 11. Time Customization of Prices: The Long Term

1. The Justice Department raised antitrust concerns about the Microsoft acquisition. In the face of a long legal process, Microsoft eventually withdrew its offer.

2. E. Berndt, L. Bui, D. Reiley, and G. Urban, "Information, Marketing and Pricing in the U.S. Anti-Ulcer Drug Market," Massachusetts Institute of Technology working paper (1994), provided the data on which this figure is based.

3. An interesting presentation of the global battle between Tagamet and Zantac is in: R. Angelmar and C. Pinson, "Zantac (A)," INSEAD Case 592-045-1, Fontainebleau, France.

4. A brief description of this theory is found in R. Winer, "Behavioral Perspectives on Pricing: Buyers' Subjective Perceptions of Price Revisited," Chapter 2

in T. Devinney, *Issues in Pricing: Theory and Research* (Lexington, MA: D. C. Heath/Lexington Books, 1988).

5. A. Doob, J. Carlsmith, J. Freedman, T. Landauer, and T. Soleng, "Effect of Initial Selling Price on Subsequent Sales," *Journal of Personality and Social Psychology,* 11:4 (1969), pp. 345–50.

6. Blattberg and Neslin, *op. cit.*

7. The underlying theory here is Prospect Theory. See Winer, *op. cit.,* for a brief description. More detailed description can be found in D. Kahneman and A. Tversky, "Prospect Theory: An Analysis of Decision Under Risk," *Econometrica,* 47 (March 1979), pp. 263–91, or R. Thaler, "Mental Accounting and Consumer Choice," *Marketing Science* 4:3 (Summer 1985), pp. 199–214.

8. R. Sultan, *Pricing in the Electrical Oligopoly,* Vol. I, *Competition or Collusion* (Cambridge, MA: Harvard University Press, 1974), p. 185.

9. R. Dolan and A. Jeuland, "Experience Curves and Dynamic Demand Models: Implications for Optimal Pricing Strategies," *Journal of Marketing,* 45 (Winter 1987), pp. 52–62.

10. G. Brock, *The U.S. Computer Industry: A Study of Market Power* (Cambridge, MA: Ballinger, 1975).

11. Sultan, *op. cit.,* p. 190.

12. B. Isaacson, "Goodyear: The Aquatred Launch," Harvard Business School case 9-594106.

13. P. Carroll, "Prices of Memory Chips Slide as Output Proliferates," *Wall Street Journal,* February 14, 1996, p. B4.

14. F. Scherer, *Industrial Market Structure and Economic Performance,* 2nd ed., (Chicago: Rand McNally, 1980), p. 240.

15. L. Stern and T. Eovaldi, *Legal Aspects of Marketing Strategy* (Englewood Cliffs, NJ: Prentice-Hall, 1984), p. 257.

16. H. Simon, *Price Management* (Amsterdam: North-Holland Elsevier, 1989).

17. S. Sherman, "How to Prosper in the Value Decade," *Fortune,* November 30, 1992, p. 93.

18. L. Ingrassia and W. Carley, "Rolls-Royce's Victory in Landing Engine Job Highlights Industry Ills," *Wall Street Journal,* January 2, 1996, pp. 1ff.

19. B. Bayus, "Dynamic Pricing of Next Generation Consumer Durables," *Marketing Science,* 11:3 (Summer 1992), pp. 251–65.

20. J. Steffens, *New Games: Strategic Competition in the PC Revolution* (Oxford: Pergamon Press, 1994), pp. 228–29.

Chapter 12. Organizing for Power Pricing

1. See S. Hyde, "Navistar International," Chapter 10 in D. T. Seymour, *The Pricing Decision* (Chicago: Probus Pub. Co., 1989), pp. 225–240, here p. 233.

2. See B. Atkin and R. Skinner, *How British Industry Prices* (Old Woking: The Gresham Press, 1976).

3. Hyde, *op. cit.,* p. 233.

4. L. Miller and G. Stern, "U.S. Car-Rental Firms Neglect Core Business, Often Skid Into Losses," *The Wall Street Journal Europe,* February 19, 1996, p. 1 and 5, here p. 5.

5. L. Mohan and W. Holstein, "Marketing Decision Support Systems in Transition," in R. Blattberg, R. Glazer, and J. Little, *The Marketing Information Revolution* (Boston: Harvard Business School Press, 1994), pp. 230–252.

6. C. Moorman, G. Zaltman, and R. Deshpande, "Relationships Between Providers and Users of Market Research: The Dynamics of Trust Within and Between Organizations," *Journal of Marketing Research,* 29:3 (August 1992), pp. 314–328, report that the trust between line managers and market researchers is extremely critical for the acceptance and application of the research results.

7. See B. Atkin and R. Skinner, *op. cit.,* p. 236; "Welche Rolle spielt der Preis?" in *ASW–Absatzwirtschaft-Zeitschrift für Marketing* (July 1994), p. 22.

8. See also F. Cespedes, "Coordinating Sales and Marketing in Consumer Goods Firms," *Journal of Consumer Marketing,* 10/2, 1993, pp. 37–55, and Dan N. Nimer, "Nimer on Pricing," *Industrial Marketing,* March 1971, pp. 48–55, here p. 48.

9. R. Kern, "Letting Your Salespeople Set Prices (Sort of)," *Sales and Marketing Management,* 14 (August 1989), pp. 44–49, here p. 44.

10. D. Nimer, "Nimer on Pricing," *op. cit.,* pp. 48–55, here p. 48.

11. P. Stephenson, W. Cron, and G. Frazier, "Delegating Pricing Authority to the Sales Force: The Effects on Sales and Profit Performance," *Journal of Marketing,* 43 (Spring 1979), pp. 21–28.

12. Ibid.

13. K. Wiltinger, "An Exploratory Investigation of Task Environmental Characteristics Influencing the Delegation of Pricing Authority to the Sales Force," in M. Bergadaà, ed., *Proceedings of the 24th European Marketing Academy Conference* (Cergy-Pontoise [France] ESSEC, 1995), pp. 2125–2133.

14. For a detailed analysis of premarketing see M. Moehrle, *Prämarketing* (Wiesbaden: Gabler-Verlag, 1995).

15. I. Bejenke, "Bellicose TV Guides Compete in Germany," *Wall Street Journal Europe,* March 6, 1996, p. 4.

16. H. Simon, *Price Management* (Amsterdam: North Holland-Elsevier, 1989).

17. H. Simon, ibid., p. 664; see also Magid M. Abraham and Leonard M. Lodish, "Getting the Most Out of Advertising and Promotion," *Harvard Business Review,* May–June 1990, pp. 50–60.

18. See especially H. Raiffa, *The Art and Science of Negotiation* (Cambridge, MA: Harvard University Press, 1982).

19. See, e.g., J. Nirenberg, *How to Sell Your Ideas* (New York: McGraw Hill, 1984); E. N. Detroy, *Sich Durchsetzen in Preisgesprächen und -verhandlungen* (Zurich: Moderne Industrie, 1990).

Chapter 13. Becoming a Power Pricer: Check Your Pricing IQ

1. D. Collis and C. Montgomery, *Corporate Strategy: Resources and Scope of the Firm* (Homewood, IL: Irwin, forthcoming).
2. G. Stern, "GM's New Marketing Chief Seeks Clarity Amid Muddle of Overlapping Car Lines," *Wall Street Journal,* May 1, 1995, p. A3ff.
3. G. Keller and A. McGahan, "Saturn: A Different Kind of Car Company," Harvard Buisness School case 9-795010.
4. R. Serafin, "The Saturn Story," *Advertising Age,* November 16, 1992, pp. 1ff.
5. J. Case, "Customer Service: The Last Word," *INC.* Magazine, April 1, 1991.
6. R. Dolan, "Northern Telecom (B): The Norstar Launch," Harvard Business School case 593104.
7. P. Fitsch, "Monsanto Herbicide Won't die on Vine," *Wall Street Journal Europe,* February 1, 1996.
8. M. Marn and R. Rosiello, "Managing Price, Gaining Profit," *Harvard Business Review,* September–October 1992, pp. 84–94.
9. B. Shapiro, K. Rangan, R. Moriarty, and E. Ross, "Manage Customers for Profit (Not Just Sales)," *Harvard Business Review,* September–October 1987, pp. 101–108.
10. "Printing Press Importers Accused of Unfair Pricing," *Wall Street Journal,* February 27, 1996, p. A14.
11. L. Cohen and E. Tanouge, "Drug Makers Set to Pay $600 Million to Settle Lawsuit by Pharmacies," *Wall Street Journal,* January 18, 1996, pp. A1ff.

Index

ABOUT THE AUTHORS

Robert J. Dolan is the Edward W. Carter Professor of Business Administration at the Harvard Business School.

Hermann Simon is chairman of Simon, Kucher & Partners Strategy and Marketing Consultants in Bonn, Germany, and Cambridge, Massachusetts. He is also Visiting Professor at the London Business School. He lives in Koenigswinter, Germany and Cambridge, Massachusetts.